LOSING SMALL WARS

LOSING SMALL WARS

BRITISH MILITARY FAILURE IN IRAQ AND AFGHANISTAN

FRANK LEDWIDGE

YALE UNIVERSITY PRESS
NEW HAVEN AND LONDON

For information about this and other Yale University Press publications, please contact:

U.S. Office: sales.press@yale.edu   yalebooks.com
Europe Office: sales@yaleup.co.uk   www.yalebooks.co.uk

Set in Minion by IDSUK (DataConnection) Ltd

Printed in Great Britain by TJ International Ltd, Padstow, Cornwall

Library of Congress Cataloging-in-Publication Data

Ledwidge, Frank.
    Losing small wars : British military failure in Iraq and Afghanistan / Frank Ledwidge.
        p. cm.
    Includes bibliographical references and index.
    ISBN 978-0-300-16671-2 (cl : alk. paper)
    1. Iraq War, 2003—Participation, British. 2. Iraq War, 2003—Campaigns–Iraq–
Basrah. 3. Afghan War, 2001—Participation, British. 4. Afghan War, 2001—
Campaigns–Afghanistan–Helmand River Valley. 5. Strategic culture–Great Britain.
6. Great Britain–Armed Forces–Management. 7. Great Britain–Military policy. I. Title.
    DS79.765.G7L44 2011
    956.7044'3341–dc22

                                                                                2011012024

A catalogue record for this book is available from the British Library.

10 9 8 7 6 5 4 3 2
2015 2014 2013 2012 2011

Contents

Acknowledgements

I have spoken with, and taken up the time of, many dozens of people in the course of researching and writing this book. It is always difficult to do justice to everyone, but here goes.

Above all, many serving and retired veterans of Iraq and Afghanistan – ranging from private soldiers to three-star generals (or civilian equivalents) – have given me their time to discuss what to them are immediate and personally vital issues. I am particularly grateful to my former comrades in the units with which I have served. They know who they are. Similarly, I have had the privilege of hearing the views of an equally wide range of serving diplomats, civil servants and police officers. Between them, these soldiers, sailors, airmen and civilians have hundreds of years' service in conflict zones. It has been a pleasure and a great privilege to have had the benefit of their individual and accumulated wisdom.

My Afghan friends still resident in the country would, I think, prefer not to be named for now, but they have been invaluable in providing the Afghan perspective. Bob Churcher was kind enough to read and comment on several drafts. His rare combination of many years as a military officer, followed by a decade or so of assisting in reconstruction in Afghanistan, put me right on a whole raft of matters; his help was invaluable. Similarly, Brigadier Richard Iron has patiently fielded many questions and provided wise guidance. David Loyn has helped and encouraged me in writing this book from the start.

Those other incredibly brave journalists Jean Mackenzie and Stephen Grey have spent many hours outlining the view from outside the wire – which is to say the reality of life in Helmand. Bijan Omrani, an expert on the history of the country, has kindly given me the benefit of his deep scholarship on Afghanistan and has put British involvement there firmly in context. To provide a robust critique of the civilian aid effort, one could ask for no more informed or experienced a view than that of Dan Jarman.

Martin Bayly, an emerging scholar, and Colonel David Benest, an established one, have given me the benefit of their research into and knowledge of British counterinsurgency history; David Betz and David Whetham, wise supervisors both at King's College, London, have patiently listened to my often unformed views and corrected them, as have the dean Dr Joel Hayward, lecturers and cadets at the RAF College Cranwell. Professor Anthony King of Exeter has provided remarkable encouragement and a fascinating, informed conceptual angle.

Other friends and colleagues who have given of their time and patience include, but are not limited to, Cynthia Alkon, Dr Sigurd Berven, Toby Bonthrone, Professor Theo Farrell, James Fergusson, Dr John Gearson, Lara Griffith, Richard Jermy, Commodore Steven Jermy, Dr Robert Johnson, Mary Kaldor, Matthew Kypta, Walter Ladwig, Major General Andrew Mackay, Gabrielle Rifkind, David Ucko, Harry Verhoeven, Stephen Weiss, Colonel John Wilson.

Of these friends and colleagues I would like to single out Dr Michael Finn and Alex Donnelly, who have endured many days of discussion of the dilemmas thrown up in writing a book such as this.

Some (or all!) of these impressive individuals may not agree with my conclusions; whether they do or not, I trust they will accept that we share a dedication to ensuring that the mistakes of the past inform but do not infect the future.

The librarians of the Joint Command and Staff College Shrivenham and RAF College Cranwell have been particularly kind and efficient. I can summarize their assistance by stating that they are at the top of their profession.

Thanks also to Phoebe Clapham, my editor at Yale, who has patiently fielded my endless questions as to structure and content. One could ask for no better agent than the ever patient and courteous Andrew Lownie, without whom this book would not have seen the light of day.

Special thanks are due to my wife, Nevi, and my son, James, who have had to endure my immersion in recent military history. I hope to be able to make it up to them.

Introduction

Now that it was dark we were led out onto the tarmac, formed two files and trooped into the hold of the C-130 Hercules, its engines already running. We were directed, as always, to sit along the sides of the aircraft. One of the last to board, I took my place towards the back. The RAF loadmaster, like some camouflaged flight attendant, went around offering us all foam ear defenders for the flight to offset the constant roar of the engines. Ready now, he stood just opposite where I was and pressed a button for the great rear ramp to lift. As it slid into place, the aircraft began to move. The loadmaster turned the already dim interior lights off, leaving us in complete darkness. As we took off steeply into the Afghan night, I can safely say I have never felt more at home in my life. This was where I wanted to be, on my way to serve as a civilian justice adviser alongside my comrades in the British armed forces, in what I believed to be a just and winnable war.

The next day, after an exhilarating white-knuckle ride, low and fast in a Chinook over the Helmand valley, I arrived at the fort in Helmand's capital Lashkar Gah which housed the 'Provincial Reconstruction Team', or PRT, and was swept up into the urgency and immediacy of the war in southern Afghanistan. The months I spent in Helmand were the most interesting of my life, as well as the most revealing. I had arrived there a believer in the mission.

This was not like the war I had fought in Iraq as a military officer four years before. I had arrived in Basra with the mission of finding the much-touted weapons of mass destruction (WMD). It did not take long to realize that the dozens of missions we were running all over southern Iraq were really nothing more than an occasionally dangerous hunt for moonbeams, and that the British mission as a whole was losing its way. The war in Helmand was different, I thought. It was a struggle against a well-defined enemy; and not only our enemy but the enemy of the Afghan people. While I had few illusions about the role I could play – typically it takes decades for the results of justice development to become apparent – I was confident when I arrived that the British military forces had the measure of the enemy.

It took a few weeks for the doubts to take root. I began to suspect that the constant briefings we were receiving (and indeed giving) represented the war the army would have *liked* to have been fighting, rather than the one in which it was actually involved. There was constant talk of operations and strikes. PowerPoint presentations gave an account of development that I did not recognize from my own daily meetings inside and outside the wire with Afghan officials. There was talk of 'inkspots' of development, spreading (as they supposedly had in the Malaya campaign in the 1950s) from one 'secured' area to another within an 'Afghan Development Zone' that, as far as I could see, was entirely illusory – and indeed turned out to exist almost entirely in the minds of those PowerPoint briefers. It was luminously clear from the daily reports that British forces controlled only the area a few hundred metres from the barrels of the machine guns guarding our beleaguered bases.

It also struck me that this was very much a *military* campaign. Despite the rhetoric, the army ran the show; civilians – Afghan and British alike – were ancillary at best. While the civilian effort limped along with relatively tiny amounts of money and resources, the army literally blasted away millions of pounds per week in munitions, over and above the £400,000 it cost to keep each British soldier in the country for a year. Far from the 'comprehensive approach' of full cooperation between civilians and military that I had been brought to expect, this was a campaign unequivocally led and conducted by soldiers.

The dysfunctional local government we were there to support was totally corrupt and distrusted. The Afghan army, so Afghans told me, was useful primarily for protecting them from a drug-addled police force, with whose work I became very familiar. A thriving, obscenely wealthy narco-culture existed around us and in parallel both with the virtual world of constant progress we advertised to the many visitors to the PRT and with the real world of squalid poverty in which most Helmandis lived. It was little wonder that, among the Helmandis I spoke to, there was no enthusiasm at all for our presence. After all, why should there be? The constant 'collateral damage', in the form of slaughtered civilians, of refugees and of towns devastated by battles between British forces and the Taliban, did nothing to remove the impression that all this was rather too resonant of our own little Vietnam. Then there were our casualties. Every week brought its own 'ramp ceremony', when the bodies of ordinary, but quite extraordinarily brave, soldiers caught up in this war were sent, with prayers and praise, home to their shattered families.

Was this really where the blood of British soldiers should be shed? What had happened to our special skills at this, our particular aptitude at 'war among the people'? Military officers are not encouraged to look far beyond their own responsibility. When I had commanded my team in Basra I kept my doubts very much to myself, with the exception of one or two close colleagues who shared them. The overt approach always was – and must be – that we must trust our leaders. In Helmand I was beginning to see that those leaders had little or no more idea than I (or any other critically minded member of the mission) about what was happening. I also saw that once the clothing of military discipline and trust was removed there were few answers to rather fundamental questions.

I had been a company man, trained and raised to be a dedicated and very loyal servant of the British Crown. After university, I spent the first seven years of my working life as a criminal barrister in Liverpool. While there, for a little adventure, I joined the Royal Naval Reserve and learned the arts of navigation and seamanship on minesweepers in the Irish Sea. When I was commissioned in 1993, I was fortunate to be selected for what was then called the Joint Services Intelligence Organisation in Ashford. I spent very little time in Her Majesty's warships after 1995, working entirely with the land forces on campaigns very far from the sea.

After my initial training, which included learning Bosnian, I worked in what are called 'special duties' in Bosnia. (The term conjures up all manner of derring-do, but, like most such appellations, was designed to hide a rather mundane, albeit interesting job.) I was a year or so late for the Bosnian war, so my duties over the two tours I served in the peacekeeping mission centred on locating and capturing war criminals. Here I saw how the skills of the British – gleaned from decades of trial and error in Northern Ireland – were useful and effective in another Western European theatre of civil conflict. There were problems, such as language and the tendency to overlay every political and military problem with Northern Irish analogies, but these could be overcome, I thought.

From Bosnia I went straight to Kosovo as part of a military/civilian peacekeeping unit. If I had been late for the Bosnian conflict, I was right on time for this one. For nearly two years I lived in a society in the middle of a civil war, as a civilian 'international' – albeit one privileged to be at little risk of kidnap or murder. During the Kosovo war I saw soldiers on all sides, Serbian, Kosovan and NATO, each perceived as oppressors, accomplices to murder or liberators, depending on the perspective. Each force, needless to say, viewed itself uniformly as a defender of freedom. I watched the society of a town break up over those two years until it was relatively normal for my small team to be called out (there were no independent police) to investigate a kidnapping and/or murder of uninvolved civilians. From the perspective of the perpetrators of these murders, they were either taking legitimate reprisal or capturing and executing 'terrorists'.

After the Balkans, I worked for several years as a human rights officer for an international organization (the Organization for Security and Co-operation in Europe). I was based mostly in the former Soviet Union, in such places as Tajikistan, ravaged by civil war. In 2003, I was called back into regular military service in Iraq. My job was to command one of the teams of the Iraq Survey Group, which was responsible for the doomed search for WMD. We conducted patrols all over southern Iraq and assisted in 'strike missions' in the only slightly more successful search for those who wished us harm – people we called 'insurgents'. This yielded a close acquaintance with the way in which priority national policy is executed at ground level and the sometimes chaotic nature of military operations. Four colleagues were killed doing that job. Many more of those from my UK unit have been killed or seriously injured in Iraq, including one close friend. That was the last military tour of duty I undertook. I was beginning to have the insidious feeling, described by the great historian Sir Michael

Howard, that for my generation this affair 'marked our end as a *good* power, one that could be expected to act honourably' – much as Suez marked the end for his generation.[1] For very many soldiers like me, who joined to defend our country, not to invade others, this was and remains something of an existential shock. A few years after my tour in southern Iraq I was promoted to head of my branch of the service – a very small but highly operational branch. As such, I was responsible for ensuring that young men and women were present and trained for deployment to the wars described in this book. I retired as a military officer in 2009.

At the time, I put the madness of Iraq down to political, not military incompetence. After all, the British armed forces were, I thought, the finest in the world. At the front-line tactical level where I operated, I saw only brave and professional senior non-commissioned officers (NCOs) and junior officers doing their best and doing it at the tactical level extremely well. Mistakes and incompetence are, of course, everywhere to be found; but surely something of this scale could only be the fault of politicians? When I had arrived in Basra the local people were clearly pleased to see us: early in my tour some children literally threw roses. Six months later we were regularly mortared or rocketed in our bases, and were more commonly received on the streets with stones than with flowers. We were watchful for roadside bombs and shooting attacks. For armed forces that had, we supposed, invented the term 'hearts and minds' it was sobering. It became a great deal worse after I left.

Reflecting on my tours in Helmand and Iraq, I asked myself what went wrong. Where was our supposed 'counterinsurgency' inheritance? How did we get to the point that our preaching on our supposed expertise was regarded by American comrades as 'more British tripe'?[2] All too often the blame is placed on equipment shortages. There are fine accounts of the delay and corruption in that field to be found in other works.[3] I do not subscribe to the view that failure was due to inadequate or too little equipment. No doubt casualties would have been lower with better gear, but that better gear would not have turned failed missions into successes. I do not believe it was a paucity of tools that was at fault. It was not a lack of armoured cars that allowed the growth of sectarian gangs in Basra; rather it was a lack of consistent, effective strategy and leadership, very much the province of generalship.

It is important to remember that senior military commanders are human too, even though military training and conditioning is understandably designed to hide this rather obvious fact from their subordinates. As Michael Howard has said, it is not easy to train for something that may happen once or twice in a career and hope to get it right first time.[4]

Until I went to Afghanistan, I had largely been on the receiving end of life-changing decisions. In Helmand, I was stationed with the headquarters of 'Task Force Helmand', and every day I saw senior commanders take extremely difficult decisions that they knew, whatever happened, would cost lives and limbs. As General Richards, at the time commander of NATO forces in the south of Afghanistan (now chief of the defence staff and therefore head of all UK armed forces), told James Fergusson, 'Given the inadequacies and failings of our fellow man, it is much harder to be an active practitioner than to be an analyst/historian/academic/journalist etc., especially when they have the benefits of hindsight and no pressure of time and events – i.e., to do, rather than criticise others who do.'[5]

This is so. I would add that the very great majority of senior British military commanders are intelligent and professionally minded; often, not always, they are not only excellent leaders but also men (they are mostly men) who possess well-developed critical faculties. Much of what you will read in this book will come as no surprise to them. Indeed, a very great deal of this work has been gleaned from talking to such officers.

However, generals have, we are constantly told, 'broad shoulders'. If we have gone wrong, then the generals must bear their share of responsibility, since it is they who primarily govern the preparations and planning for fighting a war. And as possibly the most famous military adage to enter common parlance has it: 'Preparation and planning prevent piss-poor performance.' It follows that responsibility for the rather poor results of our forces' performance must rest with senior officers. After all, while the price of failure in finance might be the collapse of a bank, military failure has rather wider consequences. There is the irreparable damage to the victims of war in the form of dead and maimed soldiers, Iraqis and Afghans. Those costs simply cannot be quantified. Then there are the vast financial costs – the campaign in Afghanistan sucks an astonishing £6 billion per annum from British taxpayers.[6] There are wider strategic consequences: all just-war traditions have at their heart the ideal that the horrors of war should be entered into only to obtain a better peace, but we have only to look at the consequences of our campaigns in southern Iraq and Helmand to see how far we are from a 'better peace'.

I would like to stress here what this book is *not*. First, it is *not* a critique of British servicemen. War is the ultimate high-stress activity, as any old soldier, sailor or airman with combat experience will tell you. Human nature dictates that catastrophic error and simple, understandable misjudgement are very common features of what Clausewitz calls the 'friction' – essentially the chaos – of war. The purpose of training and intelligent preparation is to reduce the likelihood of such error, mistake or disaster, and to mitigate their effects. Errors, mistakes and disasters will nonetheless occur – they are inevitable. War is the very province of mistake and error. There is absolutely no reason why the residents of Europe's largest island should be less naturally disposed to failure or incompetence than any other nation at a similar level of development. In other words, military competence is not an endowment delivered with the clouds and rain. Nor is it passed down in the genes. If military (or any other) skill is to be maintained, it needs to be constantly renewed and never taken for granted. You will find in these pages no criticism of the ordinary servicemen trying to fight the wars into which they have been led, nor of the values and traditions they espouse. Traditional elements of military culture are necessary qualities, but they are by no means sufficient.

Second, at the other end of the scale, this book is *not* a critique of British defence policy; nor is it an attack on the bloated British Ministry of Defence (MoD). There are fine studies in existence or gestation on the waste and inefficiency of all the services and of their governing ministry.[7] Third, while there is a degree of narrative within, there is no detailed history of either the Basra or the Helmand campaign. An excellent account of the Basra campaign is to be found in Richard North's *Ministry of Defeat*.[8] Patrick Cockburn's masterly *Occupation: War and Resistance in Iraq* deals with the disaster of the US–UK invasion and its consequences throughout Iraq.[9] Helmand has had some of its campaigns very well covered by fine journalists such as James Fergusson, David Loyn and Stephen Grey.[10] 'Herographies' and blood-and-guts accounts of derring-do abound. However, a full account of Helmand has yet to be written. It is, of course, an ongoing campaign.

Finally, you will *not* find an explicit critique of the grand strategy of intervention in Iraq and Afghanistan.[11] Nor will I deal in detail with national strategic leadership, declared by the Public Administration Select Committee of the UK House of Commons to be seriously at fault. It is right in saying that 'Lack of consistent strategy goes a long way towards explaining why the conflicts have not gone well for the UK' in Iraq and Afghanistan.[12] Think-tanks and commentators are beginning seriously to get to grips with the acute lack of strategic thought in the United Kingdom.[13]

Academics and researchers have also begun to deal with recent failure. Professor Anthony King of Exeter University has led the way from the sociological perspective with some superb analysis of British military culture. From the different (but linked) world of war studies, David Betz of King's College, among others, has looked closely at strategic and operational failure. Both approaches are informed by close familiarity with the armed forces and their involvement in recent conflicts.

Excellent accounts exist elsewhere of the failures of pragmatism and reason that led us into these campaigns – the politics and politicking surrounding them. The book in your hand is, for the most part, set firmly within what is now often called the operational and to a lesser extent the tactical realms – where the fighting was actually done. General Sir Richard Dannatt, the former head of the army, put it this way:

> It is at the strategic level where the big thoughts are thought, where the broad ideas are conceived, and it is at the tactical level where the rubber hits the road and the bullets fly. However it is the level in between that is so critical, for this is where ideas are turned into practicalities ... this is the operational level of war. It is the level where the general really earns his pay, because it is here that a plan is formulated that turns grand ideas into...success achieved by forces on the ground.[14]

The failures at the operational level point up very serious problems at what is often called the strategic level, where politics and, more specifically, *political objectives* meet the military means to achieve them; or should meet them.

This book sets out to be one man's reasonably well-informed view of why our forces, and our army in particular, have performed so badly in recent operations. There is discussion of the strategic elements of the fighting of our recent wars, but such discussion is confined to the elements of strategy that impact directly and immediately upon that *operational* level.

The reader will also not lose sight of the fact that these were and are predominantly America's wars. The US military role in them is not examined in detail, save insofar as it impacts directly upon British involvement. The invasion and occupation of both Iraq and Afghanistan were and are US operations, with UK forces playing a strategically auxiliary role.[15] The wars of the British in both theatres, however, were fought by most soldiers in well-defined geographical areas of responsibility (AORs – the military loves three-letter acronyms): Basra and the southern provinces of Iraq, and Helmand province in Afghanistan.

Criticism of the armed forces is often stifled by fear of the dread accusation of 'defeatism' or, even worse, of undermining 'our boys'. No serving officer could write a book like this and expect to keep his commission.[16] Accounts of serving officers are and must be positive. The tragedies of Iraq and Afghanistan to a very great degree are understandably but damagingly shrouded in the flags and grief of the returning dead, commemorated in Wootton Bassett and elsewhere. One former army officer spoke to me of his fear that 'speaking out' might attract the disapproval of his former colleagues who are still fighting. If I am candid, there is more than a twinge of that feeling in me – the idea that somehow, in writing a book such as this, I am 'letting the side down'.

Like any other 'profession', there is undoubtedly within the armed forces (as within other exclusive organizations) an inherent belief that they are *uniquely* well qualified to discuss military matters. 'Leave it to us,' they say. 'We know what we are doing.' We have been happy to devolve debate about the way we conduct warfare to military men (and a very few women) in the most conservative institution in the country. They know, we still presume; leave it to them. This is simply another manifestation of British military exceptionalism. I believe discussion of military matters should not be 'left to them'. Indeed, it is not in our tradition to do so. It is only recently that military experience and knowledge have been so peripheral to the mainstream of our society. As a result, a 'stab in the back' myth has developed – that the primary fault lies with those who failed to resource the missions on which the soldiers were sent with adequate equipment and weaponry; that it is someone else's fault after all.

In seeking to move the debate away from tired questions of kit and whether the wars were 'right' or 'wrong', I will examine whether the problems facing Britain's armed forces – predominantly the army, which is far larger than the other two services combined – can be found in their mentality and approach; in other words, in their culture. The British military profession is a society apart. The armed forces are the most closed within a strong field of closed establishment institutions. This separation and exclusivity is necessary, since we ask of them the kind of service and sacrifice we demand of no other element of the public service. This separation from the 'mainstream' is evident at its most basic level to anyone visiting a military base, upon which no reader without the requisite pass may legally stray. They are secure areas, designed clearly and rightly to keep out the many and ever more varied hostile elements of the outside world. The guarded gates and barbed wire fences serve, to a great degree, also to keep their inhabitants and their ways in.

Of all Britain's professional societies, none is more defined by its different language, values and behaviour. Even the dress is distinctive. With its often strange and arcane rituals and histories, the British military is almost the ultimate example of anthropologist Clifford Geertz's definition of culture as 'the stories we tell ourselves about ourselves'. There is nothing inherently negative about any of this. The problems begin when those stories are believed and acted upon. Separation then becomes exceptionalism. There is a deep-rooted belief in the idea that anything can be done, and that the possibility of failure is not only not an option, but cannot even be acknowledged. This in turn gives rise to deeply unrealistic approaches, which may be characterized by the benign phrase 'a can-do attitude'. This is otherwise known as 'cracking on'. No other profession can afford such illusions. In the law or in medicine the delivery of unrealistic advice results in adverse consequences both for those requesting the advice and for those delivering it.

The campaigns recounted in this book are linked and must be seen together. Part One of the book contains basic narratives of the Basra and Helmand campaigns. These are not intended to be comprehensive; the idea is to provide a factual background for what follows. I would ask the reader to remember that, although the campaigns are described here separately, the key elements of both campaigns – between 2006 and 2009

– were simultaneous. The campaigns in Basra and Helmand were simultaneous and *symbiotic*. Each impacted heavily on the other. Helmand was to be, partly at the very least, the army's vindication for the failing Basra campaign. Equally (and paradoxically) the resources required to conduct the Helmand campaign, steadily increasing because of the almost complete lack of strategic thought given to it, made defeat and humiliation in Iraq almost inevitable.

Part Two looks at the reasons for the failure on the part of the British to attain their objectives or to come close to doing so. I look at the fundamental failure to apply the most basic principles of strategy to the wars in Helmand and Basra. I have no hesitation in calling the high command of the armed forces to account for what I regard as nothing less than a dereliction of duty. Yet no senior officer has been held to account; none has been dismissed; none has resigned; none has been removed from his position. In any other society, this would be termed a 'culture of impunity'. There is a growing realization that although chiefs of staff are responsible for the provision of advice to ministers, responsibility for military activities lies messily between ministers and chiefs of staff of the services. The MoD as an institution is, to a significant extent, responsible for much of the strategic dyslexia that (I argue) lies at the root of the UK's lack of success in Iraq and Afghanistan. Its understanding of strategy has largely revolved around business or departmental strategy – a managerial approach – rather than defence or security strategy.[17] Responsibility for the failure of military strategy must in reality be shared by the bureaucracy of the MoD, politicians and indeed military commanders.[18]

The stories that the army, in particular, tells itself are examined in the chapters on the ideas behind military doctrine and operational practice. I look closely at the oft-recounted stories of British prowess at 'counter-insurgency', particularly in Malaya and Northern Ireland. I try to show that the lessons from those campaigns were simply not identified, let alone learned. There are profound problems arising from an almost completely sealed-in military culture when it encounters and works, all too often violently, in a deeply foreign civilian world. Shibboleths such as the 'comprehensive approach' act merely as temporary palliatives at best.

We then go on to look at the problems of intelligence. Our services talk to themselves and like what they hear. Unfortunately, on several levels, they are rather less fond of listening to others. First, in the areas they have

been occupying, they seek to exercise influence without deeming it necessary to learn about those whom they are seeking to influence. This makes
useful intelligence gathering almost impossible. The wire fences and
armed guards around our services, both at home and abroad, stand as a
metaphor for a closed and defensive mentality.

'I don't want to hear problems; I want to hear solutions,' as the old
commanding officer used to tell his subordinates. We then look briefly at
what might be done to open the necessary networks and build what one
general has called 'the post-modern warrior'.[19] In a world of ever greater
complexity, where what is required is acute awareness, those closed and
exclusive networks need to be opened and critically broader approaches
taken.

I began this introduction with a brief account of my own first impressions of Helmand. We move now from discussion of why failure happened
to look at what happened. We begin our journey through Britain's recent
wars in the outskirts of Basra in late 2003.

PART ONE

CHAPTER 1

'Ridiculous Expectations'

You fought the battle, you won the battle and you fought it with great courage and valour. But it didn't stop there. You then went on to make something of the country you had liberated and I think that's a lesson for armed forces everywhere the world over.

Tony Blair to British soldiers, May 2003

Sir Roderick Lyne: *Call it phase IV, I don't care what you call it, it went wrong.*
General Piggott: *Wrong is too strong.*

Evidence of General Sir Anthony Piggott to the Iraq Inquiry,
4 December 2009

Venice of the east

The drive from the airport into Basra is much like that into any other developing-world city. Fast freeways take you from the airport into progressively more depressing suburbs. Huge open spaces with rotting trash, playing kids and scrap metal separate the road from the shanty flats in which a predominantly poor population live. There is a smell – burning plastic, with the distinctive tang of open sewers. Desultory males and the occasional woman, black burka flapping in the light, hot wind, wander the dirty wastelands between road and tenement building.

'Lovely place, Basra, sir. Pity you're only seeing the posh parts,' said the soldier as he drove me on my first journey into the city in September 2003.

Into the city proper and we came to road junctions with odd statues, one of three entwined fish. Another monument had at one time been a Saddam mosaic, but was peppered now with bullet holes. We wound over muddy canals and through the usual lively traffic-choked mess of an Arab city centre, all cheap hotels and travel agencies. Down long boulevards lined with fridges and cookers, new white goods and old furniture.

To the river, the Shatt al-Arab, and a half-mile drive straight down to the archway gates of Basra Palace base – heavily armed guards, sandbags and bunkers. Everyone relaxes, the 'top cover', who stand up out of the Land Rovers with their machine guns, sit down now and we all unload our rifles. Mine were the initial impressions of thousands of British soldiers. Nearly two hundred did not return alive, and many hundreds and thousands more came back as different men.

Basra is one of several cities that have been described as 'the Venice of the east'. For the initial visitor, whether or not in a military vehicle of an occupying power, the signature of Basra is its smell. The other initially striking feature is its size. Basra has about the same population and area as Birmingham. Like any old city in the world, it has a rich and fascinating history. Basra was, for example, the home port of Sinbad. It is a cosmopolitan Gulf city with a strong history of foreign influence, independent-mindedness and dissent. It is the Marseilles, the Liverpool of Iraq. Its story did not begin in 2003. Britain was no stranger, historically, to insurgency and civil war in Iraq.

'Bloody and inefficient'

They have been tricked into it by a steady withholding of information . . . The Baghdad communiqués are belated, insincere, incomplete. Things have been far worse than we have been told, our administration more bloody and inefficient than the public knows . . . we are today not far from a disaster.

These seem familiar words concerning Iraq. They were written in 1919 by T.E. Lawrence (of Arabia).[1] The British, despite some horrendous setbacks, had driven the Ottoman Empire out of Iraq by 1918. Efforts to 'appear as a benign power bent on imposing a benign administration'[2] by way of the resolution of blood feuds between tribes resulted in those tribes uniting against them.

The ensuing 1919–23 uprising against the British is still widely recalled – it was here that 'Bomber Harris' cut his teeth, dropping high explosives on civilians. These 'magnificently successful' operations were based around coercion, such that if a tribe was minded to cause trouble, a message was dropped on them. The message stated that, should the tribe not desist from its activities, the village would be bombed and destroyed – a technique known as 'proscription bombing'.[3] Squadron Leader Arthur Harris reported after a raid in 1924:

> The Arab and Kurd now know what real bombing means, in casualties and damage: They know that within 45 minutes a full-sized village can be practically wiped out and a third of its inhabitants killed or injured.[4]

In addition to this novel way of conducting operations against rebels, there was extensive use of force based on the preponderance of armed, trained soldiers. 'Ultimately it all came down to force employed in sufficient numbers . . . tempered by the idea that it should not be used excessively' – a reasonable statement of the British ideal in conducting this kind of war.[5]

While the Iraq insurgency of 1919–23 and its legacy had been largely forgotten by the British, for the Iraqis it was a key element of their history as a nation. They also remembered that when the British army originally entered Baghdad in 1917, General Stanley Maude told them they had only 'come to liberate Iraqis from the evil rule of the Turks'.[6] The Iraqis were thus familiar with the fragility of Western promises even before recent disasters. One British general was politely reminded about this early in the occupation of 2003. Once it had been made clear to him that Basrawis were happy that their city had been taken with few casualties, some Iraqi clerics made it clear to general Sir Peter Wall that:

> you are not particularly welcome here. Remember what happened when you were here last time . . . And, of course, all our forebears learned a lot about this and it would be as well if you would capitalise on that experience and get this done quickly, which was a very powerful message, but it wasn't backed up with any clarity as to how we should implement it.[7]

The aftermath

The post-combat phase of an 'intervention' operation, such as that to invade Iraq, is known as 'Phase IV'. Military planning is framed around 'phases': Phase I is the planning phase; Phase II the physical and material preparation; Phase III is the battle itself; and Phase IV the post-conflict element. Platoons of generals and their minions worked on the invasion – Phase III. Committees discussed and decided on 'force generation', deployment, operational planning and logistics. The original plan had been for the British to invade through Turkey and take control of the Mosul region. The objective had switched from the north to southern Iraq only three months before the war started: the planners were told on Christmas Day 2002 that Turkey would not permit its territory to be used as a platform for the invasion.

When the 'shock and awe' invasion began in late March 2003, Britain supplied one of five divisions involved, although its total commitment was in the region of about 40,000 soldiers. As the US 3rd Infantry Division charged up to Baghdad, the British were conducting a masterly operation – with the US Marine Expeditionary Force on their northern flank – to take Basra, the second city in the country and the capital of the Shi'a south. The divisional commander in the initial phase, Major General Brims, was faced with the prospect of an assault on a huge city, about which he knew very little. His solution reflected the best traditions of the British armed forces. Instead of conducting an all-out assault, the British took the more deliberate approach of ensuring that they dominated the physical and indeed psychological battlefield (or battlespace as it is now called). Having destroyed any demoralized and poorly led ramshackle Iraqi army formations they encountered, they moved forward to the outskirts of Basra. Instead of moving in force into the town – a move which, it was felt, would ensure heavy combat and consequently heavy civilian casualties – the British sent small armoured columns in short thrusts into the centre of the city to gather intelligence and show that the British were now in control. When the conditions were right, they entered Basra in force against almost no opposition and took up bases all across the city. The methods used in Basra proved very useful in informing the similar American success in Baghdad. It was an excellent demonstration of the use of minimum force in a major war environment, and a fine victory, albeit over a very weak enemy.

More pertinently, this initial phase was exactly the kind of operation for which the army was, and is, configured. Fast-moving armoured manoeuvre warfare was what took Basra and completely and effectively rendered the Iraqi army irrelevant. This was what the troops had trained for over the decades; this was the kind of warfare that had recovered Kuwait twelve years before. It was exactly the war the British army wanted to fight. Unfortunately, it was not the war that it was going to spend the next six years fighting.

It is now abundantly clear that after the high-intensity combat phase there was something of a 'what now?' feeling. Given that the 'what now?' feeling is exactly what military planning is intended to avoid, this was a rather major oversight. As one well-known tactical commander, Colonel Tim Collins, has put it: 'It became very apparent to me shortly after crossing the border that the government and many of my superiors had no idea what they were doing.'[8] That was so. There were however plenty of available lessons from history in how to deal with the occupation of a highly developed formerly totalitarian country.

Operation Eclipse

As early as the spring of 1941, the British high command was beginning to look in detail at how an invasion of occupied Europe might be effected. In 1945, the grinding combat machines of the British and US armies smashed their way into Germany. In their wake came echelons of units that had been given the title 'civil affairs'. There were tens of thousands of these soldiers, engineers, administrators, medical and legal experts, whose job it was to ensure that reconstruction began as soon as possible. When combat operations ended, almost immediately thousands of experts in public health, counterintelligence (to track down war criminals), ordnance disposal, civil governance and public health fanned out across the pacified areas. There was also a strong emphasis on the disarmament of former enemy combatants of all nations, and, of course, on allied prisoners of war and assistance for displaced persons. Very many of the personnel attached to these units were German expatriates, almost all Jewish, who had joined the UK armed forces.[9] Plans were made for dealing with the expected (or at least envisaged) continuing resistance by hard-line Nazis and SS soldiers.

This entire operation was given the title Operation Eclipse.[10] It was not treated as some sort of subsidiary plan or as an afterthought. On the contrary, this part of the entire operation was declared to be the 'consummation of Overlord [the invasion and occupation of Western Europe]'.[11] Its execution was by no means perfect, and there were difficulties with what military planners call 'sequencing' – the order in which operations are carried out. This resulted in some confusion as to where and when 'Eclipse conditions' (triggering the planned assistance) took effect. It should be stressed that at all times this was a *military operation*, though augmented by very many civilians. It was by no means without the interagency squabbles and rivalries that beset operations today. The results, however, were admirable. In the case of Eclipse, the *expected* insurgency against the Allies never, of course, materialized, although plans were drawn up for the eventuality.[12]

In Iraq, the situation which applied in post-Nazi Germany was reversed. The rebellion was unexpected and unplanned for – in retrospect, that is in itself extraordinary in a country with as strong a tradition of resistance as Iraq.

Needless to say, there was no lack of awareness of the Eclipse operation among planners or well-informed officers. Indeed, there is evidence that the US army sent officers to Germany to examine the lessons of Eclipse, but they were forbidden to use their findings. Certainly there is no evidence of British officers doing the same thing.[13] Wilfully failing to take on board clear lessons from other conflicts, by the way, might well be seen by psychologists as a textbook example of 'cognitive dissonance'.[14]

'None of this had really been thought through'

General Tim Cross was liaison officer to what became the Office for Reconstruction and Humanitarian Affairs, a short-lived agency commanded by an American general. It was the predecessor of the disastrously run Coalition Provisional Authority (CPA). Generals were aware of the need for a 'comprehensive approach' in Iraq, but the Americans wanted to 'get on with it'.[15] Cross was conscious that no one was looking at Phase IV. Certainly, he was not: 'Nor as operational commander should I have been.' The good general does not explain why he should not have been so concerned . . . 'but no one else was either'. In fairness, General Cross was one of the few offering the advice that 'we should not begin the campaign until we had a much more coherent post-war plan'.[16] It is the duty of a general to supply advice like that. Unfortunately no one was listening.

There was not even an agreed acceptance that the term or concept represented by 'Phase IV' was appropriate. One general who was closely involved in the planning of the operation, Lieutenant General Sir Anthony Piggott, was deputy chief of the defence staff with responsibility for 'commitments' (and thus rejoiced in the acronym DCDS(C)). He was, as he put it, the 'military strategic focus' of advice to the armed forces. He says:

> I hate the term 'Phase 4' and I hate the term 'aftermath'. And I wouldn't have invented or used either of them myself. And the phasing [*sic*] of phase 4 implies a phase 5 or phase 6 and it has got this sort of nature of going into the future and I think it is concurrent shaping all the time that was required, not phase 4 planning, let's now plan for phase 4. It's the wrong thinking.[17]

Piggott had a point: sequential thinking is not appropriate for 'stabilization' missions such as the one in which the army had found itself. The term 'Phase IV' was probably indeed not helpful. The *concept* of planning for occupation was essential. As the army and its few civilian colleagues were to find, 'concurrent shaping' – which might otherwise be characterized as 'muddling through' – was not going to work.

General Sir Freddie Viggers was senior British military representative in Baghdad from May to December 2003. While the general is particularly critical of the lack of American planning,[18] he is no more positive about the levels of British planning. There was, he says:

> [a] lack of any real understanding of the state of the country post-invasion. We had not done enough research, planning into how the country worked post-sanctions . . . *none of this had really been thought through*

[my italics] . . . there were lots of sockets and plugs [*sic*] but not too many were joined up . . . without a basic understanding of what you are going into, you have nothing but to be surprised and disappointed if it doesn't go quite as you had dreamt it might.[19]

General Petraeus, who commanded the coalition presence in Mosul (where the British would have had their headquarters, had Turkey decided to assist the invasion directly), famously asked: 'How does this end?' He received no answer. There was no campaign plan for the aftermath. The completion of the invasion was an end in itself and therefore, the reasoning went logically, there was no requirement for post-war planning. As one senior 'special forces' soldier put it to me: 'We hadn't signed up for an internal security operation. We had signed up for a link-up with the Iraqi people and then we were to fuck off.'[20]

It was axiomatic that British success in previous 'low-intensity conflict' was based, to a very large degree, on legal legitimacy and rule of law. British experience in Northern Ireland had reinforced a long-standing rule of police primacy in situations of disorder. However, the army was not short of recent experience in places where there was no police force: Kosovo had not been an easy operation from that perspective. The British contribution there had shown great innovation, and new ideas had been developed – for example, of bringing control of intelligence-gathering assets to the level where they were required, rather than keeping them as tools of higher and often remote and highly bureaucratic command structures. Intelligence and surveillance had been fused with operations in much the same way as they had been in Northern Ireland. Similarly, 7 Armoured Brigade had adopted a non-sequential approach to what now would be called 'stabilization' operations, with a number of 'lines of operation' running concurrently. By today's standards, this was a very holistic operation.[21] In Kosovo, though, there had been no large-scale breakdown of order, even in the absence of civil police, due mainly to the large numbers of NATO soldiers deployed. Those numbers were not going to be available for Iraq. The lack of any thought whatsoever as to how the army might, for example, deal with looters was to have disastrous consequences. The army was to fall into the grey area between gendarmerie and military activity. More than any other factor, the restoration and maintenance of order requires *numbers* – numbers taking the form not of clerks, cooks and staff officers ensconced in bases, but the ever-vital 'boots on the ground'.

In addition to the planning and operational requirements of the occupation of Iraq, there were the more inchoate but no less important expectations of Iraqis themselves, and Basrawis in particular. After all, the arrival of the Allies had created certain expectations on the part of the Iraqi people. Indeed, General Graeme Lamb stated that the Iraqis had 'ridiculous expectations' of what the British would achieve for them.[22] Given the rich promises delivered through the international media of a 'free democratic Iraq', and indeed given the obligations of an international legal order, about which the UK and the US had been preaching for many years, one wonders quite how 'ridiculous' such expectations really were. Whatever the Iraqis believed would be done for them, in Basra they were to be disappointed.

Early days in Basra

The degree to which the invasion of Iraq was an historical aberration is sometimes forgotten. With the significant exception of Germany in 1945, the last time Britain's army overthrew a government by force in further-ance of its own national interest and installed an occupying force for a period of years was in 1896. Then, after a series of inconclusive wars and a disagreement about payment of 'fines', the British overthrew the Ashanti rulers of the Gold Coast (now named Ghana), sent them to the Seychelles and installed their own government with a supporting military force.

Some 107 years later, on a dubious pretext, the regime of Saddam Hussein was dispatched with the considerable assistance of the British armed forces. After the initial flower-throwing honeymoon in Basra, the realization began to set in that the British were likely to be in Basra for a while. Over the summer of 2003, the British force drew down from a maximum of 40,000 to 12,000 by the autumn, and to about 8,000 by the end of the year. British soldiers patrolled Basra in soft hats. They were to be seen relaxing over coffees and hookah pipes in the city centre.

The British troops in Basra continued their 'peacekeeping' patrols in unarmoured vehicles. They were comfortable with this; after all, it was peacekeeping in Kosovo and Bosnia all over again – and the British knew all about peacekeeping. Some had a slightly less optimistic approach: mutterings began that this could be more of a Belfast than a benign Bosnia. But that, too, could be handled. There was undoubtedly a degree of professional smugness on the part of the British. The soft-hat approach reflected (so went the common wisdom) the realistic 'hearts and minds' approach at which they were so adept. The British knew how to do this; the Americans did not. Even august and often sceptical military historians bought into this story (as indeed did I at the time):

> As the entry into Basra was to prove, the British Army's mastery of the methods of urban warfare is transferable. What had worked in Belfast could be made to work again in Basra.[23]

Outside the comfort of the various bases, law and order had collapsed, with looting and destruction on a remarkable scale. As one Basrawi journalist put it:

> Since April 2003, the people of Basra have consistently been bemused by reports that they and their city enjoy a state of calm and stability under the command of the British forces, in contrast to the north of Iraq and the so-called Sunni triangle.[24]

By the time I arrived in the city as a British officer in September 2003, six months after the invasion, matters were beginning to deteriorate. After a number of fatal attacks, patrols out of the camp were fully briefed, fully armed and ready for trouble. The era of soft hats was gone, and a visit to a café would have been regarded as lunacy. The civilian mission that had hurriedly been constituted – the CPA – gave the impression of being in a constant panicking funk. With no strategic vision, and even less knowledge of the environment in which it was working, this is not surprising.[25] The situation was beginning to slide.

Matters had taken a sinister turn on 24 June 2003, when six military policemen were killed in the town of Majar al-Kabir in Al Amara province after the British had decided to search this town, which had a particular reputation (for decades) of violent resistance to outsiders. The paratroopers who had been conducting the 'sweeps' had allegedly been using dogs – an insult that added to the injury to pride caused by the raids and the weapon searches. This was regarded as nothing less than a provocation. There was a shoot-out and the paratroopers retreated. Six Royal Military Police (RMP) soldiers who had been conducting training at the police station were left behind. Due to a failure in command and control, and very poor communications, neither the group of paras nor the RMP unit knew the other was there. The RMPs had no chance.

Patrick Cockburn, who had been visiting Iraq for decades, reported that local leaders had told him: 'If Saddam Hussein could not take away our weapons, why should we allow the British to do so?' According to Cockburn, the only reason the locals could imagine for the move to disarm them was that America and Britain intended a long-term occupation.[26] As Cockburn says: 'If the British army had really learned any lessons in Northern Ireland about not provoking local communities, they had largely been forgotten somewhere between Belfast and Al Amara.'[27]

During that first summer there were several more shootings and grenade attacks, and other soldiers were killed. As one officer put it to me at the time, it was 'beginning to look like we have got ourselves a very big Northern Ireland'. No sensible British commander would have sent a unit of assault troops into the 'worst' areas of South Armagh without expecting a great deal of trouble. Of course, in Iraq no soldier had much idea of where the 'bad' areas were – or what to do when he got there. That was at the root of the killings in Majar and of much of what was to follow

This was emphatically not Northern Ireland, although the reflex of senior officers was understandably to fall back on what they knew. With no effective 'framework' intelligence system such as operated in Northern Ireland – one that took account of all areas of life, promoted acute local awareness and maintained accurate records of, for example, vehicle ownership – the British had very little idea of what was actually happening on the streets and in the buildings of the city.

Fighting the wrong enemy

At this time the Shi'a majority, with its militias and strong political parties, was apparently quiet. Despite events such as those in Majar al-Kabir, the British had taken the view that the real enemy were shadowy 'former regime loyalists' – Ba'athists with a grudge. Few could believe that Iraqis could actually be resisting the 'liberators'. 'Strike missions' were launched regularly in Basra to 'take down' these largely illusory Ba'athist terrorists – I took part in many and not a single one resulted in success. There were even reports of an Al Qaeda offshoot, Ansar Al Islam – a Kurdish organization – hatching plots against British forces. The odd Saddam Fedayeen (Saddam's Men of Sacrifice) or hard-line old regime loyalist was collared, but no one who was a significant threat. There were regular reports of 'foreign fighters' recruited by Saddam (and later by Al Qaeda) from Muslim countries to fight the Western invaders, but failed operations over many nights convinced many soldiers that the only 'foreign fighters' in the city were wearing British uniforms.

I recall one mission, involving an entire battle group of 600 men, which succeeded in arresting a group of car dealers. It was alleged they were involved in a plot to shoot down British aircraft at Basra airport, as they were transporting troops to and from leave However, it soon became evident that they were not involved in paramilitary activity of any kind, let alone a strategically significant conspiracy, and it subsequently transpired that the intelligence upon which the mission was based had been supplied by a rival group of car dealers, who were simply using the British to remove inconvenient opposition. This form of 'touting' (informants providing information to the British in Northern Ireland have long been known as 'touts') has become a pattern in both Afghanistan and Iraq, with the UK military all too often taking the role of 'useful idiots' in commercial, tribal or gang rivalries. Needless to say, this did (and does) nothing for army–community relationships. For the soldiers, these all-night 'intelligence-led' operations in the first year of occupation were tiring and intensely frustrating. Half a dozen raids were launched, for example, on one 'colonel' who was alleged to be the mastermind behind attacks on British and other soldiers in the region. It was eventually determined that, if this former officer existed at all, he was living happily in Dubai with minimal, if any, involvement in 'insurgency' in Basra.

In these early days of the occupation there was little understanding of who constituted a true threat to the force or the mission. These were not necessarily the same thing: largely ineffective and sporadic attacks on the British did not necessarily constitute a serious threat to the overall mission.

Conversely, serious threats to the mission, insofar as a coherent mission could be discerned, took the form of attacks upon the people of Basra.

Untroubled by the British, the various Shi'a militias were hard at work eliminating as many of the 'former regime loyalists' (or FRLs) as they could. These Ba'athists had enough problems simply staying alive, without attacking the British forces. The Shi'a militias' approach toward anyone with the slightest connection to the former regime was horrific torture and murder, and bodies were found daily. It must be said that there was a view, held by very many at all rank levels of the British forces, that the Shi'a were doing our job for us. They were, of course, very much doing their *own* work, clearing the way – setting the conditions – for a fundamentalist Shi'a-dominated south. In practical terms, this meant horror and fear for ordinary Sunni citizens and Christians, as well as for ordinary Shi'as, most of whom simply wanted peace and quiet to get on with their lives.

Not everyone in the units on the ground was convinced that it was the now beleaguered Sunnis/FRLs/non-existent Al Qaeda who represented the real threat. While set-piece operations searched, largely fruitlessly, for often illusory opponents, deeply unpleasant things were happening to Basrawis who did not meet the standards of the radical Shi'a militias. I remember a conversation with an infantry sergeant in December 2003. He was disturbed by having stumbled (almost literally) upon a torture chamber being used by Thar Allah (Fist of God), one of the militias operating in the city. He was concerned that this group and others like it were 'literally getting away with murder'. Infantry units such as the sergeant's were on constant patrol. They were beginning to realize that something dangerous was happening. This was a realization largely lost on the 'elite' military intelligence units operating in the city. Shi'a gangs – death squads – were not confining their attentions to former Ba'athists, or even Sunni elements. The previously tolerant society of Basra, a cosmopolitan port city, had no attractions for these men, many of whom had spent years in Iran before the 'liberation'. Alcohol sellers, women who did not wear the veil or who had spoken to foreigners, academics and Christians were all potential targets for kidnap and torture. As the police force was formed, it started to become clear to the soldiers on the ground that all was not well with it. This was not surprising: the militias *were* the police.

Senior army officers, informed as they were by a somewhat bewildered military intelligence apparatus, were largely unaware of this; or at the very least they were unaware of the *significance* of this activity. The view prevailed that looting, intimidation, rape, kidnap and murder were essentially Iraqi problems – which they certainly were. No one, however, was interested in what the Iraqis wanted or needed – or in how Iraqi (here specifically Basrawi) wants or needs related to the mission in hand. The British force existed not to protect the Iraqi population of the city: it existed largely, indeed almost exclusively, to protect itself. This was not lost on many of the soldiers, who coined a phrase for this approach: we were, it was said, 'a self-licking lollipop'.

In fairness, there were too few troops to do a great deal more. There were enough, however, to deal with some completely superfluous tasks. The unit with which I served was the Iraq Survey Group. This was a force of about 1,000 men and women, roughly 100 of them British. It was composed of intelligence officers, analysts, reconnaissance assets, infantrymen and linguists – all in great demand elsewhere. The task of this group was to find the so-called 'weapons of mass destruction' – the pretext for the whole invasion, or at least for the British component. In the detachment with which I served in Basra, our concern was with searching dozens of bombed, looted and long-deserted military bases for traces of weapons we all realized early on in the mission did not exist and had not existed for very many years. The only chemical shells – battlefield weapons, *not* WMD – that we encountered were from the era of the Iran–Iraq War. They had been uncovered by a Danish army unit and, said a Danish soldier to me afterwards, bore every sign of having been made in the United States. Had we instead, for example, used our frankly impressive technical and human resources to seek out the graves of those missing persons killed by Saddam, the people of Basra might have begun to develop the idea that the British were concerned, at least to a tiny extent, with their welfare. At the very least, those graves actually existed. But that would have required the kind of holistic approach of which we were, at that stage, incapable.

The work of the Iraq Survey Group is illustrative of the approach taken by all coalition forces in Iraq up to 2007 – entirely inward-looking. In December 2003, a senior officer in Basra said, in my presence and with some pride, that the British army was 'the biggest and best gang in Basra'. That just about summed up the developing chaos.

'If you break it, you own it'

We were not the only gang. To any soldier speaking to Basrawis, it was apparent that there was a very great deal of fear in the city – fear not of us, but of religious fanatics. The university – with which I had a great deal of involvement – was being 'cleared' of elements deemed unsatisfactory to Shi'a parties. On the streets, it became very rare to see women in 'Western' clothes such as jeans. Had the British devoted a little more effort to looking out at the people they had 'liberated', they would have seen that Basra was rapidly becoming a law-free zone. After the wholesale looting and destruction following the 'liberation', security for Basrawis remained very poor indeed. There was no police force, nor anything resembling one. Kidnappings, car-jackings and robbery were the least of the problems. The reprisal killings that were to characterize the next two years were under way. It was not long before they turned into a wholesale programme of ethnic cleansing of tens of thousands of Sunnis and Christians.

This is a hitherto unreported aspect of the war in southern Iraq. Human Rights Watch, a professional and balanced non-governmental organization, reported that no effort was made to constitute a working legal or judicial system. In view of the experience of Kosovo and Bosnia, this is an extraordinary lapse, and was to have severe consequences as soldiers found themselves in a confusing legal limbo when confronted with criminality. In an atmosphere such as that, the situation is ripe for any group to set itself up as the arbiter of justice – including British soldiers. And in due course this is exactly what happened.

Unfortunately, the atmosphere of growing lawlessness engendered by the lack of planning crept into the approach of a small minority of soldiers and some of their commanders, who took the view that there were occasions when the usual, tightly enforced rules need not apply. On occasion, sinister means were applied to those detainees who had the misfortune to find themselves in the care of, for example, the Queen's Lancashire Regiment, which suffered what has every appearance of a breakdown in military discipline after its commander told the regiment, following the death of a well-regarded officer from another regiment, that 'the gloves [are] off'. The resulting torture and death of Baha Musa continues to mire the army in innuendo and allegations that this was not an isolated occurrence confined to one unit.

This kind of behaviour, as much as the chaos on the streets, was a direct result of failure to plan and provide for Phase IV. Whether the strategy (if it can be called that) did or did not mandate planning for occupation, the law certainly did, in the form of the Hague and the Geneva Conventions.[28] These provisions might be summarized as saying (as indeed Colin Powell said to President Bush, though to no effect): 'If you break it, you own it.' That was not simply a homespun truism, as the general well knew. That these simple, effective and well-known legal provisions were ignored throughout the period of the UK's role as 'occupying power' in Iraq is a testament to the cavalier attitude of the UK and its armed forces to international law.[29] The results of this kind of law-breaking were to be found not in international litigation – this was not available – but in the damaging consequences that were to unfold on the ground of failing to allocate sufficient (or indeed, in the early days, *any*) resources to ensuring 'public order and safety'.[30] These duties are not obscure provisions, buried deep in old tomes. They are clear and uncontroversial obligations that are well known to any senior officer with even a passing familiarity with humanitarian law (law of war), let alone to the myriad lawyers employed by the armed forces and the various relevant ministries.

There seems to have been an understanding that an occupying power has legal responsibility, but less awareness of the implications. A paper was produced by the 'Defence, Diplomacy and Intelligence Team', which appears to have been commissioned by the staff of the Chancellor of the Exchequer of the time. Entitled 'Iraq – the aftermath – military options', it stated: 'There is little policy discretion [in the first three to six months]. Once we enter Iraq, our commitments will be determined by events and by our obligations under the Hague and Geneva Conventions.'[31] The paper goes on to discuss the tension between getting out quickly and the aspirations of ministers, particularly of the prime minister, that Britain should take an 'exemplary' role in the reconstruction.[32] It might be described as a thin document, comprising as it does just six pages of A4. The fact that this note was produced on 4 March 2003, just over two weeks before the invasion, speaks volumes for the priority placed on the 'what now?' question.

Despite these serious problems, until mid-2004 it seemed that matters were going far more swimmingly in the British-run south – the Multi-National Division South East (MND SE) – than in the US-controlled Multi-National Division North (MND N). This was ascribed by the British to their innate skills in peacekeeping rather than to the perhaps more plausible reason that Basra and the south were predominantly Shi'a, and therefore willing to give the army (which certainly at first was considered a liberator) the benefit of the doubt. Accordingly, the British, as ever, were willing to step in and offer the benefit of their insight. The then head of the British army, General Sir Mike Jackson, suggested that a battalion of British paratroops be sent to the capital to help: 'Part of the problem was the posture of the US army in their tanks, in their Darth Vader kit with the wraparound sunglasses and helmets and flak jackets and everything else. There was no real rapport between the US army and the ordinary citizens.'[33] Another, larger, part of the problem at that time in the American sector was the slaughter of civilians in large numbers. The Americans were initially keen on Jackson's offer, but the British then withdrew it. This was a great disappointment to the 'paras' serving with my own unit on the ground in Basra at the time, who were looking forward to showing the Americans how to deal with contemporary urban warfare. One is given to wonder whether British paratroops, with their less than stellar history in winning over the people, would have been quite the best troops for that task.

Many of the techniques developed for Northern Ireland in which all soldiers such as myself were trained before and upon deployment – and which the British were keen to pass on to US colleagues – were unsuited to urban Iraq. Take, for example, 'satellite patrolling'. This was a technique that had been developed of splitting patrols – or 'multiples' – into several four-man 'bricks'. These satellite teams operated in unpredictable patterns. The idea behind this was that it was a prime concern for Irish Republican Army (IRA) operators to get away after they had conducted their mission or 'hit'. Satellite patrolling ensured that the IRA was never able to assess where another patrol would turn up. It was highly effective. The trouble is, as one highly experienced veteran of both Belfast and Basra has put it, 'the IRA's concern over escape routes and the urban geography of Belfast, both of which led to our satellite patrolling techniques, are not necessarily reproducible when confronting Islamist insurgents in Iraq'.[34] Such insurgents were perhaps concerned more with mounting one highly effective attack than getting away with many smaller 'hits'. Indeed, having a number of relatively small patrols instead of one larger 'multiple' might – probably would – serve to *invite* rather than deter attacks. Basra was not Belfast and Baghdad even less so.

'Like a flick of the switch'

Meanwhile, as the British congratulated themselves on their acumen, the Shi'a militias were building their own forces, with the active assistance of Iran. In military terms, the Shi'a militias were 'setting the conditions' for their own return to the military scene in a rather major way in 2004. The British, ensconced in the very heartland of the Iranian-influenced south, were not interested in interfering. Instead, they reasoned, the solution to the bubbling problem of the militias would be to co-opt them into the police.

This situation continued until one particular day, the day when the consequences of a failure to grasp the civic situation became all too apparent. As General Stewart, general officer commanding at the time, put it, 6 April 2004 was a day on which, 'like a flick of the switch', the British 'moved into insurgency overnight'.[35]

Traditionally, in their successful campaigns, the British regarded the police as an essential auxiliary arm. In Northern Ireland, the police had been the single most important security force. The army, for most of that campaign, had been strictly subordinate, in keeping with traditional ideas of civilian primacy. In Basra, the police were thought of as a ticket out of the disorder that was beginning to unfold around the army. The same approach was seen in Helmand. On the face of it, this was a sensible approach; but in practice it was heavily dependent on recruiting the right people. After all, even in Northern Ireland it took eight years to build the Royal Ulster Constabulary up to a point where it could assume primacy.[36]

From 2003, the 'new' police consisted of a loosely linked agglomeration of uniformed armed groups – also known as 'militias'. This was a deliberate decision by the British, in the hope that it would give them all a stake in the new government security structure. Unfortunately, no effort was made to win over the loyalty of these militias to the new structure, and neither were mechanisms established to oversee it. The uniforms they wore were police uniforms, supplied by Britain. In permitting this, the British had legitimized the militias. Worse, they had handed over to them the job of maintaining 'law and order'. The only Western journalist living in Basra, Stephen Vincent, spent some days embedded with the UK forces. He was not complimentary about their approach. In one particular article, he reported that half of the police, supported and trained by the British army, were members of radical religious parties. The result was ever-increasing oppression of what remained of the city's less visibly devout majority. 'Hundreds' of murders of former Ba'athists were taking place every month, and many of them were perpetrated by the same police. The British were turning a blind eye to all this.[37] Vincent was kidnapped and killed on 3 August 2005, three days after that article was published.

Serious crimes

The worst of the police teams that were initially supported and trained by the British was the 'Serious Crimes Unit' (SCU) – an apt name for what was a gang of rapists, torturers and murderers who took orders not from the governor but from Muktada al-Sadr. As the years drew on, the SCU became synonymous with terror for Basrawis, and more than a nuisance for the British. In September 2005, two Special Air Service (SAS) 'special forces' men were captured by 'police' and taken to the SCU headquarters. There they were seriously mistreated – beaten up. It is now apparent that an agreement had been made to hand them on to a militia unit, where they would be held as hostages. It is highly likely that their lives were saved by action on the part of their comrades the next day. A 'senior military officer' is quoted by the *Daily Telegraph*: '[The SCU] is one of the major organs that contribute to death squads in Basra. They dress in police uniform, use police cars, police pistols and will murder just for political or criminal gain. The SCU are a significant part of death squad activity in Basra.'[38] The officer did not say what everyone knew: that they were a British creation.

Throughout the army there was a belief that, by waving the Northern Ireland and Balkans wand over Basra, things would somehow turn out well in the end. Despite the rampant criminality and civic chaos in that city, for a few months it did look as if things might indeed turn out that way. The prism through which the British were looking at this problem and making those judgements was, of course, that of casualties among *themselves*. This early period was when the war was lost by the British. During the summer of 2003 and into 2004, they failed to build a government for the city that might forestall the radical Shi'a militias, which were gradually to take control over the next two years.

At the tactical level, the threat posed by the Shi'a militias was not fully realized at the operational level until General Stewart's 'light was switched on' that April morning in 2004. This was a major failure not only of intelligence, but of political calculation. It was clear to all that the militias were gradually gaining in strength. While the British army was 'the biggest and best gang in Basra', it had assuredly lost any political credibility in a culture where power is generally expressed in a robust and unequivocal fashion. After April 2004, both in Basra and, particularly, in the highly volatile town of Al Amara, combat was intense, with militias regularly probing British capabilities. The previously intermittent mortaring of bases became a serious, constant problem, causing casualties as well as sapping morale. Most damagingly, there was an exponential increase in the effectiveness of improvised explosive devices (IEDs). Armoured vehicles previously considered invulnerable were being smashed by a new kind of roadside bomb, the 'shaped charge' or 'explosively formed projectile' capable of penetrating the best armour the British had. It is now clear that Iran, where many of these devices were made, was asserting its presence in Basra far more aggressively. By 2005, the movement of British troops in the south of the country was far more restricted and dangerous, and casualties far heavier.

Short-termism and the 'six-month wars'

As the occupation proceeded, and as one UK brigade gave way to another every six baleful, casualty-filled months, the situation gradually, inexorably deteriorated. Battalions cycled through, finding themselves less and less capable of maintaining any real form of authority on the streets of Basra. The British MP and former soldier Adam Holloway observed a correlation between the optimism inherent in the six-monthly end-of-tour summaries: 'Every six months there was a little spike of hope upwards. This reflected the departures of senior officers out of Basra at the end of their six-month tours, as it had been left on a high note – as they presented the place in better condition at the end of their tour than at the beginning.'[39] In Afghanistan and Iraq, army units served six months in theatre.[40] Every British soldier knows the routine well: one spends two months learning the job, two months doing it and two months counting the days until you go home for 'tea and medals', as the saying goes. This is another legacy of Northern Ireland. Units on long tours in the 'Province' served two years – as did the headquarters units – and were posted there with their families. Short-toured units served six months. The six-month rotation was retained for Bosnia in the early 1990s and flows on today.

'Reconstruction'

What of reconstruction? There were civilian officials in Basra, but they rarely, if ever, got outside the wire after 2004, and worked remotely. The Foreign and Commonwealth Office (FCO) maintained a small consulate, and the Department for International Development (DfID) had some staff. Until 2008, when the Iraqi army took Basra, there was little useful coordination on the ground between civilian and military staff. 'Priority' tasks identified during the very early stages of the operational planning – involving rather important matters, such as the provision of water or electricity – were literally never carried out. For example, until 2009, the British had not undertaken the 'priority' task of surveying electricity substations. It might be protested that this was not the job of the army. That may well be true, in which case it might be better to remove it from a list of military priority tasks.

The same applied to rubbish collection and the provision of water. In any event, the army is replete with highly skilled experts in these matters – both regulars and reservists – who, at the very least, would have 'reach-back' access to the knowledge required. It should be stressed that there is no suggestion that the army should build or operate any of these systems, merely support the planning. Similarly, these were tasks that the US army certainly did not feel were beneath it. While the British generals complained about the lack of civilian assistance in both Afghanistan and Iraq, some American generals rolled up their sleeves and tried their best to improve the environment they occupied. General Peter Chiarelli sent the officers of the 1st Cavalry Division to Austin, Texas, to see how the services of a town are actually supplied – sewerage, trash collection, electricity supply. In that division's tour in a ferociously dangerous Baghdad in 2006–7, Chiarelli is often considered to have been the first of the US generals to have 'got it'.

From 2004 in Basra, however, the generals were faced with having taken on too much. No British officers were sent to Wigan or Croydon to see how cities were run. Why should they have been? After all, what can you do in six months? There were simply too few soldiers to have more than the slightest occasional effect on security at a very local level. More importantly, there was little will, political or otherwise, to do so. By the end of 2006, control of the city had essentially been lost to the Shi'a armed groups. In September 2006, Basra was to all intents and purposes the domain of one of them – the Jaish al-Mahdi (JAM), the military wing of the Office of the Martyr Sadr (OMS) – and there was only the most limited involvement of central Iraqi government. This was accompanied by a wholesale 'ethnic cleansing' of Sunnis from their areas, a process in full swing throughout the country. Basra's Sunni population had been 15 per cent at the beginning of the war (of a population of about a million). By 2007, this had reduced to an estimated 4 per cent.

In an almost unreported development, the town of Al Zubayr, with its mostly Sunni population, had lost about half of its people by 2007; many of them fled either to the northern areas of Iraq or abroad to Syria.[41] These bald figures hide hundreds of thousands of horrendous stories of fear, murder threats, quick flits in the night with all a family could carry, leaving everything else behind. Against this background of increasing chaos, a drifting and failing mission, the British, too, cycling through their six-month tours and with a constant drip of casualties, were looking for an exit. A thousand miles to the east, in Helmand, a war was ramping up that the army thought it might be able to win.

Running hot

It is against this background that General Sir Richard Dannatt, the chief of the general staff and professional head of the army, gave a much-touted interview to the *Daily Mail* in October 2006, a few months after Britain's torrid introduction to Helmand: 'We are running hot, certainly running hot. Can we cope? I say just.'[42] Dannatt had very sound reasons for expressing these views.

There are between ten and twelve deployable brigades in the British armed forces – new brigades are regularly formed and disbanded as required.[43] Given that each spends about six months in a given operational theatre, it follows that every brigade will cycle though an operational area roughly every four years – assuming an operation that requires brigade-level commitment. If there are two operational theatres, this cycle is reduced to two years. The consequence for soldiers is that they can expect to be away from home, in often dangerous environments (if they are in an infantry or other front-line unit, *highly* dangerous environments) for at least six months out of every twenty-four. Or so it might seem. For the army, the reality is far worse than that. Given the requirements for post-tour leave and pre-deployment training, every tour will take at least a year from every brigade. In other words, a soldier will either be preparing for, be engaging in or be recovering from an operational tour for one month out of every two. Dannatt was making the point that this was not a pace the army could sustain. Conducting two concurrent medium-scale operations – effectively beyond the limit of the UK military's declared capability – did not happen by accident. One senior British officer, Commodore Steven Jermy, has summed up the situation:

> Basra was a political and military defeat. But at least it allowed us, in very senior military eyes, a 'better go' at Afghanistan, in a rural province – Helmand – where the conventional strengths of UK forces, including its air power, could be brought to bear clear of the urban mire.[44]

After all, Afghanistan was 'the good war'. The decision was taken to find a presentable pretext to get out of Iraq.

CHAPTER 2

'Defeated, Pure and Simple'[1]

I don't know how you could see the British withdrawal from Basra in 2007 in any other light than as a defeat.

Colonel Peter Mansoor, BBC, *Secret Iraq*, October 2010

Roderick Lyne: *To what extent was this happening under the aegis of an overall strategic plan?*

General Salmon: *We were working to a set of objectives. There was no comprehensive strategic plan that I saw.*

Evidence of Major General Andy Salmon
to the Iraq Inquiry, 20 July 2010

How 7,000 soldiers turn into 200 patrolling riflemen

By 2006, the situation in Basra had deteriorated even further. When General Richard Shirreff took over command of the British presence in Basra in June 2006 there was, as he himself said, 'no security'. Of the force at his command of about 7,000 soldiers, only 200 were available for patrolling Basra's streets. The rest were engaged in securing their own bases in the city and outside. They were 'fixed to their bases ... this was not what I had been led to expect'.[2] This did not stop the army from attempting its framework patrols; but by now these were regularly greeted with rocket-propelled grenades and machine-gun attacks. The momentum, as he said, was 'going downhill'. Some 90 per cent of the attacks in and around the city were on British forces.

The UK force in Iraq varied very little in size over the period of the British occupation in late 2003 to 2007, being consistently in the range 7,000 to 8,000. The huge majority of service personnel in Iraq, and indeed later in Helmand, never left the safety of the highly secure bases in which they lived. There were a number of such bases. The largest in 2006 was at Basra airport, where the headquarters of MND SE was located. Commanded by a British major general (who, like everyone else, rotated through six-month tours), the MND was composed of large units of British, Dutch, Danish and Italian troops.

Headquarters, especially divisional headquarters, are rarely seen on television – and for good reason. Essentially they are very large, air-conditioned, open-plan offices, with literally hundreds of desks and computers manned by staff officers or non-commissioned officers. Here is where the entire mission is administered. Those desks host hundreds of pay, administration, supply, transport, logistics, communications and technical experts. There is what amounts to a large travel agency, which deals with travel in, around and out of theatre. A civil affairs section looks at tribes and local politics – some civilian advisers may be seen here. There are blocks of desks, often with little flags attached, where the liaison officers from various contributing nations have their place of work. The operational part of the organization, the sharp end (insofar as there is a sharp end at divisional HQ) employs dozens of officers planning and assessing operations. Then there is an entire area, usually sequestered, where another few dozen intelligence analysts and planners ponder maps and computer screens. Not too far away a cookhouse bustles with activity all day and much of the night, serving meals to the thousands of HQ staff and visitors. A fully manned media and 'communications' unit ensures that journalists are properly shepherded and informed.

Outside the air-conditioned headquarters building is what amounts to a medium-sized airport, complete with staff ranging from aircraft fuellers, by way of engineers and firemen, to baggage handlers. Briefing officers and sergeants give several talks a day to incoming troops about 'pissing clear twice a day' and driving carefully. So that 'the system' knows they are there, the new men and women are 'in-processed' by data-entry clerks, who might range from dedicated administrative staff to disgruntled Royal Marines who are unfit for their infantry duties. An entire unit of RAF staff exists to ensure the smooth exit of soldiers from theatre – the much-maligned 'movers' – checking them onto flights and ensuring that everyone is present and correct, weapons and all. The base is supplied mostly not by air but by land, with fleets – convoys – of trucks moving in and out of the base, day and night, driven by some of the bravest but least celebrated servicemen. Ammunition is handled and secured by specialists separately. The whole base, of course, needs to be guarded by a force of army and RAF soldiers. It is the army that provides the gate guards. The RAF has its own regiment dedicated to airfield security: they do not stoop to such mundane duties as guarding the gates – their job is patrolling the extended perimeter. Many of these service personnel at the headquarters work on a three- or four-shift system, so in some trades, for every soldier on duty there are two or three resting.

This arrangement is replicated at ever smaller levels: a brigade of between 4,000 and 6,000 troops, a battle group (usually under 1,000), a company (about 100 troops) – all have their headquarters. Other bases might have particularly important separate roles. One, for example, might contain a fully equipped field hospital, complete with doctors and nurses and ancillary administrative and security staff. Another might house a prison which needs to be staffed and guarded.

Particular specialist units, such as the military police, engineers, intelligence (to which I belonged) or special forces might be seen regularly outside the wire on their way to or from a particular mission. But they were rarely – if ever – patrolling and directly involving themselves in securing the mean streets of Basra. Exactly the same situation prevails in Helmand, where vast headquarters soak up very large numbers of men and women in uniform. As we will see, the question of numbers is utterly crucial to the failure of both the Basra and the Helmand operations.

Operation 'Spinbad'

The security situation deteriorated with every passing six-month deployment. By 2006, Basra was under the de facto government of a gaggle of Shi'a militias, the most formidable of which was Muktada al-Sadr's JAM. In September 2006, the British occupation forces made an attempt to wrench Basra and its neighbouring towns from the control of the militias. This was

Operation Sinbad. During planning of the operation, the assessment was rightly made that the militias' centre of gravity was the police, which contained what amounted to terrorist groups, completely outside the control of any form of government. Operation Sinbad began in September 2006 with some robust operations to retake police stations and neutralize the worst of the police, the notorious SCU.

Traditional counterinsurgency methods were to be used to reconstruct areas of the city, 'pulsing' into those areas for forty-eight hours at a time. Unfortunately, there were insufficient forces to hold any area of Basra for more than a few hours, often even then under severe fire. One soldier involved in these operations described a battalion-level operation to fight its way into the target area, build a playground complete with swings and slides, and fight its way out. That night the playground was dismantled, he said – with the exception of the slides, which then provided effective launch pads for rocket attacks against the local British base. A soldier's story perhaps, with a suitable element of almost baroque black humour; but nevertheless indicative of how some of those involved perceived the effectiveness of what they were doing. Operation Sinbad – or 'Spinbad', as it was quickly renamed by the soldiery, reflecting a less than total faith in its means if not its objectives – ended on 18 February 2007. The soldiers had succeeded, with help from the few Iraqi army units that had been trained, in reducing the appalling murder rate within the city. Their achievements were soon overwhelmed by the reality that Basra was still in the hands of the militias. The original intention of Sinbad was far wider than expunging a single police unit, although it did not succeed even in accomplishing that. The SCU was fully operational again by mid-2007.

On the day the operation ended, Tony Blair announced the largest drawdown of British troops, 3,000 of the total (in early 2007) of 7,000. This was to be accomplished over the coming months. The British presence in Afghanistan was being ramped up, and the few available operational infantry battalions, the cores of the battle groups, were needed elsewhere. If any moment can be described as the moment of defeat, this was it. As one senior officer with close involvement in Iraq put it to me: 'Having shifted in 2003 to Iraq, we pulled out at the decisive moment.'[3] A British senior officer summarized the situation: 'The Americans decided they were going to win; the British decided they were going to leave.'[4]

Deciding to win . . .

Early 2007 was also a decisive moment for the Americans. For several months, a national debate had been taking place concerning what to do about the military situation in Iraq – a situation that was obviously and publicly heading towards defeat. The decision was taken (against the advice of the Iraq Study Group, which had been appointed to advise on a way forward) to focus on a major effort to win the war. General David Petraeus had replaced General Casey as 'Commander Multi-National Forces Iraq'. Casey had done a good job, the consensus ran, but not good enough; he had to go. On 23 January 2007, President Bush announced the deployment of an extra five brigades (about 20,000 men) to stabilize the situation in the centre and north of the country. The Surge had begun. In February 2007, at exactly the time Operation Sinbad ended and hopes had faded for any kind of honourable British exit, the Americans began Operation Fardh al-Qanoon (Establish the Law). The aim of this was to provide for Baghdadis what the British had failed to provide for Basrawis: security and services. These efforts were not entirely without important British help.

The beleaguered brigades of Basra were not the only UK forces operating in Iraq. Two smaller, highly effective operations were being run from Baghdad in support of the US efforts there. The first (and better known) was that of the SAS Task Force Black. Teamed with the larger US Delta Force, it was decisively effective in the destruction (for the time being) of Al Qaeda in Mesopotamia. This operation was led very effectively and with a great deal of organizational innovation by General Stanley McChrystal. The second highly efficient UK effort was led by General Sir Graeme Lamb, responsible for the Strategic Engagement Cell. Again, this was an impressive operation, dedicated to convincing potentially insurgent tribes to fight for the government.[5] What these operations illustrate is the potential effect of the application of real, as opposed to notional, resources (in this case, superbly led, trained and equipped special forces) to a coalition effort at its strategic heart (in this case, Baghdad).

The Surge and the intense special forces operations coincided with that major terrorist formation in Iraq, Al Qaeda in Mesopotamia, overplaying its hand. It had offended local Sunni sensibilities, to say the least, by kidnapping local women for 'marriage' in some towns. And its tactics of suicide-bombing Iraqi civilians had not proved popular. Groups of Iraqi insurgents now turned on the Al Qaeda groups and began to attack them. While much of the evidence suggests that this was an indigenous initiative by Iraqis, US forces were very quick to take advantage of what amounted to a windfall. They began to pay these groups, which were given titles such as 'concerned citizens', and eventually became known as 'the Awakening'. It may well be, as is believed by some critics who are very familiar with Iraq, such as Robert Fisk and Patrick Cockburn, that the 'Awakening' was incidental rather than consequential to the new US tactics of population protection. It is also true, as those same critics propose, that much of the ethnic cleansing had played itself out. What cannot be denied, however, is that the US efforts dovetailed with the new developments and certainly acted to assist, at the very least, in achieving tangible progress in security for the people of Baghdad and other cities. The Americans, under their galvanizing new leader General David Petraeus, were willing to guarantee that the efforts they were making were to be enduring:

> Instead of telling Sunni sheikhs that we would leave soon and they must assume responsibility for their own security, we told them that we would stay as long as necessary to defeat the terrorists. That was the message they had been waiting to hear. As long as they perceived us as mere interlopers, they dared not throw their lot in with ours. When they begin to think of us as reliable partners, their attitudes began to change.[6]

In April 2008, the International Crisis Group, one of the world's leading conflict think-tanks – well known for its hard-hitting, well-researched reports, and by no means generally regarded as sympathetic to military sensitivities – reported: 'US field commanders displayed sophistication and knowledge of local dynamics without precedent during a conflict characterised at the outset by US policy misguided in its assumptions and flawed in execution.'[7]

In 1943, Rommel observed of the Americans that they were fast learners, when he first encountered them in the deserts of North Africa. In their first engagements with the German Afrika Korps at the battle of Kasserine Pass, the US army was essentially defeated. It did not take them long to learn from this defeat and to adapt:

In this they were assisted by their extraordinary sense of the practical and material and by their complete lack of regard for tradition and worthless theories . . . the Americans, it is fair to say, profited far more than the British from their experience in Africa, thus confirming the axiom that education is easier than re-education.[8]

Field Marshal Rommel might just as easily have been speaking of Iraq in 2007.

Strategy and the 'Surge'

The British had found themselves at serious strategic odds with the predominantly US corps under whose command they nominally fell. Some have sought to claim that the 'problem in the south was different'. It was indeed. It was far less complex than that faced by the admittedly much larger US forces in the north. Unlike the British, who had to look in only one direction (towards the Shi'a), the US troops found themselves caught between at least two mutually hostile groups who had spent the previous years engaging in ethnic cleansing, instigated – unwittingly – by the American invasion in the first place. In the south, due to British wilful ignorance of the problem, ethnic cleansing had played itself out. There was no significant Sunni 'problem', as surviving Sunni Basrawis, and indeed the great bulk of Christians, were now largely resident outside the south, and in fact outside Iraq.

The US efforts within Fardh al-Qanoon may have been incidental rather than causative, as experts such as Patrick Cockburn consistently maintain. At the very least they did not make the situation worse. Most importantly, they linked the political ends to the strategic means: the political objective involved securing an end to the civil war by providing space for negotiations to produce an effective government; the means, in the minds of the US military planners of the 'Surge', involved trying to hold the line while that happened. This, in turn, involved neutering the Sunni resistance and preventing further civil war. The long-term effectiveness of this approach is something for historians to judge, but at the very least, the ends (policy) and means (strategy) were coherently formed and articulated.

The search for a British way out

In the southern area of responsibility there was no prospect of any kind of surge. The strategy was explicitly of exit rather than victory. The search in the south was on for a way out. It was in January 2007, with the failure of Operation Sinbad, that the next commander, General Jonathan Shaw, was deployed to command MND SE. The British military chain of command was not going to commit further troops, and the Iraqis regarded the British as more of a hindrance than a help. The first step was to move the beleaguered battle groups from their remaining bases in the city of Basra to the large headquarters at the airport ten miles out of the city – and, it was thought, ten miles from immediate trouble. This was 'redeploying' rather than withdrawal. The operation was to be called 'Zenith'. The second step was to recast the problems of Basra as criminal in nature, rather than political. As Shaw put it to the Iraq Inquiry in December 2009, 'this was Palermo rather than Beirut'.[9] Putting aside the fact that Basra was larger than Palermo and Beirut combined, and that, as any resident of Palermo will attest, organized crime has political consequences, this was nothing more than self-delusion. The reality was that by 2007 JAM was the only militia, indeed the only real power (apart from the British) in town. It and the OMS dominated the social, political and religious landscape.

Almost as a reflection of the hopelessness of trying to take the city back, or, more realistically, of establishing some form of government control, it was decided to turn from a counterinsurgency to a 'counterterrorist' profile, with an emphasis on targeted killings and 'strike operations' – meaning raids and arrests. In terms of shifting the key political ground, this achieved nothing. A new solution was posited, this one undoubtedly from the Northern Ireland playbook: if we cannot beat these militants, the reasoning went, why not co-opt them into the political process?[10] After all, it had worked in Northern Ireland.

Salvation appeared in the form of one Ahmed al-Fartusi, commander of JAM in Basra, and fortuitously a prisoner of the British in their detention facility at Basra airport. Fartusi offered a deal. In exchange for the release of prisoners, he would abandon the military avenue and lay down his arms. From now on, his would be the way of peace. 'Prove your good faith and your influence,' said the British. 'Order a three-day ceasefire on the city.' He did so, and in July 2007, for three days, Basra was quiet. No rockets smashed into the bases, and patrols went out unmolested. The beginnings of a deal emerged. The JAM would not attempt to interfere with the withdrawal to the airport in the retreat from the city's bases – the (unintentionally) ironically named Operation Zenith. Nor would it attack the British base. If it kept to the agreement, seventy JAM activists would be released from British custody and the JAM would attempt to achieve its aims through the ballot box, in the form of a political party. The British had in mind the deal done with Irish terrorists, with whom they had become intimately familiar over thirty years of conflict. But there were some key differences. First, there was the vast background of political discussion, debate and international involvement with the closely monitored prisoner releases in Ulster. Second, and even more importantly, the British negotiators (who were not army officers) in Northern Ireland had an expert grasp of the people and issues with which they were dealing. This was not the case in Basra.

By 2006–7, British strategy was driving in at least three different directions. Whitehall was insisting that force levels in Basra be driven down, while British troops in southern Iraq were still pursuing operational success, and Britain's principal ally was beginning a 'surge'.[11] Meanwhile the priority was shifting to Helmand.

'Worst in class . . . '

By August 2007, the Americans had come to the conclusion that 'the British have basically been defeated in the South'.[12] The garrison of 500 troops in Basra Palace in Basra City were under what amounted to siege. The realization was growing that Basra was not the success the British had been boasting about to their American comrades two years previously. British rule in Basra had produced 'the systematic abuse of official institutions, political assassinations, tribal vendettas, neighbourhood vigilantism and enforcement of social mores, together with the rise of criminal mafias'.[13]

US senior officers were becoming decidedly less than enamoured of the continuing arrogance of Britain's military commanders. There was still a lingering sense of 'the British playing Greeks to the American Romans . . .

whatever truth there may have been during the Second World War, and there was precious little there ... there was certainly none now'.[14] One controversial, but apparently well-sourced newspaper report quoted a 'senior figure closely involved in US military planning':

> It's insufferable for Christ's sake. He [General Jonathan Shaw – the general officer commanding British forces in Iraq at the time] comes on and he lectures everybody in the room about how to do a counterinsurgency. The guys were just rolling their eyeballs. The notorious Northern Ireland came up again. It's pretty frustrating. It would be okay if he was best in class, but now he's worst in class. Everybody else's area is getting better and his is getting worse.[15]

A senior US officer 'familiar with General Petraeus's thinking' is quoted as saying, 'The short version is that the Brits have lost Basra, if indeed they ever had it . . . for a long time they have not been engaged in Basra.'

In contrast, an atmosphere of defeatism was developing. Mark Urban quotes an unnamed senior American officer who visited Basra and asked Shaw what he could do to help:

> He told me that he didn't need any help, that he had decided to withdraw his division to the airport where it would wait the decision to pull out. I looked at him and said 'well, thank you for your clarity. You at least told me exactly what you are going to do.'[16]

An SAS man put matters a little more bluntly: 'defeatist doesn't quite cover it'.[17]

Retreating with flags proudly flying

Following up on the expressed intention of withdrawing the division to the airport, the last stage of Operation Zenith was the most difficult – getting those men out of the besieged palace in Basra City. On 4 September 2007, the 4th Battalion, the Rifles (4 Rifles) handed over Basra Palace base to the Iraqi army and drove through the city to be reunited with the rest of the force at the airport. It all seemed to go so well. Indeed, as the

Warrior armoured infantry fighting vehicles drove for the last time from the last base at Basra Palace, large Union flags flew proudly from their aerials. No attacks were made on them. What the TV cameras did not show was that not only did JAM militiamen not attack the withdrawing armoured vehicles, but it was the JAM that in fact picketed the routes – that is, they placed units on the route of the retreat to ensure that it all went off well. The British were guarded by their enemies on their way out of Basra, like the defenders of some medieval castle being given safe passage by their victorious besiegers.

For decent Iraqi officials like Jalil Khalif, a police chief appointed by the central Iraqi government in late 2007, the situation was desperate, and the British were being blamed: 'They left me militia, they left me gangsters. They left me all the troubles in the world.'[18] As the British Foreign Secretary David Miliband correctly observed, 'We are not handing over a land of milk and honey.'[19]

An accommodation was arrived at, whereby, if British patrols wished to enter Basra City, they could do so only after agreement from the JAM. In December 2007, Basra was handed over to Iraqi government control. This was, of course, a fiction, as there was a three-way fight going on between the Fadhila (the faction of Basra Governor Wa'ili), the Supreme Iraqi Islamic Council, and, of course, the JAM. When General Barney White-Spunner stated at the Iraq Inquiry, 'Despite all our efforts Basra was not functioning all that well', there was more than a little truth in it.[20]

In accordance with the agreement reached with al-Fartusi, the prisoners were released in batches of between two and five men. Each signed a solemn oath, in front of a judge, to the effect that he would renounce violence. Al-Fartusi himself was released on the last day of the year, and the last of the JAM prisoners left the detention facility on 2 January 2008. Many of these were known to have killed British soldiers. In the classic 1934 British work on small-scale war, *Imperial Policing*, Major General Sir Charles Gwynn advises that, in situations like this, 'the release of prisoners is particularly dangerous as they, as a rule, emerge more hostile than ever, and often with new plans conceived during confinement'.[21] Few British soldiers present in Iraq had read Gwynn's book – much advertised by academics as embodying the origins of a supposed 'British way'. General Gwynn was right. On 6 January 2008, the airport base was subjected to the heaviest rocket assault of the war so far. By 31 January, attacks on the British were at pre-'accommodation' level.

'Post-accommodation' Basra

The moment when the British realized that they had made a quite horrendous mistake – the 'oops moment' – came in early February 2008, when two convoys, cleared in advance by the British with the JAM, came under attack. A charity worker was killed and an American Corps of Engineers colonel seriously injured. A journalist, Richard Butler, was kidnapped by the reconstituted Serious Crimes Unit of the Iraqi police. Only its headquarters had been destroyed; the unit itself was still very much in business and was still a hotbed of thuggery. Butler was forcibly released by units of the Iraqi army during Operation Charge of the Knights some weeks later.

In defence of the British approach, there are three factors that should be borne in mind. The first was that this war could not go on forever. At some point there would need to be some form of political agreement, and the Iraqis would at some stage need to govern and to secure the city and province 'for themselves'. The British could not hold these prisoners indefinitely, and there was no question of holding on in Basra indefinitely.

Second, the British were training up the Iraqi army. Indeed, two full divisions, the 10th and the 14th, were nearing the end of their training. As General Shaw said at the Iraq Inquiry three years later, 'success was to be defined in Iraqi terms not British ones'.[22] This process was working towards an Iraqi solution, not one imposed by the occupiers. On its own terms, there was a certain consistency to the tactic of 'accommodation'. The trouble was that the insurgents had a solution of their own in mind that did not involve the Iraqi government at all. The British narrative developed for the withdrawal of all British involvement from Basra was novel. It was important, goes the line, that the Iraqis should be forced to deal with Basra. A novel idea in counterinsurgency warfare was being developed, based around the concept of withdrawal to force the host government to do something, whether or not it was capable. The chief of the defence staff, Air Chief Marshal Sir 'Jock' Stirrup, put the new policy this way:

> My advice was that the best way of changing this [the political dynamic
> in Basra] would be to withdraw UK forces from the inside of Basra and
> force the Iraqis to deal with the problem themselves or accept the fact
> that they could not control their second largest city.[23]

The truth was, of course, that the British in Basra Palace were hopelessly
besieged, and no 'advice' one way or the other would change that.

Finally, the view was taken, and formally expressed, that the British
military presence was part of the problem rather than part of the solution,
given that it was attracting 90 per cent of attacks. Unfortunately, as events
were to bear out, they were being attacked *not* by 'criminals' resisting them
because they were British, but by insurgents fighting against those they
saw as visible representatives of the national government. This was, in fact,
a true insurgency or rebellion – a struggle for political control, not a
criminal turf war. Granted, the two are not necessarily mutually inconsistent terms: one of the most successful 'anti-mafia' efforts of the 1920s,
led by the legendary Colonel Cesare Mori, used methods not at all dissimilar to those now termed 'counterinsurgency', in order to rid Sicily of its
Cosa Nostra problem (until the Allies reinstated it in 1944).[24]

At the time that British policy was being developed and implemented,
in 2006–7, the Iraqi government was weak, although it was growing in
confidence as the US Surge began, slowly, to take effect. (It also received a
fillip from the combined factors of Al Qaeda in Iraq overplaying its hand,
and the relevant religious and ethnic cleansing having run its course.) The
Iraqi government, however, even with the assistance of the main effort of
the US armed forces, could not yet control its capital. Baghdad in 2007,
despite the Surge, was in a state of de facto civil war, with most of its people
living in daily fear. What the alternative would be if the Iraqis could *not*
come to the rescue of an abandoned Basra, Sir Jock Stirrup does not state.
There was no Plan B, only a Plan A. Plan A – forcing the Iraqis to take
charge – was in fact dictated not by ideas of 'removing the training wheels'.
Rather what drove it was the strategic overstretch occasioned by the British
blunder into Afghanistan; or, as the generals put it, 'rebalance in order to
gain strategic coherence in Afghanistan'.[25] In fairness to the generals, there
was an aversion to the domestic consequences of casualties sustained in an
Iraqi campaign that was popularly seen to have failed already.

It soon became apparent to the citizens of the city that there was indeed no Plan B. As the British abandoned Basra, the Iraqi state was not yet ready to retake it. The people soon felt the consequences of allowing the JAM the run of Basra. The kind of savage pressure to which the ordinary people of one of the Arab world's great cities were subjected is illustrated in a report from the *Independent* newspaper:

Shia gunmen attacked a group of students on a picnic. Their 'crime' was that young men and women were mixing together. As the police stood and watched, one gunman tore off the blouse of a female student. Two university guards who attempted to intervene were shot. The militia filmed their attack, put it on CDs, and distributed it at the market as a lesson, concentrating on the young woman's semi-naked state. She later committed suicide. Another student there at the time, Halima, left Basra after the attack and now lives in Nasiriya. 'They picked on the girl because they wanted to humiliate females. They beat us with their rifle butts and said next time it would be a lot worse,' recalled Halima. 'The police did nothing; we never saw the British. I could not stay in Basra after that.'[26]

As anyone serving in Basra during the British involvement knows, this kind of event was common. In December 2007 alone, more than forty women were raped and murdered for wearing non-Islamic dress.[27]

The importance of Basra

Despite the dominance of the militias, now complete with the withdrawal of the British army, the 'Palermo not Beirut' narrative held a seed of truth within it. But not in the way General Shaw and others were keen to stress. Basra is important beyond its obvious position as the capital of the Shi'a south and its proximity to Iran. It had another, more strategic, importance to the coalition effort, not fully realized because of the fragmentation of that effort as a whole. Its importance lay not in religion and its status as the largest Shi'a city, but in something more profane. Basra sits atop one of the world's largest oilfields.

Whoever controlled Basra province controlled potentially vast amounts of cash. When Muktada al-Sadr, leader of the OMS and the JAM, heard

that two of his commanders from Basra were visiting, he said: 'I smell
gasoline.'[28] There was huge scope for co-option of the oil: through stealing,
siphoning or hijacking it. Aside from the oil, there were plenty of other
opportunities for heavily armed militiamen to make money. For example,
500 lorries a day drove out of Umm Qasr, Iraq's only ocean port. Each
driver was forced to pay $30 to militiamen to enter and leave the port. This
alone yielded the militia's treasury $30,000 in cash every day.[29]

Then, of course, there were the thousands of stolen vehicles smuggled
into the port (or indeed unloaded onto boats offshore) from the United
Arab Emirates. Iraqi authorities later estimated that about 80 per cent of
the JAM's money came from Basra during this period. Much of that
money was itself, of course, in the normal corrupt way, channelled to
various mini-warlords; a great deal of it, however, went to support the
JAM/OMS cause and, to a lesser extent, the other militias, the governor's
Fadhila militia and the Supreme Iraqi Islamic Council. Materials were
being bought, Iranian and Hezbollah trainers needed to be paid, and the
training camps in Iran needed extensive subvention. Attacks on British
and Iraqi forces were not cost free: the price of a single 107mm rocket was
about $450. Salvos into the base at the airport were composed of up to
twenty such rockets, and might therefore cost about $10,000. Those and
other weapons, supplied by the Iranian Al Quds force, needed to be smuggled over the border (usually by Marsh Arabs). They were then sold to
militia groups. The British could move fairly freely over Basra province
outside the city. But given that it was only with the permission of the JAM
that they could pass through Basra itself to get to the border areas, there
was little they were going to be able to do to stop this flow.

So Basra was indeed a vast centre of criminal activity. In a society like Iraq
in 2007, this was not saying very much – the government was closely involved
in levels of corruption unseen for generations in the West, even in some of
the more easy-going countries of southern Europe. This was no Palermo,
where at least people can generally walk the streets in peace and go about
their business. The influence of the financial resources raked in daily by the
JAM and the other groups went far beyond supporting the whims of a few
godfathers, as the current narrative would have us believe. A quiet Basra
meant, as one senior British officer put it to me, the huge Sadr City area of
Baghdad in flames: insurgency in Baghdad was funded by activity in Basra.

This was not fully appreciated by General Petraeus and the American command, now fully focused on a 'population-centred' strategy for Baghdad and the towns around it. They had no rubric in the early months of 2008 for dealing with Shi'a militia, which were regarded as a minor irritant, compared with the priority coalition focus on Al Qaeda in Iraq. But as far as the Iraqi prime minister was concerned, the Shi'a militias were at least as much of an existential threat to his fragile government as the Al Qaeda terrorists. Their very existence undermined the most basic principle of a government's monopoly of force. He was determined to deal with them.

As the Americans focused on Baghdad, and the British negotiated their permissions from the JAM to traverse Basra on their patrols, Prime Minister Maliki was planning his own solution to the militia rule in Basra – Iraq's second city and, as matters stood, an existential threat to his authority. Operation Charge of the Knights, the defining battle for Basra of the entire war, began on Monday, 25 March 2008. Neither the British nor the Americans had significant notice of this. Even if they had known, the divisional commander, General White-Spunner, was away on his mid-tour break, skiing in Germany. On 23 March 2008, Prime Minister Maliki arrived in Basra and gave his instructions, which came as something of a surprise to all involved, including the Iraqis.

Operation Charge of the Knights

When the Iraqi army began operations almost immediately, the British were still hunkered down at the airport. They provided very little direct support in the ensuing battle – although they did assist with reconnaissance and medical aid. For the first time, the British-trained Iraqi army divisions went into battle. An entire brigade of the 14th Division, mostly locally recruited, was mauled by the JAM in the first week. On 2 April, there was a coordinated counter-attack by the 1st Iraqi Division, heavily supported by US MITTs (embedded Military Instruction and Training Teams) and 'corps' assets such as Apache helicopters based in Baghdad. At this point, some British elements were permitted by London to join the battle. The JAM were swept away. There was a pause in the operation, during which the Iraqi government and the local sheikhs met and agreed that the JAM's days as a governing 'authority' in Basra were over.

It was at this point that Prime Minister Maliki realized that the British had been misrepresenting the situation. Like many leaders of weak governments, he had been poorly briefed by his own, and indeed by the British and American, advisers. This was no gang-ridden set of slums. Basra had been dominated by the OMS under its military wing, the JAM, and other groups violently opposed to any notion of democratic government, even the form seen in Iraq. Maliki blamed the British for allowing the situation to deteriorate so far, and was particularly incensed by the deal struck with the militias. When the commander of the British brigade visited him at his operational headquarters during the battle, the officer was left waiting outside. Maliki never trusted the British again.

Little of this was lost on the British troops holed up inside the well-fortified base at the airport. There is no doubt whatsoever that, on the part of the soldiers, there was a real sense of shame, especially when the Americans arrived. There is no doubt that in this battle the soldiers wanted to get out and do their job – which they would undoubtedly have done brilliantly. After all, this was real combat. As matters turned out, when the US Marine Corps' MITT teams appeared in their Humvees, so a British officer present at the time told me, 'People came out of their houses and cheered – the Americans have arrived! At that moment it became clear to the Iraqi commander General Mohan that the coalition weren't the problem in Basra, it was the militia, and the British should have been helping much more.'[30]

In all the dismal years of Britain's presence in Iraq, no real account had been paid to what the people of Basra actually wanted. The consequence was that the people had been lost long before the city had been sold to the JAM. James Hider of *The Times* reported the views of some Basrawis in April 2008, just after the end of the first Basra phase of Charge of the Knights:

'I think the British troops were the main reason that militias became very powerful,' complained Inas Abed Ali, a teacher. 'They didn't fight them properly and, when they found themselves losing in the city, they moved out to the airport and chose to negotiate with the militias and criminal groups as if they were legal.'

'The British Army had no role in Basra,' Rahman Hadi, a coffee shop owner, said. 'We haven't seen any achievements by them in the streets of Basra. I don't know why their troops didn't respond to the acts of these militias for long years, after seeing all the suffering that Basra people went through.'[31]

A civilian attached to the British diplomatic mission in Basra confirmed what real Basrawis had been fearing and waiting for:

> People in Basra with militiamen and drug dealers living next door were not willing to report it to us, why should they? When 25,000 of their own troops landed on Basra, then they acted, and the Iraqi Army dealt with those criminals in their own way.[32]

What the people wanted was what they wanted anywhere. Political freedom and elections are a simple abstraction in the absence of safety in which to work and live. When the British ceded what had been a relatively liberal and potentially extremely prosperous city to groups of religious fanatics, the people gave up any sense of trust. And they were never to recover it: James Wither, a professor and retired senior British army officer summarized the situation very well: 'The military's failure to provide a secure environment for the local population represented a strategic failure for the UK in Iraq.'[33] For the local population, the penny dropped when a robust operation – led by their own army but crucially and visibly supported by the Americans – swept away the militia terrorists. That it was *not* the coalition (i.e. the British) force, which was hunkered down at the airport just along the road, was all too apparent and in no way surprising.

Endgame in Basra

For the British, the remaining year in Basra wound on, with the usual desultory casualties – although by now very few to enemy action. During Charge of the Knights, the British brigade, under Brigadier Julian Free, had changed the UK military profile very quickly and effectively to adjust to the new situation. The effort was focused now on providing the training and operational support, embedded now, that was necessary for the new Iraqi army to provide much-needed security.

What was significant about the deployment of Brigadier Free and his commander, General Andrew Salmon, was not so much its effect on the overall Basra campaign – the Iraqis had dealt with that with Charge of the Knights. Rather it was the approach taken to his work by Major General Salmon, a Royal Marine, which he has called 'holistic'. He was keen to ensure that planning was not a case of informing civilians of the plan and then asking what they were going to do to help. Unlike other commanders in both Afghanistan and Iraq, if there were insufficient civilians to complete a task, he did not complain about them: he assigned soldiers to assist them. At the Iraq Inquiry, a year and a half after his deployment, he was asked whether the military had been used to do things that might better have been done by civilians:

> Well, we didn't live in a perfect world and we learned a lot over the six years of the campaign that, you know, delivering in quite a violent scenario demands short-term things to be done and you need considerable amounts of military there to enable that to happen. Some agencies are going to be able to work in that environment and some aren't, partly because of their training, their background, their skill sets; also partly because of different attitudes to risk and the protocols that exist around that issue.[34]

The kind of work he is talking about was, for example, a survey of electrical substations. This was essential in order to determine the nature and extent of the work required on the electrical infrastructure. This, along with many other key tasks, had been identified six years before in the operational planning as 'priority one'. Clearly, with a far better security situation, the general could afford to use troops in matters that should have been done years before. The question remains: why had work that had been identified as 'priority one' in operational planning not been done after six years? The answer lies in the six-monthly cycles: anything that might take longer than six months was simply not done. The reasoning was simple but ruthless. There was no credit in something that would be finished after one's time was up; and anyway, your successors may simply not follow up your task.

Missed opportunities were not confined to the building of expensive infrastructure. The Marsh Arabs, who occupied the critical border areas with Iran north and east of Basra, had been the main conduits for the import of Iranian weapons. Instead of building effective relationships with them in order to control these imports, the British had focused on sending large formations to the border, which was ineffective. In the latter half of 2008, in a simple and quick operation, British troops immunized the Marsh Arabs' cattle against tuberculosis (TB). At a stroke, this reduced the incidence of child mortality among the Marsh Arabs – predominantly caused by cattle-borne TB – by 50 per cent. As one senior officer present in Iraq at the time said to me: 'It is incredible that this had not been done before, as the Marsh Arabs were the only people who could effectively control what came through the border.'[35] Building positive and, above all, mutually beneficial and long-lasting working relations with the Marsh Arabs at an earlier stage might have significantly improved the campaign's chances of success. We will see the same lack of a wider approach to the needs and wishes of local people, and indeed to the campaign as a whole, in Helmand.

An overall strategic plan?

There was little sense of that true 'campaign approach'; instead there ensued a series of six-month urban wars. Why this should be the case from the strategic perspective was clarified by General Salmon's testimony to the Iraq Inquiry.

> *Roderick Lyne*: To what extent was this happening under the aegis of an overall strategic plan?
> *General Salmon*: We were working to a set of objectives. There was no comprehensive strategic plan that I saw.[36]

There was no overall strategic plan, after six years. The head of the PRT in Basra in 2006, the very experienced civilian post-conflict expert Mark Etherington, asked in his evidence to the Iraq Inquiry a question that, with the benefit of hindsight, seems obvious now:

> how . . . did UK – a country with considerable experience of conflict and which prided itself on its grasp of counter-insurgency – drift into a position where it had no effective joint civil–military plan in Basra until 2008, five years after assuming responsibility for the city?[37]

This was not a failure of politicians or funding. It was a fundamental failure of generalship and political leadership. As a result, as one leading academic expert on Iraq, Dr Eric Herring, told the UK Parliamentary Select Committee on Defence: 'UK forces tended to be (often uncomprehending) spectators, occasional protagonists and only rarely the centre of power and legitimacy.'[38]

When the end did come, it was not to the Iraqi army that Basra airport base was handed over on 31 March 2009, but to elements of the US army under Major General Michael Oates. With the exception of a few mostly naval assets training the Iraqi navy at Umm Qasr, the British military role in Iraq was at an end.

As a final humiliation, in July 2009 the Iraqi parliament, through 'procedural delay', failed to renew the mandate for the few mostly naval British personnel to stay in Iraq. They had to be withdrawn until parliament got around to dealing with it.

The campaign had cost the lives of 179 British soldiers; the limbs, eyes and mental health of many hundreds more; and literally (since no one bothered to count them) countless Iraqis killed and maimed. It cost something else, too. In 1942, when his battle staff told him that rescuing the remnants of the British and New Zealand divisions from Crete might cost many ships, Admiral Cunningham replied: 'It takes three years to build a ship, but three hundred to build a reputation.' In 2007, a senior American officer is reported to have said that 'there will be a stink about this [Iraq] that will hang around the British military'.[39]

The army was now to begin to try and recover that long-built reputation in Afghanistan. Some have alleged that there was more to it than this. Afghanistan was to be the 'good war' that was to make up for the perceived defeat in Basra – especially in American eyes. General Sir Richard Dannatt, the chief of the general staff and head of army at the time, said as much himself:

> there is recognition that our national and military reputation and credibility, unfairly or not, have been called into question at several levels in the eyes of our most important ally as a result of some aspects of the Iraq campaign. Taking steps to restore this credibility will be pivotal – and Afghanistan provides an opportunity.[40]

There is no doubt that this was a common view held by many, including, I am ashamed to say, myself. For the army, though, there may have been an even deeper significance: 'Getting into a fight became the purpose in itself.'[41]

In written evidence to the UK Parliamentary Foreign Affairs Committee the former UK ambassador to Afghanistan, Sir Sherard Cowper-Coles, stated:

> the then Chief of the General Staff, Sir Richard Dannatt, told me in the summer of 2007 that, if he didn't use in Afghanistan the battle groups then starting to come free from Iraq, he would lose them in a future defence review. 'It's use them, or lose them.'[42]

This comment was later strongly denied by Dannatt. If either the statement or the sentiment is true, it is a far more sinister development than the obvious 'tail wagging the dog' analogy. It comes perilously close to pure militarism, which may be defined as military institutions placing their own survival above the interests of the state they are formed to serve. A senior naval officer, Admiral Chris Parry, has stated that Helmand was regarded by generals as the army's 'Falklands Moment', referring to the war of 1982, which is generally thought to have proved the utility of the Royal Navy and saved it as a 'blue-water' world-class force.[43] There was a general feeling and a mood in the Ministry of Defence that the army's moment had come and that the future should be cast in their image. What the Falklands had done for the Royal Navy, Helmand would do for the army.

CHAPTER 3

'Where's Helmand?'

Her Majesty Queen Elizabeth the Second has sent me and my soldiers all the way from England to help you in your fight against the Taliban.
Colonel Greville Bibby, to a group of
Afghan tribal leaders, 18 August 2009

I think we just had not really spotted what it would be like in the Pashtun south.
Evidence of Sir Robert Fry, assistant chief of the defence staff,
to the House of Commons Public Administration
Committee, 16 September 2010[1]

Imperial legacies

On your way out of the Joint Command and Staff College at Shrivenham, the intellectual home of the armed forces, just to the left of the main doors, is a painting that is striking in its contemporary relevance and redolence. Lady Butler's *Rescuing the Wounded under Fire in Afghanistan* shows the aftermath of a brief and evidently ferocious fire-fight somewhere in an Afghan desert during the Tirah campaign, one of Britain's larger interventions on the North West Frontier in 1897. A trooper from a cavalry unit dismounts, grabbing his wounded comrade as his horse rears. Another cavalryman, a white headband now having the look of a bandana, is racing away, a wounded man slung across his horse. In the distance we see a group of white-clad Afghans, swords raised as they close in – charging and almost audibly yelling taunts – on yet another soldier, who raises his hand as if pleading with the viewer. No rescuer rides for him. This kind of fight is deep in the historical/genetic make-up of the British soldier, sailor and airman, each in his domain. When I served in Helmand, the infantry unit responsible for guarding our base wore shirts with the following stanza from Kipling's 'Young British Soldier' emblazoned on their backs:

When you're wounded and left on Afghanistan's plains,
And the women come out to cut up what remains,
Jest roll to your rifle and blow out your brains
An' go to your Gawd like a soldier.

There are, of course, several subtexts in this partly imagined history. This, for the British, was the land of the 'Great Game'. It was here that the army had stood at the edges of empire and faced down the Russian bear, while at the same time pacifying the fierce Pathans. For those twenty-first-century Pathans (or in the south of Afghanistan, more properly Pashtuns), of course, the British were simply sticking to their role as the regular invaders of their country. On three previous occasions they had entered Afghanistan un-invited, and, from the Afghan perspective, had been ejected on each occasion with ignominy. First had been the war of 1839–42. In this, the greatest of all British military disasters of the nineteenth century, a major British force entered Afghanistan in 1839. After a series of catastrophic miscalculations a force of 4,500 British soldiers and 12,000 civilian followers set out to return to British India through the Khyber Pass on 1 January 1842. A few days later Dr William Brydon, the sole survivor of the column, managed to reach safety at the British fort at Jalalabad. A very few prisoners were returned by their Afghan captors later that year. The follow-up 'Army of Retribution', which did exactly what it had been formed to do, is less well recalled by Afghan and Briton alike. In the war of 1878–80, despite a rather severe setback at the battle of Maiwand, the British prevailed. And then in 1919, when the Afghans tried to invade what is now Pakistan, the British managed a victory of sorts – though even with the aid of modern weaponry it was a close-run thing.

That this perceived story of almost constant British defeat was not entirely true does not in any way matter: the Afghans of the south believed it.

Unfortunately, once again, as in Iraq, the British had completely failed to appreciate that the 'liberal myth' of their essential beneficence was not equally appreciated by the people whose land they were to enter uninvited.

This time around, the British had been in Afghanistan since 2001. A relatively small British presence had secured Kabul, and for some time operated a PRT in the relatively benign northern province of Mazar i Sharif. Now, in 2006, a new British 'reconstruction' presence was to be set up in the southern province of Helmand, along with an accompanying military force. The operation was to be called Herrick IV, and it was to be part of an overall NATO expansion into the south, the so-called 'Phase 3' deployment. (Herrick was the operational title, generated randomly by computer, for all UK military efforts in Afghanistan.) Given that Helmand was said to be 'Taliban heartland' it promised to be a tougher mission.

Helmand and the 'Maiwand thing'

It was only towards the end of 2009 that the British government finally settled on an apparently consistent and settled *casus belli*: 'Our objective is clear and focused; to prevent al Qaeda launching attacks on our streets and threatening legitimate government in Afghanistan and Pakistan.'[2] Whether the objective is either clear or focused is a matter for discussion elsewhere. What certainly is true is that few ordinary soldiers could articulate it. Initially there was little understanding, even at the highest levels, of what the British were doing in Helmand in the first place. The commander of the International Security Assistance Force (ISAF) in southern Afghanistan at the time, General David Richards, said:

> we were told the Canadians had asked to do Kandahar and that we would go to a place called Helmand. And I thought, 'Where's Helmand? That's not very important. Kandahar is what matters.' And I've never yet had a good reason given me why that decision was taken.[3]

In fact, the decision had been taken at a meeting held by Ministry of Defence officials in Ottawa with their Canadian counterparts in 2005. The Canadians had volunteered to 'take' Kandahar, the key *sine qua non* of the

Pashtun heartlands. Richards, who was to become chief of the defence staff in 2010 and accordingly professional head of the British armed forces, was also distinctly ambivalent as to whether the British army was right for the job. With considerable reflective insight, he commented later:

> They [the Canadians] would have gone slower at it than the somewhat over-energetic rather macho approach the British took – partly with little alternative, given their troop numbers then you could have had a calmer and perhaps healthier situation . . . and you would have avoided the Maiwand thing.[4]

'The Maiwand thing'. Helmand may not have been important for the British generals. But for Afghans, Helmand is very important indeed. Not far from Gereshk, Helmand's second largest town, just across the border in Kandahar province, is the hamlet, now rather flyblown, of Maiwand. Here, in 1880 (the year after Isandlwana, where a British brigade was defeated by Zulus), an Afghan army under Ayub Khan defeated a full British brigade.[5] Some British commentators have presented this defeat as the victory of a force outnumbered many times by thousands of religious fanatics. This is not the case; the British were beaten by superior tactics and military art.[6] For Afghans, the battle of Maiwand has all the resonance of Agincourt; with its legends of the lady Malelai removing her green veil and exhorting the soldiers on to victory, there is also more than a touch of an Afghan Joan of Arc. We have forgotten much of this history, if we ever knew it. Helmandis certainly have not. This, then, was the heartland of Afghan pride and patriotism. Historian and journalist David Loyn has worked and travelled in the country since the very early days of the Taliban in 1994. He relates that the Taliban even today sing songs of the battle: 'My lover, if you are martyred in the battle of Maiwand, I will make a coffin for you from the tresses of my hair.'[7] More prosaically, an ex-Taliban minister and ambassador, Mulla Abdul Salam Zaeef, expressed views that are widely shared:

> Another strategic mistake was to allow Great Britain to return to the South, or Afghanistan in general. The British Empire had fought three wars with Afghanistan, and their main battles were with the Pashtun tribes of Southern Afghanistan. They were responsible for the split of the Pashtun

tribal lands, establishing the Durand Line. Whatever the reality may be, British troops in Southern Afghanistan will be measured not in their current actions but by the history they have, the battles that were fought in [the] past. The local population has not forgotten, and many believe, neither have the British. Many of the villages that see heavy fighting and casualties today are the same that did so some ninety years ago.[8]

In his book *A Million Bullets*, James Fergusson puts the case more pithily: 'To the Afghan mind the return of the Brits looked like an Allah driven invitation to a punch up. Round four of a conflict between two nations that had been at it intermittently for 170 years.'[9]

The unfortunate fact was that the British *had* forgotten their history. They would be no more welcome here than if they had returned in force to the west of Ireland in the 1950s, proclaiming peace. Afghans are far more conscious of their history than Europeans today. They have very long memories. The writer Victoria Schofield recalls an incident during the Second World War. Some British officers had gone to visit villages in the North West Frontier Province: '"Have you seen any foreigners lately?" they asked the local inhabitants. They were rather taken aback when the reply came: "Yes, two Italians".' Italy was then at war with the British Empire and there were concerns that there might be German or Italian agitators or spies in the region. This could be serious. Fortunately, 'Further investigation revealed that they were referring to two Jesuit priests on their way to Peking in the Seventeenth Century.'[10]

The problem of governance

None of this might have mattered, of course, had all the other factors been right. After all, for the previous years, American special forces had based themselves happily and generally peacefully at a base near the capital of Helmand, Lashkar Gah. The British brigade HQ was to be based in the compound of the PRT in the town itself. On the edge of the city cemetery, and guarded by a company of Spanish-speaking National Guard, the personnel of the PRT had rarely ventured out to bother anyone, and no one – Taliban or otherwise – had ventured to bother them. Very few casualties had been sustained by US forces in the years prior to the British entry. But then Americans generally had had a far happier history in Helmand than had the British. Most of the province's agriculture, since the fall of the Taliban devoted to opium, was based around an irrigation system designed by the Americans in the 1950s in one of the largest and most successful examples of US foreign aid in their history. This system was dependent on the huge Kajaki dam, itself built by the same engineers who had constructed the Hoover Dam in Colorado. In other words, much of the useful infrastructure in the province had been built by Americans. The rest had been constructed by the Soviets. On the face of it, without any further or better information, one could have been forgiven for saying that this might be a three-year mission with no shot fired. This, of course, is exactly what UK Defence Secretary John Reid did say. What is less readily recalled is the pained expression of the Afghan general standing alongside him once he realized what Reid had said. At its higher levels, the British had no further or better information. In the words of the chief of joint operations of the time, 'We knew very little about Helmand Province.'[11]

Give or take a thousand square miles or so, Helmand is the same size as Bosnia and about two and a half times the size of Wales. This in itself is unimportant. Far more important is the fact that its population is probably (no one knew then and no one knows now) somewhere over a million – slightly smaller than that of Kosovo. When British forces entered Bosnia and Kosovo in the mid- and late 1990s as 'peacemakers', they were part of forces about 60,000 strong. It is important to bear in mind also that both Bosnia and Kosovo were essentially benign environments, at least for foreign forces. Not a single peacekeeping soldier was killed in combat in either place after the entry of NATO forces. Furthermore, it does not take a geographer to point out that the Balkans are in Europe, implying short lines of communication. Being European countries, there was a strong infrastructure – most importantly from the military perspective, good roads. In Helmand, outside Lashkar Gah there are few metalled roads, and those that exist are easily cut or blocked. The population is dispersed into small settlements, most of which are little more than a few clustered 'compounds', as the soldiers call them; others might simply call them houses. The British deployed a brigade of 3,300 to Helmand, with limited transport capability, long lines of communication and almost no local awareness.[12]

Then there is the rather distasteful element of local governance. The Taliban had brought an end to the 'days of the gun' that had prevailed from

1992 to 1996 and had enforced their version of the law effectively. The roads were safe to drive on, and there was almost total security from the previous chaotic Hobbesian world of the warlords and gangs who had run amok in Helmand and the rest of the country.

After 2001, the province had been taken by one of those warlords, Sher Muhammed Akhundzada – known to foreigners as 'SMA'. He, too, kept some form of order, based not, as with the Taliban, on religious and national sentiment, but rather on money and patronage. No one could describe SMA as a man dedicated to the principles of democratic partici-pation and human rights. Moreover, there had been the matter of the nine tonnes of opium allegedly found in his house. There are two sides to every story: SMA asserts to this day that he had impounded this devilish substance and was on the verge of handing it over to the authorities. Those very authorities (essentially the US Drug Enforcement Agency and its Afghan proxy force) say that he was carrying on the family business started by his uncle to assist in funding his fight against the Soviets. His was a seriously powerful family, commanding respect. SMA's uncle, Qasim Akhundzada, had indeed led thousands of mujahedin against the Soviets. In view of later events, it was interesting that his major battle, a defeat, was fought in Musa Qala in the north of the province in 1983, against a full brigade of Soviet soldiers. In 2007, it took a full brigade of British and American troops to prise it back from the Taliban, many of whom had at one time worked for SMA. James Fergusson, in his fine book *Taliban*, says that many of the fighters against the British were the *same people* who had fought the Soviets.[13] Musa Qala was a name with which the British and American forces were to become very familiar over the next few years.

Either way, with the British leading the counternarcotics effort – each nation had taken on an aspect of 'nation building', and the British had volunteered to 'take' counternarcotics – it was something of an embarrass-ment for them that this well-known drugs baron, or 'narcokhan', was running 'their' province. In late 2005, they prevailed upon President Karzai to get rid of him, much to American displeasure (and indeed Karzai's, as SMA was close to both the president and his brother). What the Americans saw and the British refused to recognize was that this man was the devil you knew. SMA himself has said that it was with regret that he had, in his own words, sent 3,000 of his men to the Taliban as he could no longer afford to keep them.[14] The only Western journalist who worked in Helmand without the protection of the British was Jean Mackenzie, the head of the well-regarded Institute for War and Peace Reporting (IWPR) agency, which trains local journalists to cover their own countries. She takes a firm view:

> The British should not have tried to impose their views without knowing what was going on . . . SMA was unsavoury but effective. Although it is true that he took 75 cents on the dollar of 'taxes' the population in general saw something out of the remaining 25. When he went, his men were left with lots of weapons and nothing to do. It was a field day for the Taliban.[15]

A senior British officer closely involved at the time told me that removing SMA 'was the key act which created the chaos'.[16]

To anyone with the slightest acquaintance with the history of UK involvement in Helmand, the divergence of approach between the UK and the US is plain. It continues. From the start, the US took the entirely pragmatic approach that some people were simply not going away. The obvious (but not the sole) example was SMA, as described above. The British approach might essentially be summed up in the phrase 'we want nothing to do with such people'. This approach continues, although the realization is growing within the British government that a sniffy distaste sometimes has to be overcome if advances are to be made in the larger mission. Once again, as in Basra, the British found themselves trapped by the 'area of responsibility' syndrome, where larger strategic issues were subsumed by local questions of convenience or, indeed, in Helmand, abstract principle.

Partly because of this approach, the British counternarcotics agenda worked directly against its military effort in the world centre of opium production. On occasion, British soldiers in villages would find themselves literally stumbling upon opium, which represented the only income the community was going to earn for the year. Invariably they were instructed to impound it for destruction – a noble victory for the anti-drugs mission, but a serious setback for soldiers trying to build positive relations with those same villagers. Afghan farmers asked why their livelihoods should suffer because the British could not control their own youth. The situation was made worse by the fact that the US was perceived to be undermining British policy. Jean Mackenzie has strong views as to the wisdom of this approach:

> spearheading counternarcotics without having an earthly clue what they were doing while being undermined by the US who were still in bed with warlord drug dealers. Being lead drug nation *and* Helmand security 'responsible nation' was the worst possible combination of circumstances.[17]

SMA's replacement as governor was one Engineer Daoud, a small-scale Helmand landowner – and by all accounts a decent man. Daoud was related by marriage to the minister for narcotics. The British took the view that, since they were in the business of building 'good governance', Daoud was the right sort of man. From that early perspective they may have been right. But from the military perspective – and any realistic, more traditional, truly pragmatic assessment based upon containment – this was a crucial mistake. His successor, Governor Waffa, was worse – an unreconstructed tribal satrap. His unfortunate combination of autocracy and ineffectuality did not assist the situation later in the mission.

Time spent in reconnaissance is never wasted

So goes the famous military saying. It was wasted in Helmand. For, aside from US involvement, there was a good deal of British knowledge within certain circles about Helmand before the collision of the 3rd Battalion the Parachute Regiment (3 Para) with the province in 2006. Indeed, the first serious ground action fought by any UK–US coalition force against Al Qaeda was in the far south of the province in November 2001, before the Northern Alliance took Kabul or the famous battles of Tora Bora. An SAS regimental task group, made up of a tactical HQ, A Squadron and G Squadron, raided a guerrilla base on the slopes of Koh-i-Malik mountain, on 22 November 2001. This was a very intense five-hour battle, fought without effective air support, during which the SAS killed nearly a hundred enemy combatants and suffered several serious casualties itself. This battle followed a number of weeks of raiding against Al Qaeda and narcotics targets in southern Helmand. The commander of the mission was one Lieutenant Colonel (as he then was) Ed Butler.

Over the next three years, SAS forces operating with an Afghan counternarcotics force (which they trained and mentored) conducted frequent raids into the province, closely coordinated with the ISAF-led PRT effort, which aimed to assist in creating the conditions for the building of a non-narco-based economy, while improving the political link between the province and the new government in Kabul. These part-time SAS efforts were later reinforced, in 2004, by the New Zealand SAS, which patrolled northern Helmand in support of the US PRT efforts. During this period, the SAS teams and the US PRT gained a close familiarity with the province and its people, via a combination of 'hearts and minds'-focused patrolling and precise counternarcotics raiding, which focused on the traders/businessmen rather than the poor farmers. They supported their missions with a field hospital, complete with specialist staff (as well as the occasional intelligence specialist), who offered medical assistance to Afghans – a programme known as MEDCAP.

As one British special forces soldier who was extensively involved in these operations told the journalist James Fergusson, this approach was said to have won over many Helmandis: 'the people would find us through the bush telegraph. Wherever we went, we'd attract a line of burkas two hundred yards long.'[18] As an example of looking at matters from the perspective of the host population, it could hardly be bettered. It was also an essential complement to the counternarcotics efforts (which could have alienated the population, given their dependence on the poppy crop), and furthermore it connected to the early attempts at 'Taliban reconciliation' being championed by intelligence agents and staff at HQ ISAF in Kabul. This whole subtle, careful and low-profile effort, operating in unison with the very well-resourced US PRT, worked well and denied the Taliban the opportunity to ignite any anti-coalition movement in the province.

When it was proposed that the UK forces take over the PRT from the US in Helmand, the SAS was tasked by Permanent Joint Headquarters (PJHQ – the operational headquarters for all UK operations overseas) to conduct a regimental operation in Helmand from April to May 2005, in order to gain up-to-date insight into the province, as well as to achieve some temporary disruption of the narcotics business there. The operation was conducted by A Squadron 22 SAS, with a task group/regimental headquarters above it. It ended in June 2005, in time for a report to be submitted to the MoD and PJHQ in advance of a key FCO-chaired meeting that would decide on the purpose, scale and resources for the Helmand mission.

Crucially, it is believed that this SAS report expressed concern about the UK's ability to carry on the effective work of the very well resourced US PRT without a significant uplift in the amount of civil aid money being made available. Any reduction in aid effort would not be welcomed by the people of Helmand. The report also recommended that the provincial governor, SMA, should be allowed to remain in power, given his influence over all the factions within the province. The report stated in clear terms that the small UK force needed to remain within the central populated zone of Helmand only, leaving the northern and southern areas to be screened by US special forces, in line with the previous 2001–4 operational design, in order to ensure that popular support could be maintained and that the tiny UK force could protect itself.

This last recommendation was critical, as the lightly armed and small UK force – 16 Air Assault Brigade, which was to be based around one battalion, 3 Para – clearly did not have the communications, tactical mobility, troop numbers or offensive support assets to be able to maintain any operational presence in the areas beyond the central zone. The SAS also noted that the very small numbers of casualties taken by the US PRT and its security teams were from land-based IEDs, similar to those seen in Iraq, and that this would be the main threat to conventional land-based operations in the central belt.

The SAS recommendations about the tactical deployment structure were endorsed in all their essentials by Colonel Gordon Messenger of PJHQ, who led the 'advanced force' for the UK deployment in late 2005, although the force still deployed with vulnerable 'Snatch' Land Rovers, no real counter-IED capability, not enough helicopters, no air-to-ground fire capability, and only a very limited ability to gather intelligence or conduct offensive operations against any emerging insurgent threat. This made it a very weak and blind force, and one that would depend entirely on the goodwill of the population (and its leaders) for its mobility beyond its bases – and even for its existence within them. If the people and their leaders liked the force, it could move; if they didn't it would be stuck in its bases and slowly destroyed. This was a very risky position to take, given the warnings of the SAS, the reduced PRT civil aid budget, and the UK's increasingly aggressive stance on counternarcotics. It was one that was made much worse by the sacking of the provincial governor, whose militia had kept control of all malign influences in Helmand (including the Taliban) up to that point. Once he had been removed, the weak, poorly resourced and blind UK force had no way of knowing what was happening outside its compounds, no way of keeping the Taliban at bay, and no way of controlling events. The mess that the British were about to find themselves in was rooted in their meddling with local governance that they neither understood nor had the capacity to control.

Airborne assault

The problems of the reputation of the British, derived from their unfortunate history in the area, were compounded by the perception that they were supporting a chronically corrupt, totally incompetent and thoroughly discredited government. The police, who had replaced the warlords in preying on those who used the roads, were arguably the worst aspect of government. Most police posts had their 'fun boy' – child catamite – and the British estimated that over 80 per cent of policemen were regular smokers of hash, with 67 per cent using opium either additionally or instead. Rape by police officers on children was common. When I visited a very senior police officer in Lashkar Gah as part of my job, I asked, only half-seriously, whether it was true that the police were responsible for 90 per cent of the crime in the province: 'That is an appalling lie – a ridiculous idea. No . . . I think it is only about 85 per cent!' replied the commander. I was not at all sure he was being as flippant as I was. Certainly, few of the Afghans I spoke to would have disagreed with the chief's assessment.

Into this chaotic world crashed the paratroopers of 16 Air Assault Brigade. Brigadier Ed Butler, a highly experienced and intelligent officer whom we last met as a lieutenant colonel leading the SAS raid on Koh i Malik, commanded the British forces in Afghanistan.

The chain of command he had been given was, as one senior officer said to me, 'floppy'.[19] It was described by journalist Stephen Grey as 'about as clear and neat as twigs in a bird's nest'.[20] He answered, in no determined order, to President Karzai through Governor Daoud, and the British ambassador – in theory the senior British official in the country. PJHQ in Northwood also had its line down to him, as did ISAF (the NATO formation which, when Butler and his 16 Air Assault Brigade arrived in spring 2006, was commanded by one General David Richards).

Making matters no better was the fact that Butler was forced to command the operations in Helmand remotely, from Kabul. His deputy, Colonel Charlie Knaggs, was deputed to command the day-to-day operations of the brigade in Helmand. Of the 3,500 troops being deployed from 16 Air Assault Brigade, only one battle group, about 650 men, consisted of fighting soldiers. The core unit around which this battle group was constructed was 3 Para, commanded by Lieutenant Colonel Stuart Tootal, a brave and dedicated officer. He has commented later, however, that '3 Para felt that their combat talents had been wasted' in the past in deployments to Iraq, among other places.[21] 'All they wanted to do was to go on operations and be tested in combat.' They 'suffered from a concern that the impending deployment to Afghanistan would turn out to be a disappointment.'[22] They were certainly not to be disappointed – at least in that respect – during this six-month tour. Other units were to include companies of Gurkhas and Fusiliers, as well as armoured and artillery support. In his descriptions of the preparations made by the battle group, Tootal tells of the 'poring over maps', the familiarization with the terrain that took place and the tactical preparation. Nowhere is there mention of any serious engagement with what the American army was beginning to term 'human terrain'. In other words, although Tootal and his team realized that they were about to be engaged in, as he puts it, 'a battle for hearts and minds', the necessary preparation for 'war among the people' seems to have been ignored.

No senior officer went to Helmand looking for a fight. However, if one were asked to choose the most appropriate British brigade for a peace-enforcement mission, one would be hard pressed to think of a less likely candidate than 16 Air Assault Brigade. These are the shock troops of the army, and of all British military units surely the last soldiers to be placed in an environment that required subtle and measured activity. Here we encounter the Byzantine politics of the British armed services. Within all services, there is a continuous bureaucratic fight for resources and equipment. The army had recently procured – at very great expense – several squadrons' worth of Apache helicopters,[23] designed originally (like almost every other piece of army equipment) for exceedingly destructive, highly 'kinetic' anti-tank warfare on the plains of northern Germany. As instruments of the Cold War 'manoeuvre warfare' doctrine, they were formidable. These attack helicopters (or AHs) were attached, for complex bureaucratic reasons, to 16 Air Assault Brigade. The army was very keen to demonstrate the utility of this 'weapons system', so the decision was taken to deploy that brigade.[24]

As to the strategy for the deployment, one very senior officer closely aware of the planning process put it like this: 'There was no strategy. This was a pure example of capability-led planning. The thinking went something like this; what have we got? Now what can we do with what we have? We have this new airmobile brigade battalion, and a new helicopter[25] system. They need to be used, or we may lose them.'[26] The same applied to the perennially threatened infantry battalions, once again under critical scrutiny pending the expected defence review, which eventually took place in late 2010. The institution and its preservation superseded any rational deployment.

The Helmand Plan

Any paratrooper will proudly proclaim that it is the function of the airborne forces to take land deep in enemy-held territory and to hold it at all costs until help arrives. History has shown that the training and ethos required for the aggressive spirit needed for this military role is not conducive to the traditional 'minimum force' principles necessary for success – whatever that means in a war without any adequate strategy – in 'wars among the people'. As events turned out, taking land deep in enemy territory and holding it until help arrived is exactly what the paratroopers found themselves doing. The problem was that, as matters turned out, there was no 'help' available. The airborne ethos need not necessarily have been a major problem, had there been a workable plan.

A plan had been drawn up on the basis of the SAS report by experienced civilian and military experts over several months. This became known as 'the Helmand Plan' – the idea of building an Afghan Development Zone in the relatively developed areas around the major towns of Lashkar

Gah and Gereshk, which, fortunately, were within thirty miles of one another and thus potentially allowed for mutual support of units and a concentration of effort. Into this area, the plan posited, would pour development aid and good governance. By all accounts it was a good, workable plan, developed by people with a realistic outlook derived from years of experience. However, as the legendary German general Helmuth von Moltke famously said, 'Plans do not survive first contact with the enemy.' This one did not get even that far. Poor intelligence, combined with pressure from Afghan authorities, led a misguided 16 Air Assault Brigade and its commanders to take a very different course of action. Intelligence had ascertained that the Taliban had 420 men in the province. This looked to be a manageable number.

Butler had found himself faced with a serious dilemma over what to do about the towns to the north of the province: Sangin, Musa Qala, Now Zad. None of them was to be garrisoned, according to the Helmand plan. This did not meet with the approval of Governor Daud.

Over the years, Brigadier Butler has come in for a great deal of criticism over the decision to move out of the area of the 'Helmand Plan' and into what became known as the 'platoon houses' of Musa Qala, Sangin and Now Zad. He over-extended the forces available, and the rest of this chapter describes the disastrous consequences of that decision. He did exactly what the recommendations of the SAS and Colonel Messenger had warned against.

Butler was not the only general, and certainly not the senior general on the spot, who was aware of, and involved in, the discussions and decision-making process. A very senior officer, now a three-star general, was present when these matters were being fiercely debated in the brigade headquarters. Despite the senior officer's presence, it is Brigadier Butler who has received the blame for what ensued. It is to his lasting credit that he has never sought to evade responsibility, despite the appalling political pressures placed upon him and the lack of any real support. It might convincingly be argued that he was placed in an impossible situation and in the circumstances had little choice.

At this stage, the concern of the Afghan government was that the Taliban could not be seen to have control of any part of the province. In fact, the Taliban controlled 95 per cent of it.[27] The British had several thousand men, and Daoud believed that something could be done about this. Unfortunately, in common with many, Daoud never understood that 3,500 troops did not equate to 3,500 men with guns available for operations. It was not only Afghans who found this puzzling. 'What are the rest of our people up to?', wrote one front-line officer.[28]

The modestly framed and realistic 'Helmand Plan' was shelved. The advice to the effect that the support for these garrisons was simply not available was ignored, and a 'we're going anyway' attitude developed.[29] The paratroopers would deal with Helmand in their own way. Over the six months of the deployment in mid-2006, at the request of the Afghan government, the battle group was scattered around the province to the towns of Now Zad, Sangin and Musa Qala.

All of these towns were to become famous names in Britain over that long, hot summer (although at the time they were competing for attention with the slightly less formidable antics of the England football team at the World Cup). The declared aim of what were to become known as 'platoon houses' (see below) was to provide support to the units of Afghan police and a very few army units.

In fact, the numbers were far worse than anyone thought: to reiterate, 3,500 troops does not in any way imply that 3,500 soldiers are available for deployment on the streets. Just as the 3,500 of the brigade could, at the time, generate only one battle group's worth of combat troops, the single battle group led by 3 Para itself had to guard and administer the positions it had taken. Even that battalion was not to receive its entire fighting component until July, fully four months into the deployment. One senior officer in General Richards' HQ had done the sums. He told the general that 'on a good day and with a following wind after a good deal of planning', once HQ and communications staff had been taken into account, and if the guard roster was doubled (i.e. halving the raw numbers required to do guard duties and man the 'sangars' – small, temporary, fortified positions – around the clock), 'we can find 168 combat troops to conduct operations from the entire Brigade'.[30]

With those numbers, the district centres – government buildings usually comprising the equivalent of council offices and a police station – were soon turned into small forts manned by the few superb infantry of 3 Para, the

Gurkhas, the Fusiliers and other companies that made up the battle group. These became known as 'platoon houses' – a platoon usually consists of about twenty-eight men. There were often other attached personnel, such as signallers or the occasional dozen or so reinforcing infantry.

'Prodding the lion'

Attracted by the prospect of taking these precariously held forts, hundreds of Taliban attacked. This series of engagements, described in a number of British accounts, was a serious tactical defeat for the Taliban, leaving hundreds of them dead. For the British, it was scarcely less destructive. On several occasions platoon houses came very close to being over-run. This was prevented only by dropping heavy bombs on the villages concerned and by subjecting them to gunfire and missiles from the Apache helicopters. Rather than 'taking the fight' to the Taliban, the army became involved in engagements that it had not expected and for which it had not prepared, but in which the Taliban was only too ready and willing to participate. The army had, in fact, lost the initiative. This was the very obverse of how this kind of warfare should be waged. The Taliban applied its strength against its enemy's weakness, collapsed its cohesion and moved with determination and speed – 'tempo' – to seize the initiative. In terms of 'find, fix and finish' it had no trouble in 'finding' the British and it 'fixed' them'. It was only due to the basic fighting skills and raw bloody courage of the British infantrymen that it did not 'finish' them. It continued to find and fix the force well into 2010.

Furthermore, there had been absolutely no construction or civil assistance of any meaningful kind. On the contrary, there was destruction and injury on a vast scale. This series of little 'Rorke's Drifts' resulted only in piles of dead Afghan and Pakistani young men – and uncounted civilians – along with forty British soldiers. As Jean Mackenzie put it to me, 'If you are not equipped you have no business being there.'[31] That statement must surely apply both in the intellectual and in the physical sense.

The tactics involved, whatever the rhetoric, were more Vietnam in the bad old days than Malaya in the good ones. The reaction was, in the words of the head of the army at the time General Sir Richard Dannatt: 'rather similar to prodding the lion who was otherwise kipping in the corner minding his own business . . . In the early days we probably wound up – maybe still are – killing lots of farmers.'[32] The reasoning was that the enemy was being drawn onto the guns, artillery and air strikes of the British. The impression that this was a mini-reprise of Vietnam was reinforced by the use of body counts, a highly unfortunate practice that was once again redolent of the worst of Vietnam. The whole approach revealed a total failure of understanding of the concepts of control and security.

An area does not become secure because of the proximity of soldiers. In the presence of large numbers of 'Taliban', this simply serves as a magnet for would-be martyrs, and that is exactly what these platoon houses became, with British soldiers only too willing to assist them in their aim of violent death. The heavy bombing resulted in trashed town centres – such as Sangin, which became a huge problem for the hugely reinforced British stationed there over the next four years – and, most seriously, in thousands of displaced people.

Sangin in particular acquired something of an iconic status for the British land forces, the army and marines. The appropriately named 'break-in battle' was intensely bloody and savage. Hundreds of 'Taliban' fighters were killed as they tried, by means of human wave attacks, to take the district centre, where the platoon house of 3 Para was besieged. No one at the time had troubled to determine what was really happening in local politics. Stephen Grey describes the situation thus:

the chief of Helmand's secret police [Dado] . . . had turned Sangin into his private fiefdom . . . Dado had started a private jail, was always drunk or stoned, had raped boys and women and was systematically stealing from the population . . . as far as . . . most were concerned, the British were there to prop up Dado and his cronies. Many of the fighters were local villagers.[33]

Dado was one of a large network of drug warlords – exactly the sort of individuals that the Taliban had removed only a decade before, thereby achieving initial popular success. Now the British were seen to be supporting these criminals' return: 'There were some who began to wonder darkly if Britain's military was being drawn into what was essentially a drug turf war.'[34] At no point did British intelligence get a real grasp of the links between warlords, 'narcokhans' and the Taliban. In fact, Sangin was one of the world's centres of the heroin trade, with the complexities and undercurrents of a Medellín further compounded by tribal and regional politics. Bereft of useful intelligence and at sea strategically, the British forces were already finding Sangin becoming something of a quagmire. They had become involved in a drugs turf war.

The British were obliged to spread their tiny force around the province to defend themselves in towns that had been taken without any consideration of the question 'what now?' This represented a serious operational problem for the British to which all too little thought had been given. Once again, as in Iraq, through a failure of planning the British had trapped themselves into the 'self-licking lollipop' syndrome – capable only of defending themselves, and scarcely able to resupply at all, given the small deployment of helicopters. So much for the principle of 'securing the base areas' (a major precept of operations in Malaya), which in this case would be the provincial capital of Lashkar Gah. Manning restrictions ensured that the capital, a city of 200,000 people, was patrolled by about eighty British soldiers, although there were never more than twenty on the ground at any one time. One intelligence officer I spoke to put the problem pithily: 'we judoed ourselves'.[35] The British had got themselves in a pickle: withdraw from the platoon houses and give the Taliban a victory, or stay and continue fighting, with no clear idea of how matters could be progressed. An impossible dilemma.

Dan Jarman, a civilian adviser to DfID with extensive experience in Helmand and Iraq, one of the very few deployed to the province at that time, assessed the problem from a different perspective:

16 Air Assault thought they could beat the Taliban. They couldn't care less about what was planned. The original joint plan? I think the paras just ignored it. Int told them there were just 420 Taliban so the thought was – 'let's go and kill them'. We are living with that analysis now; no one thought, hang on, we can't secure an area the size of Wales with 5,000 people. Only it wasn't 5,000 people. It was 650 combat troops. The original plan, the Helmand Plan ... It was a measured and realistic response, but it just went by the wayside.[36]

So much for the tactics of dispersal to, and 'holding' of, small district centres. This approach set the tone for the war for nearly four years. These small garrisons were condemned to an existence of constant patrols out of their forts into largely hostile areas. On regular occasions there would be shoot-outs with Taliban that would, because the soldiers were outnumbered, almost inevitably result in air or artillery support being called in, with attendant civilian casualties. David Loyn, a BBC journalist, writer and Afghanistan veteran, is reminded of similar scurrying raids made during the days of frontier warfare under the British Raj: 'Military adventurism for no good end – it sounded like the campaigns waged on the frontier a century before mocked then by the soldiers fighting them as "General Willcock's weekend wars".'[37]

'Setting the conditions . . .'

This approach of (effectively) actively seeking combat made it ever more difficult to gain, let alone retain, the trust of the local people, who were not initially disposed to welcome foreign occupying soldiers who had brought nothing but trouble. Only after three years, with the arrival of US marines in force, did numbers become sufficient for the military forces involved to begin to move from what amounted to a series of besieged forts to a more secure and coherent approach. The later approach was, ironically, not too dissimilar to the plan adopted before the arrival of 16 Air Assault Brigade.

Others saw it differently. As Colonel Stuart Tootal, who had commanded the main fighting unit of that brigade, put it: 'Our achievement lay in the fact that we had fought a testing break-in battle which permitted the UK to make its entry into Helmand and set the conditions for subsequent British forces to build on.'[38] That is a fair assessment as far as it goes. It did indeed 'set the tone' for the subsequent three disastrous years. However, there was certainly no intention, prior to the deployment of that brigade, of having to fight a 'break-in battle' at all – hence Defence Secretary John Reid's famous remark. What had happened was that, far from 'manoeuvre' techniques of speed and aggression 'getting inside the Taliban's decision-making cycle', the reverse had happened and the British had played perfectly to the Taliban's strengths. They had dispersed in small numbers, used very heavy weaponry to make up for numbers, destroyed several town centres and created the perfect human environment for rebels to thrive. The consequences of the military misjudgements of those early months are with the mission in Helmand still. Whether by luck or design, the Taliban had succeeded in diverting the British paratroops from what they saw as 'counterinsurgency' to fighting a high-intensity battle, destroying and depopulating town centres. In so doing, the British had fulfilled exactly their historic role as most Helmandis saw it – that of aggressive and destructive invaders.

Protecting the people?

What then of the civilians whom the British were supposedly in the province to 'protect'? Even a year later, when I served in Helmand as a civilian element of the British mission, no one quite knew where the civilians who had previously lived in these towns had gone. Some to the desert, it was thought; others to nearby, so-far untouched towns under the control of the Taliban. Very many have ended up in refugee camps in Kabul, where they scratch the slightest living in the already filth-poor environment of the notorious 'police district five'. No provision had been made for them, because not the slightest thought of them had appeared in the planning process. Dan Jarman again:

> When we asked for operations to be amended or even postponed to allow for other, more constructive activities to take place, the requests were refused. I remember when the operation to take and hold Sangin was being planned that a medical charity was conducting polio vaccinations in the region. This operation would halt the vaccinations. We asked the army to consider the thousands who would otherwise not now be vaccinated. 'They can get them some other time', was the reply. Of course they could not. The programme had been designed to deal with expertly calibrated disease vectors. Timing was critical. Was it for that reason that polio began to be seen shortly afterwards? Tough decisions sometimes need to be made. The point is, there needs to be real consultation.[39]

This entirely echoes my own experience, working as I did in a similar capacity a year or so later.

A UK civilian aid official recalls:

> ... when the 'ring of steel' closed around Sangin – the perimeter held by
> the British army – the Afghan police and army were allowed in to 'clear'
> the 'insurgents', I received phone calls from terrified civilians who were
> having the police and army tear through their town raping and robbing
> inside that ring.[40]

That was the reality. The *virtual* reality, in which the military HQ lived, was
that this was a well-run cordon-and-search operation. Clearly this was no
way to win hearts and minds, howsoever defined. David Loyn, who famously
spent some time with a Taliban unit, reported that, in one village he visited,
people were too angry to speak to him because he was British: 'One merely
pointed to the torn and bloody women's clothing left in the ruins of the
house and said bitterly, "are these the kind of houses they have come to build
– the kind where clothing is cut to pieces?"' NATO sources, said Loyn,
claimed that the Taliban had defended the village and fired on British forces
attempting to land from helicopters.[41] One would not have to enquire to
determine who was thought to be protecting whom in that encounter.

The attitude to civilian assistance among the troops of that first deployment is revealing, and certainly set the tone for subsequent problems. The
problem was encapsulated in the famous washing-machine incident.
Gereshk is the second-largest town in Helmand, and a unit of paratroopers
was based there in 2006. These soldiers thought it might be a good idea to
connect a washing machine that had been provided some months before
by USAID to alleviate what they believed to be a problem with cleanliness
at the local hospital. They applied to the DfID representative in Lashkar
Gah for money from the 'Quick Impact Projects' fund to sink a well in
order to provide water for the machine. After a short delay the request was
refused, on the grounds that the hospital was part of the national healthcare framework and was being run by an Afghan NGO. To assist in this
way might compromise the NGO's neutrality.

On the face of it, this was an entirely reasonable and humane proposal,
and one might be forgiven for taking the view, which Colonel Stuart Tootal
has expressed regularly, that this was an example of civilian inertia and
obstruction. As so often in such situations, however, matters are more

complicated than they appear initially. First, due partly to the fighting, the electricity supply to the hospital, and indeed the entire town, was intermittent at best. More importantly, washing the sheets in the hospital – which was, by Afghan standards, reasonably clean – gave employment to six women, who would, of course, be rendered unemployed in the (unlikely) event that the washing machine could be made to work. As for the neutrality issue – whilst this may be a niggling formality to soldiers, it is literally a matter of life and death to aid workers everywhere.

The criticism levelled by senior officers from the time that the 'civilians were nowhere to be found' was, in the circumstances, absurd. Even had there been all the civilian experts in engineering, healthcare and justice that the army could have dreamt of, they could have done nothing. The centres of Sangin, Musa Qala and Now Zad, most of Helmand's larger villages, were almost entirely destroyed. For the next four years, and indeed up to the present day, no Westerner – soldier, policeman or development worker – could consider entering these towns without at least a company of British soldiers as escorts. This was a very different world from the experience of the SAS with their mobile clinics (MEDCAPs) prior to the arrival of 16 Air Assault Brigade.

The legacy of Herrick IV

In one of the last acts of 16 Air Assault Brigade, a deal was struck with the local community of Musa Qala, brokered by the then governor, Daoud, under which British forces agreed to withdraw from Musa Qala district centre, and local elders promised to keep the Taliban away. The rationale behind this was that supporting the garrison in Musa Qala was simply too costly. As the British troops withdrew, under the sullen looks of the locals who had endured months of battle in their town, they did so in hired trucks – 'jinglies', the ubiquitous trucks of southern Asia covered in brightly coloured paint and lights. To the observer, it looked very much like a surrender. A few months later, in February 2007, the Taliban reoccupied Musa Qala.

The deployment of 16 Air Assault Brigade had been nothing short of disastrous. Bereft of insight or perspective of any point of view except the most radical form of traditional 'cracking on', they left a legacy of destroyed towns, refugees and civilian casualties. Admittedly, they had inflicted hundreds, possibly thousands, of casualties on Taliban forces, but the 'body count' rationale for operations had surely been discredited during the Vietnam War. They had set a pattern of dispersed forts, difficult to defend and even more difficult to support or supply. From them British soldiers dashed out on their daily missions to face not the 'human wave' attacks (which the Taliban had come to realize led nowhere), but snipers, desultory engagements and ever more lethal IEDs.

Even more damagingly, they had reinforced the image of the British as destructive invaders, whose 'come in peace' narrative was literally incredible. This was a 'story' which the British soldiers' opponents were keen to tell. Furthermore, they had created a security void. Most of the towns of Helmand continued to be no-go areas for government, and the Taliban was able to exploit this with the creation of its own version of 'government'. For those few areas under (proper) government control, in the words of a report of the International Crisis Group, a think-tank well known for its presence on the ground in areas upon which it comments: 'a culture of impunity was allowed to take root in the name of "stability" with Afghan abusers free to return to their old ways as long as they mouthed allegiance to the central government'.[42] In those circumstances, the Taliban was welcome back. When I arrived in mid-2007, as justice adviser to the UK PRT and task force in Lashkar Gah, Taliban courts were well established in all these areas. As the courts expanded, so did their legitimacy, with the result that most Helmandis preferred to have their disputes resolved there, rather than by government courts.[43] The Taliban had exploited the failure of the British to create a credible 'security zone', as had been envisaged earlier, before the staff of 16 Air Assault Brigade tore up the plan. The failure once more to see that the real civilian need for simple security (rather than an illusory 'protection from the Taliban') had to be appreciated and addressed had been a disastrous error. Matters were not significantly improved for several years, by which time it was too late.

CHAPTER 4

'A Bleeding Ulcer'[1]

The British intervention in Helmand Province has been not only a blundering catastrophe, but a violent tragedy.

Leo Docherty, *Desert of Death*, p. 185

We didn't bring them to our way of thinking.

Unidentified marine, BBC *Today* programme, 20 September 2010, speaking about the results of the British occupation of Sangin

The six-month syndrome that had proved so damaging in Basra was in full swing in Helmand, with each successive brigade defining its own objectives irrespective of what went before or what was to happen afterwards. While six months may be more than sufficient for fighting soldiers, crucially the headquarters elements were also on a six-month rotation.[2]

It was 3 Commando Brigade that took over from the paratroopers. The Commando Brigade is composed of probably the most highly trained infantry soldiers in the world – the Royal Marines – and their support services. This brigade was rather better prepared, having seen what was required during the tenure of 16 Air Assault. It took a more flexible approach to operations, with 'Mobile Operational Groups' (of course nicknamed MOGs) – very similar to the Long Range Desert Group in concept and indeed look, with vehicles festooned with machine guns, manned by soldiers swathed in ammunition and Arab-style white *dishdashas*. Very many 'enemy' fighters were killed. As always, every battle was won. As always in civil wars (such as this was), that was irrelevant.

After six months, 3 Commando Brigade gave way to 12 Mechanized Brigade, commanded by Brigadier John Lorimer. It was he who, somewhat unfortunately, coined the phrase 'mowing the lawn' in connection with his regular sweeps over territory that had been reoccupied by the Taliban.

'Stratcomms'

The influence of 'media ops' on both campaigns, especially the Afghan effort, was critical. The 'narrative' took a far more important place than anything that was really happening on the ground. The cross-departmental Afghan communications unit, which some might view as a rather Orwellian title for what amounts to a large press office, governed a great deal of what happened on the ground, with journalists directed to where acceptable action was taking place. Those journalists not perceived to be 'friendly' were simply denied permission to accompany troops.

The constant need for 'good stratcomms' (strategic communications) drove operations to a great degree. It is no coincidence that, as it deployed on its rotation, each brigade had a signature event, a major operation or technique that was intended to define it.

The six-month rotation schedule means that a brigade, and especially its senior officers, have only a limited time in which to make its mark. Cynical observers may point out (indeed have pointed out) that the only way medals are won is through 'kinetic' operations. It is demonstrably the case that every single brigade deployed to Helmand has had a signature operation – whether actually required or not. The idea of a brigadier making his plans and deciding that during his tour there should be no signature operation, and that instead there should be consolidation, is unthinkable. It has certainly never been tried. As the former ambassador to Afghanistan put it:

Each brigadier would say that he understood the 'comprehensive approach', and planned to work with DfID and the FCO, as well as with the Afghan authorities. But each brigadier would launch one kinetic operation, before returning with his brigade to Britain after the best six months of his professional life. And then the whole cycle would start again.[3]

Fiercely titled operations (often in the northern Afghan language of Dari, not spoken by Helmandis)[4] to 'retake' various villages continued every six months until 2010, when rather less glorious withdrawal operations characterized British deployments. This tended to produce a baleful six-month cycle of expectation, event and return that overlaid the usual 'two months learning, two months doing and two months counting the days home' pattern of each rotation. That the media drove operations is not necessarily a bad or destructive phenomenon. To steal an idea from Clausewitz, war nowadays might be said to reflect the old mediaeval 'trivium': the *logic* of war (its purpose – at least at first glance), the *grammar* of war (the means used to attain that purpose) and the *rhetoric*, which has a central role, both in the fight 'in theatre' and on the equally important 'home front'. General Rupert Smith took the view, when he commanded the British force in Northern Ireland, that he was fighting on four fronts: the military and political struggle in Northern Ireland; the Irish media; the national media; and the international media. This is an entirely realistic approach, since rebels and insurgents have been doing exactly the same thing themselves since the early twentieth century. Most recently, the Kosovo Liberation Army used the international media to power its country to independence. It is the job of 'strategic communications' to direct that part of the campaign, selecting, promoting and maintaining a narrative. Signature events were part of the narrative of each brigade. The advantage to the NATO participants in these operations was that they were an excellent vehicle for the provision of tangible purpose to an operation that was in a state of drift, chaotically bereft of credible strategy. For the Afghan civilians caught up in them, the reality was, of course, very different.

In the absence of credible measures to counter the tactics of the Taliban and its effectiveness in forming its so-called 'shadow government' strategy, NATO and the UK in particular needed to establish and feed a narrative of constant, steady, positive movement forward. Stephen Grey observed, 'Endless reports from both the military and the diplomats had poured forth a stream of stories of progress. Yet the facts on the ground were at odds with these reports.'[5] What the military had imported to Afghanistan from Iraq was what amounted to a martial version of the 'culture of spin' that dominated Whitehall during the New Labour period. Negativity, even when amply justified by 'facts on the ground', was not acceptable. In military terms it took on a sinister light, as it was, of course, open to the charge of 'defeatism' – a word laced with poisonous, insidious and, indeed, for military officers *treacherous* undertones. The former British ambassador to Afghanistan, Sir Sherard Cowper-Coles had himself experienced this:

> One of the most moving experiences for me as Ambassador was in Helmand, when a young and very courageous officer in the Grenadier Guards came up to me and said he'd been at school with one of my sons. He said, 'Can I have a private word with you, Sir? The strategy isn't working, but whenever I try to report that up the line, my superiors say I'm being defeatist and I must re-work my papers, because cracking on in Helmand is what it's about and success is coming.'[6]

In a similar reflection of a virtual world, the supposedly classical virtues of 'counterinsurgency' were preached. Almost every day VIP guests trooped through the briefing room of the PRT to be given PowerPoint presentations by army officers, showing 'inkspots' growing and governance being nurtured. Civilian contractors could afford to be less positive, but for the staff officers dissent was not known. As the rhetoric on 'counterinsurgency' poured out, the reality was that the officers, trained into the 'manoeuvrist' ideas of moving large groups of soldiers about on maps, did what they were trained to do: arrows with unit markings indicating cavalry or reconnaissance units found the enemy; a blocking force would hold or fix the enemy; and another arrow would ruthlessly strike down to 'finish' him. In the words of two highly experienced British officers, Major General Andrew Mackay and Commander Stephen Tatham, these represented 'a more industrial scale of conflict which involved large clearances but without the force levels to subsequently hold and build'.[7] No one even addressed the possibility that the real inhabitants of Helmandi villages might not want the assistance, in any form, of alien troops or civilians. One expert, an architect who had worked in development in Afghanistan since 1989, put the problem of 'clear, hold and build' like this: 'It is so patently clear at the village level – my life is in the Afghan villages . . . that outsiders cannot do that. Even if you can clear, you are unlikely to hold and you certainly cannot build.'[8]

Taliban strategy

The Taliban had begun to realize that there was no future in standing and fighting or in attacking British positions with human wave assaults. It was beginning to adopt other, more subtle strategies, building on its strengths. Most importantly, unlike the US and UK, it was (and is) extremely clear on its objectives. They are twofold: first, and a pre-condition for any talks, the expulsion of foreign forces; second, the establishment of a truly Islamic regime (although it has indicated that the nature of such a regime is a matter for negotiation).

The Taliban was not and is not bereft of strategy. In fact, it has adopted an old and tried strategy, known in the West as 'Fabian', after the Roman general Fabius Maximus, known as '*cunctator*' ('the delayer'), who was faced with an overwhelmingly competent and powerful enemy. Since he was fighting on his own ground and his enemy was far from home, he decided that the best policy was simple: refuse direct engagement until it was on his own terms. He would delay and prevaricate, attacking when it suited him and aiming to tire his opponent. For the time would certainly come when the invader would tire of chasing and trying to engage an enemy who would simply not comply. His eventually defeated opponent was arguably the greatest of all ancient generals – Hannibal. The similar Taliban strategy is often articulated in the well-known, allegedly Afghan aphorism: 'You have the watches; we have the time.' Dr Sajjan Gohel put it another way in evidence to the House of Commons Foreign Affairs Committee: '[The Taliban] believe they have the strategic advantage, durability and resources to outlast the West in Afghanistan ... success in defeating them militarily any time soon appears remote.'[9]

The tactics used to enable this strategy are straightforward, and in the circumstances sensible and effective. They were ably summarized by the prime minister of the time, Gordon Brown:

> What happened after 2006 is that the Taliban changed its tactics. Before, they were in a one-to-one confrontation with us. They couldn't win that armed battle so they took to explosive devices, guerrilla warfare and we had to respond to that, as all our allies had to do.[10]

The Taliban did exactly what any sensible guerrilla group would do. As well as attacking enemy weakness, it looked to its own strengths. These included the ability to bring public goods, such as security and justice with clear integrity. If a police post was extorting money or torturing captives, Taliban teams would attack that post and kill every policeman in it, to the general approval of the local people. One former Royal Ulster Constabulary officer recognized a familiar, ominous pattern: 'this is like the IRA of 1921'.[11] Since the IRA of 1919–21 mounted the single most successful rebellion against British rule anywhere, this was bad news. The single most effective selling point of the pre-9/11 Taliban was justice. The Taliban commander Mullah Dadullah rightly pointed out, before he was killed by British special forces, 'during our rule Afghans enjoyed what occupation troops from forty-two countries have not been able to offer'.[12]

Now it was rebuilding that reputation. A Helmandi woman with whom I spoke, educated and highly articulate – someone, in other words, with plenty to lose if the Taliban were to return in their old form – told me that she walked past the stadium in Lashkar Gah, the capital of Helmand, and reflected: 'In the old days on Fridays, the Taliban activists would carry out the *huddud* punishments [amputations, executions, and so on] there; sometimes I wish we could have that back. At least we could walk the streets safely.' Some may see this as an Afghan equivalent of the old Italian refrain 'at least Mussolini made the trains run on time'. For most ordinary people, the reality of day-to-day life in Helmand was fear of the predations of the police or criminals (as we have seen, often the same thing) in the form of kidnap, rape, extortion and murder. Not only did the British have insufficient troops even to begin to consider providing such security, but the 'security forces' they were supporting and sustaining were themselves part of the problem.

A new approach: 52 Brigade's tour

The perspective of the Afghan people themselves had not been at the forefront of the highly traditional, kinetic, 'mowing-the-lawn' type of activities of the British. The latter's traditional, old-style clearance operations, combined with the media-driven necessity of 'keeping up appearances', meant that any intrusion of 'realities' other than their own was distinctly unwelcome. On one occasion, I was part of a planning briefing for an operation. After the briefing, questions were invited. I asked whether any thought had been given to the inevitable refugees that would be displaced from their homes by the fighting, or indeed by the mere possibility of fighting, occasioned by the British presence. The response was nonplussed expressions from around the table and a brief, 'They'll probably go to the desert or find some family. Next question.' The attitude was very much that this was not the army's problem

A steadily worsening situation was temporarily retrieved by the arrival of 52 Brigade in October 2007. This was a new formation, initially created for the purpose from a tiny staff whose previous UK-based responsibilities had been administrative. In army parlance, it had been a 'Category B brigade'. Its commander was Brigadier Andrew Mackay, an officer known for his interest in, and experience, of 'stabilization' – the term given to bringing some degree of normality to formerly war-racked regions. Mackay was not one of the army's hard-driving, fiercely competitive 'combat' officers. A deeply thoughtful and reflective individual, he had led his brigade staff into looking at their task from the perspective of the people, who, he said, 'were the prize'. The brigade staff were required to conduct extensive study prior to their deployment – particularly on the concept of 'influence'. It rapidly became clear that there was, in the UK defence world, as Mackay and Tatham put it, 'no corpus of text or body of military experts to provide appropriate advice' on how to offer 'influence' in non-kinetic forms to the kind of 'audience' represented by the Afghan population of Helmand.[13] So the brigadier and his staff did their best to study these matters themselves. The approach of 52 Brigade can be summarized in one of the more memorable orders I heard Mackay give in his early daily command meetings in Lashkar Gah: 'The next officer who mentions a body count to me will be on the earliest available flight home.'

The six-month tour of 52 Brigade and Brigadier Mackay has been defined by the recovery of Musa Qala, the town in the north of the province that had been surrendered a year previously. They did this with panache. But there was far more to their tour than that. While the idea and practice of 'protecting the population' may have its limitations, it was a significant advance on what had gone on before, and the 52 Brigade approach was, while not exactly a step change, demonstrably effective.

Even from the perspective of UK casualties, the situation was a great improvement. With thirteen fatal casualties, the rate of death was less than a third of the brigade that went before, and half of the one that succeeded it. 52 Brigade, the 'Category B' brigade led by a man supposedly destined never to command his brigade in combat, had sustained the lowest casualties of any brigade deployed in Helmand. Was that a coincidence? Perhaps.

Unfortunately, shortly after the retaking of Musa Qala, the six-month rotation cycle kicked in again.

'A task of epic proportions': the Great Turbine Debacle

The successor to 52 was 16 Air Assault Brigade – the 'paras', deployed to Helmand once more after an eighteen-month respite. Ideas of 'population protection' were again confined to the domain of rhetoric. All that was regarded as 'fluffy nonsense',[14] and old, tried and failed approaches, such as body counts, appeared again. The signature operation this time was not an occupation or a battle, but the transportation of a single turbine to the dam at Kajaki. This was accomplished in a 24-hour operation, named 'Eagles' Summit' (in Pashto '*Oqab Tsuka*'), and involving 4,000 troops, most of them British. The embedded *Times* journalist was clearly impressed with this tactical masterpiece of deception and British guile:

It was a task of epic proportions, inspiring comparisons with *Commando* magazine, *Mad Max*, the Battle of Arnhem in 1944 and the relief of the Siege of Mafeking in 1900. The mission was to take 220 tonnes of turbine and other equipment, worth millions of pounds, across 100 miles of some of the most hostile and heavily mined territory in Afghanistan. At the climax of the Taliban's fighting season. Without anyone noticing.[15]

Certainly some people noticed, and paid for it with their lives: 16 Air Assault Brigade reported that the Taliban had lost 200 men. Clearly the body counts had started again. The intentions of the mission were noble. The official MOD publication stated:

With the delivery of the turbine complete, work can now begin on its installation and the much larger programme of the rejuvenation of the

electrical distribution network needed to pass the extra power to the
areas of Sangin, Musa Qaleh, Kandahar and the provincial capital of
Helmand, Lashkar Gah. The new turbine is capable of producing
18.5MW of economically viable, renewable energy, which will be in
addition to the dam's current 16.5MW output.

The additional electricity it will eventually provide will light up class-
rooms, allowing Afghans across southern Afghanistan to learn to read
and write in evening classes; farmers to store their produce in chilled
storage, allowing greater export opportunities for the booming wheat
markets; and clinics to offer improved health services.[16]

These splendid dreams were unfortunately destined not to be realized, for
a variety of reasons. First, the Kajaki dam is not equipped to provide electricity to Helmand, as the cables did not (and indeed do not) exist to
enable electricity to be conveyed south to Helmand itself at any significant
level. If the turbines – two are already installed, although one does not
function – worked properly, the dam would provide power mainly to
Kandahar. But unfortunately, the third turbine hauled to the site by 16 Air
Assault Brigade has, in any event, not been made to work, and it sits where
the paratroopers left it, beside the turbine hall at the dam. The materials
required to install it have not arrived and will not arrive for some considerable time. Even when they do, the task of supplying, guarding and
transporting the skilled labour, which will need to come from Pakistan,
will be a considerable one. As matters have turned out, the breathy
comparison to Arnhem is apt: a journey requiring much effort and planning, over a long and hostile route, with no significant positive outcome
whatsoever. One soldier who had been involved in the swashbuckling
clearing and holding of the hills around the road to Kajaki for the turbine
to make its way forward put it to me rather more bluntly: 'It was a complete
waste of time.'

In June 2008, 16 Air Assault's commander, Brigadier Mark Carleton-
Smith, offered himself as a hostage to fortune: 'The tide is clearly ebbing
not flowing for them [the Taliban]. Their chain of command is disrupted
and they are short of weapons and ammunition . . . I can therefore judge
the Taliban insurgency a failure at the moment . . . We have reached the
tipping point.'[17]

This proved a premature assessment. After the end of his tour, in October 2008, Carleton-Smith was less bullish. In the tones of someone who had found himself subject to a 'reality check' he said that military victory over the Taliban was 'neither feasible nor supportable'.[18] There was no tipping point during that six-month iteration, of course, and the brigade deployments flowed on through their cycles, each with new initiatives, strategies and fiercely titled campaigns to 'retake' villages. The leading sociologist and commentator on military affairs Anthony King, who had seen the British army in action in Afghanistan, observed: 'Commanders had to be seen to be doing something appropriately military, even if their actions have not contributed to – or have even jeopardised – long-term goals.'[19] Claims of imminent 'tipping points' and 'crucial years' have been and continue to be made annually.

By the summer of 2009 it was clear that the British army simply could not handle Helmand alone, even with the help of a Danish battle group, plus some Estonian and Czech troops:

> There have not been sufficient troops in Helmand to secure the population. The British army, which had primary responsibility for Helmand, was, frankly, forced into a strategy of what the troops call 'mowing the lawn'. They would clear and leave. The insurgents would scatter, would go the hills, and then when the British troops left, they'd come back down and terrorize the population again.[20]

There was precious little 'hold' and 'building' had not happened. Clearing was, for the moment, out of the question.

The long-time resident of Afghanistan and writer, and now a British politician, Rory Stewart, summed up how matters stood in mid-2009:

> [Here is a] snapshot of Helmand . . . In the beginning of 2005, there were about 200 [foreign] soldiers . . . U.S. Special Forces [were] sitting in a base in the Lashkar Gah. Broadly speaking, internationals could move around that province . . .
>
> The objective then had nothing to do with the Taliban. It was just about the fact the economy wasn't functioning and there wasn't enough security, and the governor seemed to be in league with the drug lords.

The troop deployments initially were all about dealing with those things, trying to improve the government for Afghan people.

But what then happened is we found ourselves facing an insurgency. It's a matter of debate whether deploying those troops caused that insurgency, provoked that insurgency, or whether it was just a coincidence.

The bottom line is we've gone from 200 troops in 2005 to nearly 20,000 today, and there has been no improvement in governance; there's been no improvement in economic development; there's no improvement in security. The people of Helmand are worse off in 2009 than they were in 2005. And in addition to no improvement in those governance factors, we're now facing a Taliban insurgency.[21]

On the ground, the British were repeating the same kind of operations for no gain or perceptible effect. A former major in the Special Air Service Regiment put it starkly: 'I don't think we have even scratched the surface as far as the conflict goes . . . We hold tiny areas of ground in Helmand and we are kidding ourselves if we think our influence goes beyond 500 metres of our security bases.'[22]

The British bailed out again?

After three years of savage fighting, little had been achieved, save for the destruction of large parts of what little remained of the province's infrastructure. As in Basra, the US Marine Corps provided one solution, in the form of numbers and combat power, as the 2nd Marine Expeditionary Brigade took responsibility for much of southern Helmand. In 2008, it had taken over Garmsir, a town under permanent siege since 2006. The marines were cheered as they entered Garmsir. Not because they were American, but because they were not British.[23] Now they were to spread far more widely until, in 2010, there were substantially more US troops in Helmand than British.

By early 2010, with very little initial publicity in the UK, the British effort in Helmand was subsumed by the sheer combat power and numbers of President Obama's 'mini-surge'. The British had found themselves out of their depth and without the numbers to deal with the absolute necessity of bringing about the security that (arguably) their activities had so damaged. Those early 'break-in' battles, in which the platoon houses were held by small groups of valiant, if extremely violent, young men, had brought misery to very many people and had set the tone for subsequent years. The feelings of many Helmandis were summed up in the words of one man, filmed talking to a gaggle of British soldiers during Operation Panther's Claw – that rotation's signature operation – in the summer of 2009: 'If you want to bring us security, go and live in the desert. You can fight the Taliban from there.' Another man simply wanted to get on with his life: 'You come and ask where the Taliban is. They ask me where the British are. I just want to look after my sheep.'[24] The refugee camps of Helmandis in Kabul grew.

In both Iraq and Afghanistan, what the 'population' wanted was security. For Basrawis this meant having a semblance of protection from religiously inspired militias and gangsters; for Helmandis it implied not being subject to the predations of government and police, at least as much as of the 'Taliban', who were, in any event, often young men fighting the foreign invaders who had come to 'protect' them. As one BBC reporter framed it: 'Protection for the British means "intervention". Protection for Afghans means being left alone.'[25]

One very significant mistake of Basra had been repeated. The acute desire for the people of Helmand for basic *real* security had been ignored. Instead of providing real and substantial protection (all too often from their own police) and meaningful security for them the British were focused on going after the Taliban. Moreover, the 'counterinsurgency' lessons of the old campaigns of British imperial history had been ignored. There was simply no attempt to formulate a clear strategy in pursuit of a cogent policy. That said, as we have seen, there were visionary commanders, or at least one such commander, in the shape of Andrew Mackay, a man often considered to be a dangerous radical. Other brigade commanders 'got it', realized that what the people wanted was security in a wider sense than merely security from the Taliban and acted upon that realization. For example, Brigadier James Chiswell, the commander of 16 Air Assault Brigade in its third six-month tour in early 2011, placed hunting down and engaging the enemy as fourth on his unit's priority list. First on that list was ensuring security for the ordinary people in their day-to-day activities. Needless to say, there was no guarantee that the subsequent commander would take a similar view. As we have already seen, the six-month cycle is not conducive to a consistent approach.

Structure and strategy

The 'classic' campaigns of Malaya, and even Northern Ireland, are a distant memory now. The reasons for Britain's failures in Afghanistan and Iraq are deeper than merely a failure to abide by atavistic (and in any event seriously misunderstood) 'traditions' of adroit counterinsurgency practice. Those reasons go deep into the structure of the army.

From the beginning, the British army was determined that it was going to 'take' Helmand. That was to be 'its' province. From the theatre – which is to say Afghan-wide – perspective, this meant that the British were focused not on the overall mission, but on their little aspect of it. In both Basra and Helmand, the British adopted an 'area of responsibility' – an AOR. One retired senior special forces officer told me, 'The army loves AORs – it's tidy. But it fixes you to the ground.'[26] This fixation to the ground derives from the profoundly conservative approach that the army takes to military operations. At the time of writing, this remains the case, although the US has taken over the bulk of the area responsibilities, as we have seen, because the British army proved incapable of deploying sufficient resources to do it itself. The British AOR is now roughly what it was originally planned to be in 2003, in the original 'Helmand Plan'.[27] This dearth of 'boots on the ground' resulted in heavy weaponry being used to compensate for insufficient troops, with a consequent increase in civilian casualties. Instead of focusing on what it does well, the British army continues to believe that it can somehow succeed, where six years of experience have shown that it will fail. This 'regionalist' attitude is partly driven by the army's structure, based as it is on large manoeuvre formations. This attitude played ideally into the Taliban's national strategy of delay and resistance, combined with the effective provision of public goods.

In the civilian world within which the UK army has been operating, the 'clear, hold, build' approach is essentially a fiction. Once again, this approach is rooted in a Cold War sequential approach to operations. Once again, this suits the Taliban's approach of providing public goods such as justice quickly and cleanly, unlike its opponents: the Afghan government, supported and guarded by foreign occupying forces, is simply not capable of supplying these goods in any sustainable fashion.

Brigades are planned to deploy until 2016, by which time there will have been no fewer than twenty brigade rotations. 'This is the way we do things; it is the way we have always done them; and it is the way we will proceed' – that is the attitude taken. In other words, the structure is driving the strategy, rather than vice versa. Until the Helmand campaign, this approach was termed 'reinforcing failure'. The central plank of the whole British strategy in Iraq and Afghanistan, although largely undeclared, has been to demonstrate to the Americans the strength of the British commitment to the 'special relationship'. If Basra damaged that arm of the policy, Helmand destroyed it. As a well-regarded academic has put it, 'we're no longer the ally of first resort that we once were because of performance in Iraq and Afghanistan'.[28]

One senior retired military intelligence officer, a former colleague, who has served many tours in a very front-line role indeed in both Iraq and Helmand, told me:

> It's like we offered the Americans an aircraft carrier, something they have plenty of themselves, to do a particular task they have better and bigger resources to do themselves. As times go on they find that not only are people constantly falling off it and need to be rescued, there aren't enough aircraft, it runs out of fuel and bumps into things. In the end it needs to be replaced entirely at great cost to the Americans. What must they think? Every time the British offer help now, they are going to put their head in their hands: 'Oh no, the British are here!'

It would have made more sense to offer the Americans something worthwhile, like the special forces, and have left the rest of the troops at home. But those battalions were there, and they therefore needed to be used. If we didn't use them, we might have lost them, as we saw above.

A strategy?

As for the 'strategy', which, as we have seen, shifts regularly, very few informed commentators see it as either cogent or useful. It was only towards the end of 2009 that the British government finally settled on an apparently consistent and settled *casus belli*: 'Our objective is clear and focused: to prevent al Qaeda launching attacks on our streets and threatening legitimate government in Afghanistan and Pakistan.'[29] British MP and former soldier Adam Holloway put the problem thus:

> The Government seems to give a different strategic goal every few months depending on the political mood in Britain. Last year it was 'providing security so that development can take place', then it became 'fighting the terrorists there, so that we don't have to fight them here', and as of now we are focussed on 'protecting the people'.[30]

He recalls how 'an army officer ended a PowerPoint presentation in Helmand with the words "and this is why we are here": the last slide showed a picture of Afghan girls in school uniforms. If the British public are confused, imagine what the soldiers who are fighting and dying must feel.' This point has now been grasped at the national political level. The UK Foreign Affairs Select Committee reported in early 2011:

> between 2002 and 2008 the Government provided a series of reasons for the UK's presence in Afghanistan. In 2009, partly in a bid to stem dwindling public support for the war effort, and also to ensure consistency with the US's approach, the previous Government opted to return to a single 'narrative', that of the threat to the UK of Al Qaeda returning to Afghanistan.[31]

The journalist and expert on Afghan affairs James Fergusson told the Foreign Affairs Committee:

> [There is] absolutely no evidence that al-Qaeda even want to come back or that the Taliban would have them back if they did. I've had this conversation so many times in Afghanistan and I have not come across one Afghan who gets this justification for our presence there at all. They do not believe it.[32]

The committee concluded: 'in reality, there is a strong argument to be made that Afghanistan, and the Taliban insurgency, does not currently, in itself represent an immediate security threat to the UK'.[33] Not a single

'Al Qaeda' activist has been captured in Helmand, and Western intelligence agencies have estimated that there may be 'at most' fifty to a hundred Al Qaeda members in Afghanistan.[34] In contrast, Britain is said to be host to the largest presence in the Western world.[35]

Furthermore, any residual notion of Karzai's government having democratic legitimacy evaporated in the Afghan presidential elections of 2009. In those circumstances, it is perhaps not surprising that at least one study showed most British officers to have a limited notion of the reasons why they are fighting in the country.[36]

Exit strategy

The current exit strategy relies upon training the Afghan security forces to secure their own country. This could prove exceedingly difficult. The police are widely regarded to be at best a disparate group of drug-addled rogues. Rather more commonly they are seen as criminals in uniform preying on the decent citizens of Afghanistan. The Afghan army has a different problem. One Helmandi politician told me, 'The best thing about the army is that they protect us from the police.' The problem with the army is not that the Afghan soldiers are incapable, corrupt or have an unsustainably high desertion rate, though all of these issues arise. Rather the problem lies in who those soldiers actually are. A friend of mine served in Helmand as an OMLET (Operational Mentor Liaison Team) leader, responsible for training and mentoring Afghan soldiers. He related an incident in which his men captured some Taliban fighters. They were taken to the patrol base where, being the middle of the afternoon and the appropriate time for doing so, the Afghan soldiers began to pray. One of the Taliban asked a British soldier guarding him, through an interpreter, what these men were doing. The soldier told him that they were praying. 'Why are they praying?' asked the Talib. 'They are Russians, aren't they?'

The Afghan soldiers were not, of course, Russian. Nor were they Pashtun. They were Tajik, Hazara and Uzbek, from provinces very far from Helmand in every sense. One or two may have been Pashtun, but if so they were probably Pashtun from a different region of the country. How can one be so sure? Because, significantly, less than 3 per cent of Afghan army soldiers are southern Pashtun.[37] 'In other words,' as one British official put it to me, 'they are as foreign to Helmandis as we are.' Sir Sherard Cowper-Coles, former UK ambassador to Afghanistan, made the point even more clearly in his evidence to the UK Parliamentary Select Committee on Foreign Affairs: 'The Afghan Army is almost as alien to the farmers of the Helmand valley as the 3rd Battalion, the Rifles or the 82nd Airborne Division of the United States Army.'[38] That is indeed the case. In fact, the average Helmandi Afghan would be unable to communicate with these soldiers, any more than with British soldiers, as most Helmandis do not speak the Persian dialect of Dari, the language spoken by most northern Afghans.

Historically, Afghanistan has always harboured what might charitably be called 'difficulties' between its constituent groups: the relatively urban north against the traditional tribally based south. Matthew Hoh, a former US marine and civilian political officer in the province of Zabul in eastern Afghanistan (an area similar in ethnic make-up to Helmand, although probably less traditional), resigned his post, stating that he did not feel that US blood and treasure should be spent on fighting what amounted to a thirty-year civil war:

> the US and NATO presence in Pashtun valleys and villages, as well as Afghan police and army units that are led and composed of non-Pashtun soldiers and police, provide an occupation force against which the insurgency is justified. I have observed that the bulk of the insurgency fights not for the white banner of the Taliban but against the presence of foreign soldiers and taxes imposed by a non-representative government in Kabul.[39]

As an expression of the simple idea of insurgents fighting for a cause that is at the very least cogent and understandable, Hoh's letter is as fine an example as it is possible to find. Very few aware and experienced officials who have spent longer than a few months in the country would privately disagree with Hoh's sentiments. To them, it is merely a statement of the obvious.

When asked how long he would stay if the British and Americans were to leave, one Afghan officer replied, 'About twenty-four hours.'[40] As for the police, no hope whatsoever can be placed in them. For most Helmandis, these men are a source of real fear and distrust. While the senior police officer's quip to me that his men were responsible for 'only' 85 per cent of crime in the province was amusing at the time, it exposed a very real problem. For Afghans, the consequence of this 'problem' is kidnap, rape, theft and, occasionally, murder by those who are ostensibly paid to protect them.

One day the British and Americans will leave, as the Soviets did before them. Whether the Afghan army will last for another three years, as it did in the early 1990s, time alone will tell. In the early 1990s it was a trained, armoured and well-equipped force with a significant remnant of the old professional army of pre-Soviet days. Once the Soviet forces left, the incentive to fight foreigners vanished and the levels of violence decreased substantially, at least for some considerable time. In other words, the foreign troops were the problem then as, largely, they are now. As Hoh implies, the Taliban itself may not have very much traction. But given the choice, few patriotic Pashtuns are going to prefer foreign troops (or non-Pashtun-speaking Afghans) to their own ethnic brethren in the Taliban.

Lessons from recent predecessors?

As far as Westerners are concerned, the Soviet legacy in Afghanistan is one of fire and the sword – a litany of massacres, bombings and indiscriminate oppression. This is the account we were given throughout the 1980s, and undoubtedly, as far as it goes, that is what happened. But it is not *all* that happened. In his book on the Russian experience in the Afghan War *Afghantsy* former senior British diplomat Sir Rodric Braithwaite takes the view that 'there was no grudge against the Russians' on the part of Afghans.[41] On the contrary, he recalls a visit to Afghanistan in 2008 when he was 'told by every Afghan that he met that things were better under the Russians'.[42] Braithwaite believes that this lack of animosity may derive from the appalling chaos that ensued following their departure in 1989. That chaos was ended by the Taliban in 1996. In many parts of the country it has now returned.

While serving in Helmand as a civilian adviser to the justice system (such as it was), I too was struck by how little animosity there was towards the Russians. Almost every day I attended the offices of Afghan police, prosecutors and judges. There was one particular senior police officer that I used to visit about twice a week, whom I shall call Abdul (not his real name). The interpreters working for us were young and sometimes not quite up to the task. Occasionally Abdul and I would speak Russian, a language Abdul spoke perfectly and I speak very poorly. Nonetheless, my Russian was slightly better than the interpreters' English. 'You come to see me twice a week, and your visits are useful,' Abdul commented one day. 'It is nice to talk with you about our work; but when the Soviets were here, your equivalent would sit here alongside us, he would work here, have his desk and we would speak of every case we were dealing with. That is the best way to cooperate. Why can't you do that?'

All civilians were accompanied at all times outside the gates of the fort that houses the PRT by a group of heavily armed bodyguards. The reason for this is that there was a perceived risk to us. I explained this to Abdul. 'I would guarantee your safety,' he replied, and I believed him. I asked whether Soviet advisers had had such bodyguards. 'They didn't need them and pretty much came and went as they liked – at least here,' he answered. 'They would cordon towns and secure them. Within the cordon, there were few problems.'

This is classic counterinsurgency and is exactly what the British did in their various campaigns, and indeed what was regularly done, very successfully, in Iraq by some American officers.[43] The Soviets had inherited a well-functioning and reasonably competent army when they invaded the country. Consequently, the manpower available to them was far greater. There was no army at all when NATO invaded in 2001 – and what army there is now is seriously compromised by desertion and drug addiction. The most NATO has managed is to 'secure' villages such as the famous 'city' of Marjah, into which the 'government in a box' was inserted. UK forces have barely managed to 'secure' three district centres. It is axiomatic that in Afghanistan, government control extends six kilometres from the district centres. In the case of those 'secured' by British forces, that radius is reduced to the range of the weapons on the perimeter of the district base.

The Soviet technique of cordoning towns was not very far from what had originally been planned prior to the initial UK deployment in 2006 under the 'Helmand Plan' – shelved de facto by the activities of 16 Air Assault Brigade and their successors. Abdul went on to say that we (the British) needed to think about what the Soviets did: 'at least they left us some bridges'. Bridges, of course, were not their only positive legacy. Once again, all this is dependent on having the resources and on committing them.

My friend Abdul spoke such good Russian because, at the time of the Soviet occupation, he had been taken to the Soviet Union for three years to train as a police officer, a time he spoke of with great fondness. He was by no means unusual. About 25,000 Afghans were taken to Russia or the other Soviet republics every year between 1979 and 1989 to train as doctors, lawyers, police officers, army officers, prison officers – indeed all the officials a modern state needs in order to function. The investment in training nearly a quarter of a million people – of both genders, as women's rights and equality were high on the 'socialist' agenda – was immense. Almost all the lawyers, police officers and prison officers I dealt with spoke perfect Russian and had good memories of their time in the USSR. Rather surprisingly, to me, they often worked closely with colleagues who had fought them as former mujahedin. There were two exceptions to this uniformly Soviet-trained cadre, and both of them were judges. One was a former Taliban judge, the other a flagrantly corrupt old man trained in the 1960s, who had spent a very great amount of time outside the country.

Soviet investment in civilian development went both ways. In addition to training and educating many tens of thousands of young Afghans, large numbers of Soviet civilian advisers were posted for years to Afghanistan, of whom very many were killed – despite the efforts at security.[44] Why? The reason, unpalatable as it is now for NATO countries, is that the objective of the USSR was similar to that of NATO – stabilization. Afghanistan represented a threat to the stability of its Central Asian republics, and it was a national priority to remove that threat. A great deal of construction was carried out. Similarly, of course, the army was mentored in exactly the same way as it is now. Films of the period by journalists embedded with Soviet army units are remarkable in their similarity to those we see today.

Abdul had been sent to Russia for years to train, but the best the British could offer him, assuming he behaved and did as he was told, was a two-week course in Kabul. Ensconced as he was in what he rightly regarded as a highly dangerous backwater – for most Afghans, Helmand is truly a remote and distinctly unique province – he was very keen to do such courses. The point here is that NATO's efforts are somewhat less than half-hearted. If there is to be a 'total effort' then let it be total. If national interest dictates that this effort is worth the lives, limbs, eyes and mental health of young British men and women, then surely it is worth applying the same level of aid as the reviled Soviet Union considered necessary. Of course, the USSR failed. But Afghan memories of the Soviet time are not by any means as negative as one might presume, especially as they are coloured by the even worse predations of the mujahedin warlords whom the Taliban overthrew, to general acclaim. Instead of making a serious effort to stabilize the country, the piecemeal efforts, particularly of the British, attracted little but contempt.

Helmand's history and occidentalist expectation

Afghans are not enamoured of British efforts. They take the view, however, that the British failure can only be deliberate. After all, they reason, this is not Russia. This is the free West. These people, the British, can achieve great things. Yet what have they done here? Bizarrely to the Western ear, the reason commonly believed in Helmand is 'revenge for Maiwand'. Why else would a powerful, rich country fail so disastrously to fulfil promises of security and development? Journalist Jean Mackenzie explained:

> This is not an opinion held by one or two people. I never met an Afghan who did not hold the view that the British were in Helmand to screw them. They hate the British viscerally and historically. Even if they were competent, there was no chance the British were going to do well there. But when they came in with gobbledegook about 'robust rules of engagement' and started killing Helmandi civilians, that was it.

Another well-connected official told me that the idea that the British were failing deliberately is held not only by country folk of Helmand, but by President Karzai himself.[45]

That Afghans assume that the British are (or should be) competent is interesting in itself. It is a facet of what Mary Kaldor has called 'occidentalism', the mirror image of 'orientalism', the 'West', and for present purposes the British army, is a competent and technically capable entity. The corollary of this misconception is that, when promises are made that are not fulfilled, assuming the predicate of competence and capability is accepted, there is only one possible explanation: the promises were deceitful and the failure must therefore be deliberate. Of course the British army believes itself to be competent: it has shown itself capable of killing great numbers of Taliban efficiently (along with large numbers of civilians). It is not unreasonable, therefore, that the host population should see failure to deliver on the other promises as deliberate.

Far more even than the embarrassment of Basra, Helmand has demonstrated the bankruptcy of post-imperial 'counterinsurgency' in countries without adequate or entirely supportive government. As in Basra, the most basic fundamental requirement is security. In this context that means freedom from the threat of violence – from whomsoever that violence may come – and roads not preyed upon by intensely corrupt police with whom the British are closely associated.

The British army has failed to understand the basic concept that a host population will, at the best of times, treat foreign soldiers with circumspection. These are not the best of times and the British was certainly not the best of armies to have been inserted into the single most difficult and radically traditionalist of all Afghan provinces. When that initial historical disadvantage is coupled with an excessively violent ('kinetic') operational profile – a consequence of the fact that the troops are overstretched and so lack of troops on the ground is made up for by the liberal use of heavy weaponry, with concomitant extensive civilian casualties – an occupying army has a serious problem.

The British army has now been in Afghanistan longer than the Soviets. Its declared objective in 2006 when it entered Helmand was to provide security in the province's fourteen districts. Five years later a force three times the size of the initial deployment clings on to three districts, and even in those the situation is appallingly difficult. In early 2011 a soldier, who understandably preferred anonymity, wrote to the *Independent* newspaper, 'We are told British troops will be home soon. You'd think things must have drastically improved. The troops here can't patrol any further than 3 km without coming under attack. Hardly a drastic improvement . . .' He was not optimistic about how matters might end: 'Afghanistan will be the next Iraq, forgotten and ignored. It certainly won't be a success story, though I'm sure the Americans and the British will move the goal posts to make the pull-out look like a victory.'[46] Time will tell.

An inability to collocate talk and action has resulted in an almost irretrievable security situation. The British generals – it is very difficult, of course, to establish which ones – had entered Helmand with 3,500 troops, with the aim, presumably, of being sufficiently manned to fulfil their plan. By late 2010, some 30,000 foreign soldiers (20,000 American and 10,000 British), plus several thousand Afghan troops and a few other assorted NATO contingents, struggled to hold down the province. By any standards – by any measure at all – this was a complete failure. In the opening words of this chapter, penned by Leo Docherty, himself a veteran of Helmand, the campaign was not only a 'blundering catastrophe but a violent tragedy'.

The responsibility for this must rest squarely with the generals, who are charged with providing sound, realistic advice to their political masters. We look now at how an apparent lack of strategic awareness on the part of those generals set the army up for the mess in which it now finds itself. 'It was always obvious that it was going to turn to rat shit quickly,' one senior former army officer put it to me – restating the Clausewitzian idea of friction – 'because it always does. The fact is that armies get it wrong. This is not hindsight. Coping with this is the task of the contingency planner and the responsibility of the general.'[47]

PART TWO

PART TWO

CHAPTER 5

Dereliction of Duty:
The Generals and Strategy

Commanders have consistently failed to link the resources available to them with overall campaign objectives or the long-term sustainability of the operation.

King, 'Understanding the Helmand campaign', p. 324

At times the Chiefs of Staff seem to have forgotten that they exist to represent the military to government, not the other way around.

Leader in *The Times*, 7 July 2010

From the day an officer enters basic training, the notion of taking responsibility is presented as central to the very idea of having a commission. In the oldest armed service in the world, the Royal Navy, this idea is written into the law. If any mishap befalls a ship – a collision, perhaps, or a running aground – the commanding officer is held almost automatically responsible, whether or not he is actually to blame. A recent example of this was the removal of the commanding officer of Her Majesty's submarine *Astute* after it (rather publicly) ran aground off the island of Skye in October 2010. Similarly, the commanding officer of HMS *Cornwall* was removed some months after the kidnapping, in extraordinary circumstances, of thirteen members of his crew by Iranian forces in 2007. These are, of course, relatively junior officers.

Nonetheless, this traditional practice collocates two different notions: of responsibility and of fault. It does so for good, human reasons that, until recently, did not need elucidating – a commanding officer will take care to ensure that those under his command are competent and well trained if he knows that he will have to carry the can for any mistakes they make. The idea of holding commanders responsible for events for which they are not to blame was carried to its extreme with the execution of Admiral Byng for 'failing to do his utmost' to prevent the loss of Minorca to the French in 1757. His ships were in disrepair, and his forces were far too few to defend the island. Nonetheless he was executed '*pour encourager les autres*', as Voltaire said of the incident.

The obverse of this approach is to identify a relatively junior officer in proximity to the questionable action and 'hang him out to dry'. This would appear to have been the approach taken in response to the confusion of the initial Helmand deployment, when Brigadier Butler was held responsible for the decision to disperse forces, despite the presence on or near the scene of at least one senior general. This, in military parlance, would imply a 'sloping of shoulders' on the part of more senior officers, who were in fact both responsible and culpable.

Another expedient adopted against taking responsibility for failure is the simple technique of denying that it occurred. This strategy is no longer tenable in either Iraq or Afghanistan.

A very great number of chiefs . . .

How many generals (or officers of general rank, such as admirals or air marshals) are there in the UK armed forces? One might, in a perfect world, begin by assessing how many are needed. Let us take the army, as an example. A brigade, the basic formation employed in both Iraq and Afghanistan, is commanded by a brigadier. Such officers were formerly known in the British army as 'brigadier generals', and they are still called that in most NATO armies. They are 'one-star generals'. There are between ten and twelve brigades, and so one might presume that twelve brigadiers are required. We might add some who have not been promoted and stay on the books, and others who are preparing for command, say thirty or so altogether. In fact, there are 190 – twenty more than in 1997.[1]

There are, at a stretch, two divisions in the British army that might, with a great deal of notice and a following wind, be deployed as actual fighting divisions – 1 Armoured Division and 3 Division.[2] Divisions are commanded by major generals. There are forty-three major generals. We have a single army corps (the Allied Command Europe Rapid Reaction Corps), but sufficient lieutenant generals to command seventeen army corps, a force that the British army, even when millions strong, has rarely if ever possessed. Crowning the lot, we have five full generals. Remember, these figures are *only for the army*. The other two services are equally richly accoutred, proportionally. The three armed forces are scaled for no fewer than 500 general officers – that is brigadier or above.[3] In other words, there are sufficient officers of 'flag rank' to crew three modern destroyers or to provide almost a full battalion for deployment.

To put these figures into perspective, there are far more generals in the British army than there are helicopters,[4] or operational tanks.[5] There are considerably more admirals than ships, and about three times as many RAF officers of one star or above than there are flying squadrons..

Surely the US has more?

These figures, though, are surely meaningless if we fail to compare them with their equivalents elsewhere. The US Marine Corps has far greater battlefield combat power than the British army and the Royal Air Force combined.[6] As a sea-going service, it has at its disposal a capable amphibious navy with more aircraft carriers than the Royal Navy has had at any time since the 1960s. At about 210,000 strong, it is slightly larger than the three UK services combined, including reserves. It gets by with eighty-four general officers of all ranks.[7] The US army – about five times the size of its UK equivalent, and exponentially more complex and combat capable – is limited in its numbers of generals by statute,[8] and manages to command itself with a mere 302 generals, compared to the UK army's 255. The number of generals in the truly vast apparatus that is the US armed forces is 963 – less than twice as many generals as the UK armed forces employ.[9]

The Israeli Defence Forces (comprising army, navy and air force) of about 170,000 – similar in size to the UK's – find themselves able to function reasonably effectively with only one lieutenant general, twelve major generals (or equivalent) and about thirty-five brigadier equivalents. This highly capable force finds no requirement for any four-star officers at all. There are, proportionately *eight times* more generals in the UK armed forces than there are in the US Marine Corps, four times as many as in the US army, and an astonishing ten times as many as the Israelis have.

Have there always been this many senior British officers? It seems not. Even looked at from a historical perspective, the figures are astonishing. In 1910,[10] almost exactly a century ago, the army fielded (if that is the word for such officers) nineteen full generals,[11] thirty lieutenant generals and eighty-one major generals – figures comparable to today. Or so it would seem. In fact, this figure hides some rather large factors. First, the rank of brigadier (190 today) did not exist. Command of brigades resulted in the temporary appointment of full colonels as brigadier generals.[12] Those same generals of 1910 were also responsible for the Indian army of the time (composed of about 155,000 men). The army in Britain alone comprised no fewer than eighty-seven infantry regiments, each with more than one battalion (today there are thirty-six infantry battalions), not including myriad artillery, engineers, cavalry and reserves. The army of 1910 also had worldwide commitments that in numbers, complexity and nature far exceeded today's.

With more generals than helicopters, and almost as many as there are operational tanks, can it be that the UK army simply promotes too many officers to general rank, with a commensurate reduction in quality?

In-fighting

As always, the answer is 'it's not as simple as you think'. The reason there are so many very senior officers is closely tied to the perennial bureaucratic battle between the services, which expend an extraordinary amount of effort in trying to steal a march on each other. In the vastly bloated bureaucracy of the British armed forces, each service grabs the opportunity to promote as many of its people as possible – very often, of course, beyond their capability.

Three four-star officers exist simply to keep each of the services separate and to fight their corners at equivalent levels.[13] Below them in the MoD are echelons of two- and three-star officers doing administrative jobs that in any other army of comparable size, or any rationally constituted organization, would be given to officers of far lower rank or civil servants. Then there are the various service headquarters, administrative and operational, all of which require flag or general officers to command them. The MoD provides employment for platoons of major generals and brigadiers (and their equivalents). Then there are the richly ranked organizations, such as PJHQ, which at least has the benefit of providing command and guidance to soldiers who actually work on operations. Various NATO commands take up several dozen others. One might be forgiven for asking why the armed forces need four grades of general officer anyway. Why not three, or, heaven forfend, even two?[14] In pre-First World War days there were only three grades of general, with one of those reserved only for the most senior command. The 800 or so full colonels (or equivalent) today command nothing; it is a pure staff rank. Those who do manage to jostle their way to the top do so via a promotion system almost designed to sustain an attitudinal status quo. Those who reach brigadier rank or above are intensely competitive and driven men, particularly those graded as suitable for operational command (by no means all brigadiers). The trouble is that the system ensures that they are cut from the same cloth as those more senior officers. Mavericks or 'dangerous eccentrics' do not prosper.

This must be so, as it is those more senior officers who are doing the selection. It is a fascinating and instructive fact that the most revolutionary of all those who commanded in Afghanistan, Brigadier Andrew Mackay, was, as we saw above, *not* initially selected to command a brigade on operations. Certainly, he was not cut from the 'kinetic' manoeuvre cloth of high-intensity, high-pressure, constantly moving warfare. It is no coincidence that his brigade was the only formation that looked seriously at new ways of conducting warfare – methods considered little short of radical by his peers and, unfortunately, not adopted generally until it was far too late.

Responsible officers

Fourteen brigadiers and an equal number of major generals commanded in Basra during the occupation. As of the beginning of 2011, there have been at least ten British brigadiers and four major generals involved in commanding in southern Afghanistan, not including far, far greater numbers of generals (of various ranks) attached to the various ISAF and NATO headquarters in Kabul and Europe that deal with Afghanistan. It is, in fact, difficult to determine how many generals are involved in a given operation, let alone who is responsible for the operation itself.

Each brigade commander, as we have seen, has brought his own focus and emphasis to the campaigns. Each has fought, as we have seen, his own six-month war. Incidentally, there has been only one brigadier who has commanded his brigade in both theatres: John Lorimer, who took 12 Brigade to Iraq in 2005 and commanded his unit again in Helmand in 2007.

What, though, of even more senior commanders than operational two-star officers? Is there any more clarity to command responsibility at the highest command levels? Not really. Since 2003, there have been four chiefs of the general staff – the professional head of the army,[15] and the same number of chiefs of the defence staff – the title given to the head of the armed forces.

To give some idea of the diffusion of responsibility, at least thirty-one generals of two stars or above gave evidence at the Iraq Inquiry. These numbers do not include the dozens of brigadiers involved at all levels in command, planning and administration. The words of leading journalist Stephen Grey, speaking of the operations in Helmand in 2007–8 resound deeply: 'The real problem with this mess was that when things went wrong, everyone could blame everyone else. No-one felt they were truly in charge. Or had the authority to take real risks. Or show moral courage. It was a set-up for muddle-headed thinking.'[16] One retired general put it to me this way: 'The trouble is that a lot of people want the authority, not so many are keen on the responsibility.'[17]

The hugely bloated nature of the UK military is not confined to its general officers. There are no fewer than 5,500 officers of full colonel or lieutenant colonel rank (or equivalent) in all three services,[18] and 9,550 officers of the rank of major. In other words, about 8 per cent of all servicemen are ranked at a level that traditionally would command a company of a hundred or so, or a reasonably large ship.[19] An entire division, with all its ancillary support, could be manned by army officers over the rank of major. Their naval equivalents could crew an aircraft carrier, escort it with a couple of fully manned frigates – if such could be found – and RAF senior officers could cover it all with a couple of fighter squadrons, complete with all necessary support, maintenance and guard force.

Once senior officers leave behind the rank of army major or equivalent the majority of them never see any kind of command or true leadership role. There are simply not enough such roles for the numbers involved. Instead, they are absorbed into administrative jobs, largely within the much-reviled (ironically, especially by military officers) MoD. Although cuts in such jobs were announced in August 2010, it is highly unlikely that these will work through the system within the next three to five years.[20]

Rewarding success

Leadership is crucial, central to the success of any military operation. One striking feature of the militarily successful (for the British) nineteenth century was the consistency with which certain generals were summoned to lead expeditionary wars. Reading of these often forgotten campaigns now, it is truly extraordinary how often the names of a few generals appear – Wolseley, Roberts, Kitchener and several members of the remarkable Napier family.[21] Command of large, important or high-profile missions was a matter of very great prestige. However, governments also appreciated that it was vital to have proven victors in control of important operations. Responsibility for the success or failure of operations lay squarely with the commanding generals, and there was never any doubt as to who, in any given situation, that would be. The chain of command was also clear.

The constant rotation of commanders within different formations rotating through operational theatres has been described by a senior officer to the author as 'akin to work experience for generals'.[22] Of course, with 500 general officers on the books today, a very great deal of work experience is required. This approach would have been regarded as unthinkable by the Victorians, who understood instinctively that, while success has many fathers, failure is an orphan. They were keen to ensure proper reward for the successful and deserved obscurity for the failed. Failure (or perceived failure) resulted in quick dismissal and equally quick dispatch into the world of gardening leave. Success was rewarded with pensions (Napier received the vast sum of £70,000 for taking Sindh), knighthoods and peerages. General Gordon was referred to by the sobriquet 'Chinese' due to his heroics in the wars of the early 1860s, Earl Roberts received his peerage with the title 'Kandahar'; Kitchener of Khartoum and Baron Napier of Magdala (a cousin of Napier of Sindh) had the well-deserved status of national heroes.

Into the twentieth century, the practice of ennobling senior commanders continued. In the First World War, now forgotten officers, such as Lords Byng of Vimy or Plumer of Messines, ranked alongside better-known generals such as Allenby of Megiddo (otherwise known as Armageddon) or Earl French of Ypres. The Second World War gave the House of Lords Montgomery of Alamein and Alexander of Tunis. Although Gerald Templer never received a peerage, there can be little doubt that the sobriquet 'Tiger of Malaya' was well earned. Success brought recognition.

Equally, during the Second World War, Churchill and even more so the chief of the imperial general staff Field Marshal Alan Brooke, had little hesitation in firing generals whose performance was considered inadequate.[23] One of the better known of many such cases occurred in 1941–2 in the western desert of Egypt, when, in July 1941, Auchinleck replaced Wavell as commander in chief (Middle East) after a lacklustre performance. Auchinleck removed two successive commanders of the Eighth Army before himself being fired. His place was taken by Montgomery who, some say, took much of the credit due to 'the Auk' for the later victory at Alamein. The point to be drawn from this is that when generals were clearly failing, they had to go.

All must have prizes

In June 2010, with the accession of a new British government, it seems that Air Chief Marshal Sir Jock Stirrup was asked to resign a few months before his intended retirement date, not for operational failure but because he was (allegedly) too close to the previous government. The new government stated that his departure was 'amicable'.[24] Other than Stirrup, a good man who accepted his fate with the dignity expected of one of his seniority and distinction, not a single senior officer has been dismissed or has resigned for any operational reason whatsoever during the two recent campaigns. It is invidious to select examples, although a former British general with extensive relevant operational experience told me that he had found it very difficult to explain to majors and lieutenant colonels how one general could depart for his leave (to which he was, of course, entitled, like everyone else) three weeks after he arrived, during a vitally important period of the operation in Basra. He placed it in context: 'All I have to do is imagine a US two-star general at the beginning of a major tour doing something like that. It is just inconceivable.' Not only was the general concerned not censured in any way, he was promoted. Another general was absent on leave in France when a crucial raid was launched on a police station.[25] He, too, was promoted.

While few senior officers are dismissed, almost all are decorated. Not a single general officer commanding has returned from theatre without being awarded an operational honour. Clearly the likelihood of a decoration is significantly improved if one has undertaken one of the regular 'signature' operations described above. Six of the twelve divisional commanders in Basra have so far been promoted[26] – not, so far, including Major General Andrew Salmon, who ensured a far more dignified withdrawal than could be expected in the circumstances.

In seeking a constructive solution, one can do no better than to quote Major General Andrew Mackay:

A cull should be instigated of the senior commanders not fit for their role in the war at hand and who may have played (*sic*) an unhelpful contribution to the unsuccessful conventional-orientated campaign so far; promotion systems need to be torn up and replaced with those apt for a war; those fit for command should not be kept waiting to assume responsibility.[27]

In a military world shot through with conformity, one wonders who might instigate such a cull. One should not hold one's breath waiting.

Those fit for command in a war against the armies of the Soviet Union are not the same as those fit to lead in the current form of struggle. Undoubtedly, many of the senior officers leading in Iraq and Afghanistan would have made fine commanders in other theatres – indeed in traditional 'expeditionary' wars. The war in Afghanistan and the squalid fighting in Iraq are a different form of conflict, requiring entirely different skills and attitudes – not all of which are taught at the Staff College at Shrivenham or cherished within the strongly conservative institutions of the army, navy and air force. After all, the greatest of colonial generals – heroes such as

General Redvers Buller – who were highly successful in fighting traditional 'stand up and shoot' wars against traditional colonial foes, such as the Zulus or Sudanese, proved disastrous when put up against a new kind of enemy – the Boers. In those days, however, failure was quickly followed by dismissal. Now the 'wrong people' are prospering.

This problem is well-known. A serving senior officer put it to me this way: 'In the old days, when a general did badly, he was fired. If he did well, he got a viscountcy. That is a tradition we should begin again.'[28] The danger is, of course, that in a culture where failure is without a father, this might produce rather more viscountcies than firings. Winston Churchill, so often exasperated by his military advisers (as they were with him), once expressed the view that: 'The best thing would be to form a Sacred Legion of about 1,000 Staff Officers and let them set an example to the troops in leading some particularly desperate attack.' That 'Sacred Legion' has become untouchable.

The 'stab in the back' myth

By 2010 it was clear that the British army's reputation for 'small wars' and counterinsurgency was a thing of the past. Valiant attempts by academics were made to reconstruct – or indeed deconstruct – the two campaigns as post-modernist attempts to find a way through the confusion of 'counter-insurgency'.[29] This, in turn, was compounded by a chronic, overriding lack of strategic coherence.

All who have followed the wars in Afghanistan and Iraq are familiar with the allegations of betrayal and underfunding of our forces by politicians, resulting in substandard or non-existent equipment, notably a lack of helicopters and adequately armoured vehicles. There is no doubt that there was a critical lack of helicopters. When I was in Helmand, spaces on Chinooks needed to be booked many days in advance. If, as happened regularly, an airframe went 'U/S' (unserviceable) or was 'hit by a pterodactyl', as was reported on one occasion, there might be no aircraft available for any missions whatsoever, except casualty evacuation. Up to 2008, when matters improved slightly, British VIPs often visited on American Blackhawk helicopters, there being no British aircraft to spare.[30] The chaos surrounding the procurement of appropriate armoured vehicles for both theatres is a matter of public record.

These undoubted deficiencies provided an ideal pretext for senior command, supported by a sympathetic media, to apportion blame for sinking missions to this essentially peripheral symptom, and therefore to the reviled politicians. As one former British army officer who had the valuable perspective of having also served with the Canadian armed forces, has said: 'professional soldiers tend to look at themselves as part of a select order, upholding the highest moral and professional standards, while seeing politicians as self-serving hypocrites'.[31] This approach tends, of course, to support the dangerous 'stab in the back' myth – the true message of which is 'it was all someone else's fault'. The many controversies concerning equipment played well into this narrative.

The responsibility of the politicians for failing to set any (or any adequate) policy or end-state for either campaign is beyond question. Their failure to fund adequate equipment cost many lives, but did not influence the failure of either operation. To them belongs the lion's share of responsibility for the shameful position we find ourselves in at all levels, and that responsibility should not be minimized in this book or anywhere else.

Nonetheless, generals are apt to blame everyone except themselves for the operational and tactical results of their own decisions. They are very prone to excoriating politicians for failure to fund equipment.[32] Those same generals are less inclined to declare that the procurement decisions giving rise to shortages, by and large, were taken not by reviled civil servants within the MoD, but by senior military officers. Many thousands of staff officers – some of them, indeed a great many of them, of very senior rank – are employed within the ministry staff precisely to make those sorts of decisions. The reason why there were no adequate armoured vehicles and few helicopters is that priorities set a decade ago by those officers and their civil servant colleagues resulted in decisions to fund high-end missiles, tanks and jet aircraft, rather than less shiny but far more useful transport and protection.

At the higher, theatre, level, a series of parallel strategic narratives is developing to explain British performance in these two wars of choice: That these were, in fact, successful campaigns, that Iraq was a 'strategic success' and Afghanistan is stabilizing. Ignoring any objective assessment of military performance, and the fact that US forces took Basra from a numerically and conceptually challenged British presence, the story being driven through by generals is that the results were planned all along and, though a close-run thing, matters have worked out in the end.

A long way to the east, in Afghanistan, the new story runs something like this: the British were not bailed out after a catastrophic overestimation of their own capabilities; rather, the American presence in Helmand, which vastly outnumbers the old British presence, is a testament to just how skilfully the British forces managed to hold out for so long. The British were the Spartans at Thermopylae – valiantly holding the line, while the Americans, in their role as the more numerous and better-funded Athenians, prepared to strike the decisive blow.

The one thing the British did not do was fail. Failure is bad for careers. This method of dealing with defeat, by simply denying that it happened, is not an approach welcomed, for example, in Israel, where military failures in recent years have resulted in senior politicians and generals at all ranks being fired. Repainting defeat as victory, a trait British generals have found useful, is not acceptable in Israel, where defence is a matter of vital national concern. British inquiries into national embarrassments have had a generally ruminant quality, often being led by solid establishment judges or civil servants,[33] and almost always willing to give the benefit of the doubt to senior public servants. Indeed, the Iraq Inquiry, which has turned up so much in the way of interesting information, and which is due to report in mid-2011, will not apportion blame – merely identify lessons.[34] The conclusions reached by the Israeli Winograd Inquiry into the 2006 Lebanon War – that the army was 'unprepared', the goals were unachievable and the execution was poor – would be almost unimaginable in a British context. In a society where almost every Jewish citizen has served in the armed forces, there is no room for special pleading and little sympathy for senior officers who fail.

Aside from these essentially cultural ingrained problems, there was one omission that made success in Iraq and Helmand not only unlikely but effectively impossible: the failure to articulate a strategy. This arose from a lack of coherent policy guidance and a total failure to have the slightest appreciation of the possibility that, in the words of one senior officer who had been involved in the planning of the First Gulf War, 'it might all turn to rat shit'. It was here that the generals should have jumped in and asked the right questions – or indeed *any* questions – and demanded answers.

The need for strategy

No-one starts a war – or rather no-one in his senses ought to do so – without being clear in his mind what he intends to achieve by that war and how he intends to conduct it. The former is its political purpose; the latter its operational objective. This is the governing principle which will set its course, prescribe the scale of means and effort which is required, and make its influence felt throughout down to the smallest operational detail.[35]

Every well-trained staff officer in the Western world will have encountered this precept at some point. Its central idea has been digested into a very simple aphorism that constitutes the first 'principle of war', taught to every young officer – 'the selection and maintenance of the aim'. All officers are encouraged to ask at all stages: 'What is the end-state, what am I asked to achieve?'

That is the policy. The strategy is how you get there. 'Strategy', to quote a famous maxim, 'is the art of matching ends and means.'[36] Freedom in Iraq may be the policy objective. Invading Iraq and removing its leader, and the methods required and planned to achieve that outcome, will be the strategy.[37] The number one requirement for success in achieving a policy objective is a sensible, well-thought-out strategy; without it, failure is inevitable.

The degree to which generals failed in that duty to articulate a coherent strategy has come to light with the evidence given to the Iraq Inquiry. Streams of generals appeared before this august grouping to confirm the worst: that almost no thought was given to the aftermath; that there had been no coordination between relevant government departments. The blame for this failure was put squarely on the shoulders of politicians, who did indeed bear the major responsibility. However, it was never explained, at the inquiry or elsewhere, why the military commanders had failed to make any provisions of their own or to advise strongly that failing to plan for the aftermath rendered the war an even more dangerous undertaking than it already was.

The leading strategist and academic Colin Gray describes the relative duties of generals and politicians in simple Clausewitzian terms. It is for the politicians to articulate the 'logic' of a conflict. The generals must devise and execute its 'grammar'. 'Politicians', he says, 'are promoted to the stratosphere of senior policy making, membership in war cabinets, and the like for many reasons, but demonstrable skill in strategy is unlikely to be among them.'[38] There is a gulf between politicians' understanding of war and generals' comprehension of policy. He goes on to say: 'The policy maker wages war, while the military commander fights battles or campaigns; between those realms, though drawing from them both lies the bridging zone of "strategy".'[39] It is a zone that is fraught with difficulties. This excerpt from an exchange between Field Marshal Ironside, chief of the imperial general staff (CIGS), and Minister for War Hore-Belisha in late 1939, just after the outbreak of the Second World War, illustrates the tensions that can arise:

> I said, 'Now, Mr Belisha, I have formed a better opinion of you during the last few weeks. You have behaved extremely well during this crisis, and I have changed my mind about you. But understand this – and let us be quite clear about it – I never asked to become CIGS, and I accept it only on condition that you are perfectly frank with me, that you never go behind my back, or speak contrary to or without my advice on any military matter. If I find you doing that, I will have you out, or I will go. These are my terms, and you must accept them.'[40]

There is little doubt that, were a chief of the defence staff to take that attitude today with a secretary of state for defence, he would be shown the door in short order. It is equally certain that no officer with an approach such as Ironside's would have progressed to be considered for the position. It is the duty of generals, however, to give unambiguous, impartial professional advice to their political masters: 'Politicians and the country as a whole have a right to expect senior military professionals to speak military, and hence probably strategic, truth to political power.'[41] There is no evidence that British senior commanders ever took to heart this most serious of duties – that of advising *and challenging*.

A US soldier-scholar, H.R. McMaster, wrote a landmark book in the late 1980s about a similar failure of the US chiefs of staff to take on their political masters. He called his book – somewhat controversially at the time, since he was (and is) a serving officer in the US army – *Dereliction of Duty*.[42] US army rumour has it that his promotion was stalled for some years, until General Petraeus chaired the promotion board. Brigadier General McMaster, as he now is, carried his independent mind into Iraq, where he served with distinction.[43] As we shall see, officers such as 'HR', as he is known, are rare indeed in the upper reaches of the British army.

The approach taken by senior British commanders reflected more of what might be called a 'Yes, Prime Minister' culture than the required application of professional critical thought, let alone a will actively to challenge their masters. 'We've allowed ourselves to be politicised, and to be too acquiescent in rolling over to political bidding,' admitted Major General Andrew Mackay. 'In this atmosphere of "protecting ministers" or devoting enormous energy to "getting the message right" the wrong people prosper.' This resulted in the army going into Helmand with 'their eyes shut and fingers crossed'.[44] It was not always so.

The failure of strategic thinking

At the outset of his time in Malaya, the legendary General Gerald Templer made it abundantly clear that he required guidance from government, specifically Winston Churchill, the prime minister of the day, as to exactly what was the strategic objective:

> The general object is obvious – viz to restore law and order and to bring back peace to the [Malay] Federation. In order that this object may be achieved I am clear as to what must happen from the military point of view. I am not at all clear as to what [HM Government] is aiming at from the political point of view . . . I must have a clear policy to work on.[45]

Templer received a detailed and clear reply in the terms he had requested,[46] outlining the policy of the government for the development of a Malay nation, with full citizenship, 'partnership' and democracy for all its races. This required the defeat of Communist 'terrorism' and a 'worthy and continuing British involvement in the life of the country'. This constitutes what would now be called a 'desired end-state'. It was the policy towards which Templer's strategy would strive. In turn, his tactics were closely informed by the strategy derived from that policy. It implied a firm commitment also to ensuring that the political, rather than the military, aim was paramount. In other words, it answered the question: 'What am I fighting for?' No finer simple formulation of a request for strategic guidance exists.

That kind of vision was seriously lacking in the first decade of the twenty-first century. There was a fundamental misunderstanding of the fact that the political objective and military strategy are not the same and never will be. The political objective, the policy, was simple but totally misguided. Few now doubt this. As Hew Strachan, one of the world's leading authorities on strategy, puts it: 'Strategy is a military means; freedom in this context is a political or even moral condition. Strategy can be used to achieve freedom, but can freedom be a strategy in itself?'[47] The answer, of course, is 'no'. General Rupert Smith, author of the highly influential work on strategy *The Utility of Force*, summarised the strategic problem of Iraq: 'Setting the conditions for a free and stable Iraq might have worked as a policy – not a strategy – but that was not the declared policy. In the Iraq War, as in any other, the military strategic objective is achieved by military force, while the political objective is achieved *as a result of* the military success'.[48]

Too important to be left to generals

In *Supreme Command*, a highly influential exposition of the problems relating to the political–military relationship, Eliot Cohen stresses the vital importance of constructive and close engagement by political leaders in military matters:

> 'It is always right to probe', as Churchill wrote. 'During the war ... I forced long staff studies of various operations, as a result of which I was usually convinced that they were better left alone.'[49]

It may well be that Prime Minister Churchill is being somewhat selective in his memory, as the consistent recollection of his chief of the imperial general staff, Field Marshal Alan Brooke, was that, rather than the commissioning and study of staff papers, it was many hours of plodding argument which dissuaded Churchill from some of his own more madcap ideas, such as aircraft carriers made of ice or the invasion of Yugoslavia.[50]

In what Cohen calls the 'normal theory' of civil–military relations, generals are allowed to get on with what they are good at. He relates a fictional brigadier quoting one of Cohen's heroes, President Clemenceau:

'He said "war was too important to be left to the generals". When he said that fifty years ago, he might have been right. But today, war is too important to be left to politicians. They have neither the time, training or the inclination for strategic thought.'[51]

The speaker? Brigadier General Jack D. Ripper, the crazed officer in Stanley Kubrick's *Dr Strangelove or: How I learned to stop worrying and love the bomb*. While, as Cohen acknowledges, there are few such officers in any service today, the sentiment persists. It is, he argues, a fundamentally false idea: 'On the contrary, the truth is that when politicians abdicate their role in making these decisions, the nation has a problem.'[52] When the generals are also failing in their duty to advise, or indeed to ask for clarification, a problem can turn into a defeat. It is a classic symbiosis. With politicians who were not engaged and a senior officer cadre for whom the word 'obsequious' is entirely appropriate, success was unlikely.[53]

We have seen from the very beginning in Iraq that at least one general involved in the planning 'saw no evidence of a relatively clear strategic level end-state for post-war Iraq or an overall campaign plan for how we would get to that end-state'.[54] General Cross, who was given the responsibility of planning for the aftermath, was unique in that, much to his credit, he offered a view that 'we should not begin the campaign until we had a much more coherent post-war plan'.[55] The chief of the defence staff at the time, Admiral Lord (Michael) Boyce, opined that 'there was a danger that we would be pulled into military planning while there was something of a policy vacuum in terms of our perception of what the Americans were actually doing'.[56] He did, however, wish to ensure that there was 'full engagement with the [American] policy machine, as it were, on the military net', whatever that means.[57] Exactly the same, of course, could and should be said of Helmand.

Far from the generals warning of inadequate resources, Kevin Tebbit, the permanent secretary to the MoD and the country's senior civilian defence official, stated:

The Chief of Staff view was that they could do it and were satisfied that they could manage that deployment within the resource [*sic*]. We had a meeting with the Chiefs of Staff. I was concerned. The weight of the views of the Chiefs of Staff themselves was in favour, and since it was they who would actually have to ensure they could do this, I did not press my concerns further.[58]

There was little coherent or formal advice given on potential problems, nor at any point – either in Iraq or in Afghanistan – does the kind of strategic clarity sought by Templer in Malaya appear to have been sought. At the Iraq Inquiry, one of the members asked Admiral Boyce, at the time responsible for the armed forces in his capacity as chief of the defence staff:

> *Sir Lawrence Freedman*: Were ministers given a paper, as they were in the Falklands about operational risks, things that could go wrong?
> *Admiral Lord Boyce*: That's a continuous process really and they were aware of what our plans were and what the pluses and where might be the pinch points.[59]

It is important not to understate the level of failure on the political front, the self-delusion that accompanying the US into Iraq might provide leverage and a ticket to the big league. Two accomplished and successful officers put it less politely in a report in late 2010 about the future of defence, in which they spoke of an 'almost pathological national ego-based problem with operating as a junior partner'.[60] The misgovernment, chaos and dereliction of duty towards the armed forces on the part of New Labour (and indeed politicians of other parties) are well known. None of this alters the duties of military commanders. Instead of standing up to their political governors and giving what might have been unwelcome advice, the approach taken has been far more 'crack on regardless'. History, and its accompanying releases of classified documents, will reveal exactly how unrealistic was the advice given to politicians. An idea of the tone can be gained from the former ambassador to Afghanistan, Sir Sherard Cowper-Coles, who told the UK Parliamentary Select Committee on Foreign Affairs:

> I'm not in any way blaming the military . . . but I saw in my three and a half years papers that went to Ministers that were misleadingly optimistic.

Officials and Ministers who questioned them were accused of being defeatist or disloyal in some way.[61]

In his first appearance before the Iraq Inquiry, Prime Minister Tony Blair summarized the situation in his own distinctive style:

> the very first thing is I ask the military for their view, and their view in this instance was that they were up for doing it and that they preferred being right at the centre of things.[62]

Very much the same sentiment was expressed by John Reid on the subject of Helmand. He made it limpidly clear that he was concerned about over-stretch, but that the chiefs of staff had told him – and stressed – that deployment to Helmand would have little impact upon the Basra operation: '[Chief of the defence staff] confirmed to him that our current commitment in Iraq would be sustainable when set against a deployment to Afghanistan'[63] – a breathtakingly blasé approach to take. Given that the chiefs of staff were in possession of excellent advice concerning the intensely complex environment and the inadequacy of envisaged military resources thanks to the SAS and the advance mission conducted by Brigadier Messenger (see Chapter 3), the view might well be taken that Blair's words on Iraq – 'they were up for doing it' – applied in equal strength to Helmand. The reasons for that were examined above.

Strategic success?

The way the 'narrative' of the Iraq War was played at the time (and indeed continues to be played) is that the Iraqi interest was the British interest, and we left Basra better than we found it. In January 2010 the chief of the defence staff, Air Chief Marshal Sir Jock Stirrup, told the Iraq Inquiry that the British had achieved 'strategic success':

> [There] is also still, I think, a prevailing sense in some of the reporting one sees that the British military, the British army, somehow has some-thing to be a bit ashamed of in Basra. Nothing, in my view, could be further from the truth. Again, as I sought to demonstrate, what we did

in Basra, the reposturing in Basra was a deliberate plan to force the Iraqis' hand politically. The British army did all of this brilliantly.[64]

This is demonstrable nonsense to the Sunni, large numbers of bereaved Shi'a, and the entire Christian population of the province. To many British soldiers or informed commentators, it displays a remarkable degree of cognitive dissonance. In the words of one senior officer, to hear the professional heads of the armed forces refuse to deal with reality in this way was 'the biggest kick in the teeth in thirty-four years of service. They were and are more interested in avoiding embarrassment for themselves and their ministers than in winning wars.'[65] Colonel Tim Collins put it this way: 'We need to learn from our mistakes and our successes but let's not kid ourselves and dress it up as a victory.' Echoing the senior officer furious about the 'kick in the teeth', Collins said that much of the failure could be attributed to British generals' 'lack of aggression and obsequiousness towards the Government . . . For too long we have celebrated mediocrity and when you look at the Americans there is nothing mediocre.'[66]

A senior officer who was based in Baghdad contrasted the British and US approaches. The British in Basra 'never escaped the collective cynicism of a professional group that had gone to Iraq thinking it knew better, and then blamed others for its failure'.[67] Finding itself out of the 'comfort zone' of peacekeeping or internal security, the British army was confused and nonplussed. It reacted by hunkering down and waiting for the end.

And on to Helmand

While it is certainly true that Iraq was a war of choice at the strategic level, the armed forces were more than willing to enter Helmand. Helmand was, from the start, intended to 'make up for' the disaster of Iraq. Its conduct was entirely directed by generals, the operation founded entirely on military decisions. Helmand was the army's war in the way that Iraq, ultimately, was Blair's. Whether it was the 'Falklands Moment' that some of the army's senior officers hoped it would be is open to serious question. Once again, the excuses being offered for matters not having gone as planned are underpinned by the notion of a lack of political support in Helmand. Once again this is mendacious.

The Iraq Inquiry has revealed that, at the highest levels of command, the only Cassandra in the decision-making process concerning Helmand was Sir Kevin Tebbit, the permanent secretary and therefore the senior official in the MoD:

I think the deployment of our forces to Helmand from the north was a different matter. I was apprehensive and felt that this could be a mission too far and I made my concerns known to my planning staff and to the Chiefs of Staff. I think their view was that they could do it and it was manageable.[68]

This accords entirely with John Reid's recollections. There is no record whatsoever of any senior military commander at that stage expressing doubt about the wisdom of beginning a brigade-sized operation in Helmand. Why should they? After all, this was to be the 'good war'.

The problem here should not be misunderstood. The responsible generals know what strategy is (although some regard it as the preserve of the MoD). As the assistant chief of the defence staff, General Sir Robert Fry, said to a parliamentary committee concerning Helmand:

In so far as I believe that strategy is the reconciliation of ends and means moderated by the ways that you employ, I was acutely aware that our means – the military and other resources available to us at the time – were limited and heavily engaged in Iraq. Therefore the judgment about how much could be transferred from Iraq to Afghanistan and the timing of that transfer became very, very important.[69]

The timing was only one of very many, very important factors about which judgement was to be exercised. Force levels and their relationship to the somewhat opaque objectives were perhaps even more important.

The 'can-do' problem: punching above our weight

Aside from the antiquated structures of the army both materially and (just as important) intellectually, there was a background of conviction that, even if conditions might not seem propitious for an army to take and occupy either Basra or Helmand, Britain's was no ordinary army. For this was an army which, as had been shown time and time again, from the Falkland Islands campaign through Northern Ireland and the peace-keeping in the Balkans, 'punched above its weight'.

As the historian Max Hastings has argued: 'Throughout its history, Britain has repeatedly sought to ignore the importance of mass on the battlefield, dispatching inadequate forces to assert moral or strategic principles.'[70] There is nothing heroic in deploying too small a force to get a job done. A former commanding officer of the Special Air Service Regiment, Richard Williams, put the matter concisely: 'Punching above your weight in the military, tactical sense is likely to get you killed.'[71]

It is the task of a commander to apply the right level of force, and anything less than adequate force represents failure. One should not find oneself in need of heroism in order to make up for poor planning. Equally, it is incumbent on generals to tender advice, however unwelcome, that wars should not be started unless there is a clear end in mind. In any other field, managers negligently deploying too few resources, or advising that insufficient forces were in fact enough for the task, would face dismissal. This is not the case in the UK armed forces. The consequences of such complacency are felt not by those generals responsible, but by the soldiers 'on the ground' and by the civilians killed by the heavy weapons that must be used to compensate for lack of a functional security presence.

It is worth recalling that in Malaya, now less spoken of than it once was, the British deployed up to 40,000 troops alongside a largely trustworthy force of police and auxiliaries numbering over 100,000. At the time, this meant the proportion of troops/security forces to civilians was approximately one to thirty. The available police were largely reliable, commanded as they were by the immensely capable former commissioner of the Metropolitan Police, Sir Arthur Young. There are reliable police in very few places in Afghanistan, and certainly not in Helmand. It should also be recalled that the vast majority of the (maximum) 10,000 troops that were deployed at any one time in the province were *not* men with guns on patrol. As we have seen, this was an acute failure of command and generalship. A failure properly to address (or even to display an awareness of) the necessity for deploying sufficient security forces impacted decisively on the need to use relatively indiscriminate force to compensate. This was little more than a failure of application of basic professional knowledge.

Regardless of the limited relevance of the hallowed 'counterinsurgency' operations two or three generations before Iraq, the British had no shortage of experience in the recent occupation of post-conflict states and in the levels of manning required to sustain even basic levels of security. After all, the British had been doing little else for the previous decade. There was no excuse whatsoever for failing to understand the relevant requirements.

The Quinlivan studies and numbers

This application of 'troops to task' is an absolutely central aspect of planning – in other words, 'How many people do we need to do this task?' Of course, that question presupposes that the 'task' has been identified. As we saw above, that was itself far from clear either in Iraq or in Helmand. It is the job of senior officers to assess required troop levels. The failure to complete either task competently is now appreciated, admittedly in the merciless glare of hindsight. Under the rather more merciful questioning of the Iraq Inquiry, one general – speaking only of Iraq, although his thoughts are entirely applicable to Helmand – reflected somewhat ruefully on the disaster that was to unfold: 'I can't recall having done any calculus about the sort of force densities we were going to need. I think it is fair to say that there was still an expectation that we would be welcomed as liberators.'[72]

Others, as should have been well known, had done precisely such a 'calculus'.[73] In a series of articles for the RAND organization, James Quinlivan studied the proportion of troops to civilians that is required to ensure a stable peacekeeping environment. Looking at several theatres – Bosnia, Kosovo, Sinai, Malaya – he concluded that a figure of about twenty per thousand is adequate, declining to ten per thousand after a period of continued relative security. In Basra, this would approximate to a requirement for a total of 20,000 troops in Basra City alone. Crucially, this presumes that Basra was a stable peacekeeping environment, and, while it may have been that just after the British invaded, within a short time it most certainly was not.

There was no such security in Helmand. The population of the province is in the region of one million (no one is quite sure, as the last census was conducted in 1979). Quinlivan's figures would imply a force level of approximately 50,000 for a province the size of Helmand. His case studies, however, are largely posited on 'peacekeeping' models. Helmand was neither a 'peacekeeping' situation, nor was it treated as such by 16 Air Assault Brigade, the first major British unit in the province. Patrick Mercer, an MP and former commanding officer of an infantry regiment, said the British plan was a nonsense, and that if it had been presented to him, as a staff college instructor, the student presenting it would have been failed 'and failed comprehensively'.[74]

One aspect that Quinlivan did not consider was the effect that a top-heavy organization such as the British military might have on such numbers. In 1942, Winston Churchill wrote to Alan Brooke: 'Pray explain to me how it is that in the Middle East 750,000 men always turn up for their pay and rations but when it comes to fighting only 100,000 turn up. Explain to us exactly how the remaining 650,000 are occupied.'[75] If the army today could turn out one fighting and patrolling soldier for every six deployed, matters might be slightly improved. Unfortunately, the proportion of 'tail to teeth' is all too often far, far higher.

Of the 8,000 British soldiers present in the Basra region, very few actually placed 'boots on the ground' – that is to say, patrolled outside the wire of the various fortified bases. One general reported that, of the 8,000 or so servicemen under his command, only about 200 were actually available for patrol.[76] The infantry available to patrol the streets of Basra, a small fraction of the troops deployed, covered not only Basra itself – similar in size and population to Manchester – but also several surrounding towns, some of them (such as Al Zubayr and Al Amara) both troubled and dangerous, with populations exceeding 100,000. Clearly, soldiers were to have enough problems securing themselves.

This in turn tended to reinforce the idea of the soldier and civilian regarding each other as 'the other'. As General Rupert Smith says, in circumstances such as this 'the opponent among the people is gaining advantage every day'.[77]

Exactly the same 'calculus' applied in Helmand at the outset of the operation, so that when the calculation was made of how many combat troops were available for operations, a force of 3,500 produced a dramatically small number – 168.

The six-month tour

Numbers were not, of course, the only problem that senior officers had it in their power to tackle. The lack of continuity in operations due to the 'six-month war' syndrome was (and remains) critical. Twice a year, the entire personnel of the occupying force is changed, with obvious and highly damaging effects on any sense of continuity of mission. After all, why start something that may take several years, if you will neither get to finish it nor get the credit once it is completed? In any event, your successors may well simply decide, for whatever reason, that your priority is not theirs. A culture of short-termism has developed, achieving its most damaging form in Afghanistan between 2006 and 2010, when, as we have seen, brigades would seek a defining engagement during their period in theatre. In Iraq, this short-termism produced an institutional procrastination.

The British army takes the view that more important than continuity is 'brigade cohesion', an idea drawn (once again) from Cold War concepts of fighting. Yet Afghanistan is not a war of brigade-sized units (5,000 men), or battalion-sized units (600); it is a war in which 100-man companies are the defining 'manoeuvre units'. Mackay believes, rightly, that these can be trickled in and out of the theatre of operations without damaging the overall effort. What does damage the military effort is the staccato nature of planning and of execution of those plans, which is the concomitant of the constant switchover in command and planning. As of 2010 very senior officers and their staffs now serve one-year tours. The central problem of the 'tour' approach to campaigning nevertheless remains. Two leading academics, David Betz and Anthony Cormack articulate it succinctly: 'The plain fact of the matter is that if the next General Templer was Helmand Commander he would be rotated out once the clock ticked down and even if the next person in line was the very model of grey mediocrity, he would be rotated in'[78] and the cycle would proceed.

With no clear idea of either the policy or the purpose of the wars being fought, the strategy could not but be flawed. In both campaigns there has been a diffusion of responsibility and accountability (which, if it existed at all, was largely devolved downwards); a virtual culture of immunity combined with a destructive lack of appreciation of basic strategic principles. Poor resource planning, based on astonishingly unrealistic assumptions of force requirements and on outdated and ossified practices, such as the six-month rotation of all personnel, ensured disaster. Above all, these errors were founded upon and compounded by, an (at best) fragile understanding of what the missions were there to accomplish in the first place. Even worse, there was an evident reluctance on the part of the most senior levels of command to challenge political leadership, as successful commanders throughout history have always sought to do.

The original sin, perhaps, was failing to heed Clausewitz: 'The first, supreme, the most far-reaching act of judgment that the statesman and commander have to make is to establish ... the kind of war on which we are embarking ... this is the first strategic question and the most comprehensive.'[79] The enemies in Afghanistan were eminently clear as to their political and military aims (as we saw above): their objective was, and remains, primarily the expulsion of foreign forces. For the British, the answer to Clausewitz's question was never clear.

There was, and is, an abiding feeling throughout the armed forces that they can achieve any job they are given. In his second appearance before the Iraq Inquiry, Tony Blair said, 'The thing about the military is that they are just fantastically good people in the sense that, if you ask them to do it, they will do it.'[80] This is a key thread winding through all military cultures. The British call this approach 'cracking on'. It is one thing to have such a can-do attitude when attempting an assault course – or indeed attempting a realistically planned assault on an important position. But it is profoundly damaging when this approach is applied to national strategy or to sending thousands of men to conduct operations for which they are ill equipped in terms of numbers, training, approach and attitudes.

CHAPTER 6

Cracking On: British Military Culture and Doctrine

The only thing harder than getting a new idea into the military mind is getting the old one out.

Basil Liddell Hart, *Thoughts on War*, 1944

In current military parlance, the conduct of battle takes place at the so-called 'operational and tactical' levels. Even a flawed strategy can be mitigated if not remedied by superb operational and tactical acumen. Unfortunately, as we will see in this and the next chapter, the approaches governing the conduct of the fighting belonged to another age.

Those ideas and approaches are developed and inculcated at the United Kingdom Defence Academy at Shrivenham. The academy sits in a valley, deep in the classic southern English county of Wiltshire, not far from the nondescript town of Swindon and about halfway between the dreaming spires of Oxford and the military exercise areas of Salisbury Plain. It is a pleasant campus, quiet save for the occasional overflying helicopter or explosion from military-related activities in the grounds. The Joint Services Command and Staff College (JSCSC), part of the academy, is the jewel in the crown of British military education. This is where those officers selected for promotion to the heights of the three services are brought to learn the trade of staff work, the art and science of organizing and deploying armed force. This relatively new institution, the heir to the three single-service army, navy and air force colleges of the past, is housed in a fine, modern, purpose-built complex, architecturally very much more Silicon Valley than Sandhurst. The building was consciously designed by the architect Chris Liddle to break with the country-house paradigm of the three individual service staff colleges that this remarkable new structure and institution replaced.

The visitor, allowed in after polite enquiry by a security guard, enters a large, spacious rotunda, under a dome naturally lit from above – this is the 'forum'. Around the rim of the dome hang the flags of the hundred or more nations that have sent officers here for training. On the hour, the student officers pass through on their way to their classes and seminars. The atmosphere here is reminiscent more of a highly disciplined and regulated public school than of a university or college. Around the walls of the forum are a dozen or so paintings depicting episodes from a glorious military history. All services are represented: Royal Navy ships of the line, ensigns flying, batter Napoleonic French battleships; in the air, rickety biplanes immolate German fighters over Ypres; on land, Wellington points the way to triumph at Vittoria, the distant red lines of his infantry sweeping aside Napoleon's legions on the hot plains of Spain – the ultimate British tactical planner on the way to yet another victory. The painting next to it portrays the Heavy Brigade's cavalry charge uphill into the wavering ranks of Russian horsemen at the battle of Balaclava during the Crimean War – a testament to calculated courage and the effects of surprise when applied with discipline and aggression. Rather less calculated was the Charge of the Light Brigade at the same battle, commemorated a few metres away. These, surely, are the kind of images entirely appropriate to an institution that exists to promote efficient planning and ruthless execution – inspiration and warning side by side.

Cross that echoing entrance hall and pass along a short corridor in the evening and you will find the student officers at dinner. As in officers' messes and wardrooms anywhere in the UK, the young officers are in smart 'civvies' – suits or jackets and ties. These are the mid-career officers selected for advancement in the British armed forces. 'Any officer selected for either course knows that it's a sign he is going places,' as one former academic at the college put it.[1] They represent the best of their profession, selected for their potential to reach the highest levels of their service – Royal Navy, army or RAF. For most of them, the year at Shrivenham is the only chance they will get in those often rushed and fraught years to reflect upon their profession.

Military culture

Securely enclosed within a wire fence picketed by guards, and surrounded by representations of those 'stories we tell ourselves about ourselves', the officers from the three services share common attitudes and assumptions to a remarkable degree. There is a significant homogeneity of approach among British military officers. In other words, there is a 'culture', as there is in any professional group. Understandably, the military services, like any other profession, attract to their ranks men and women who will fit in, and the services ensure that their training and formation develop them in, as it were, their own image. Those in tune with that culture will succeed and advance; those out of tune probably will not.

Legends exist of 'rebels': men such as David Stirling, who founded the SAS; Orde Wingate, who formed several groups of irregular fighters; or, above all, T.E. Lawrence. Unfortunately, such men would not prosper today. The scruffy, bumptious T.E. Lawrence – whose military training consisted of a stint in the Oxford University Officer Training Corps – was detested by the regular army of his time. The free-thinking maverick Lawrence would not have felt at home in the quiet, conformist confines of Shrivenham Staff College, with its homogeneous and clean-cut cadre of students. Indeed, one is given to wondering what the response might be today to the notion of a learned, scruffy, homosexual Arabist, with some Territorial Army service and a gift for languages, giving the army the benefit of his ideas at the tender age of twenty-eight. Lawrence, of course, was himself a guerrilla who was not averse to terrorism when it suited his purposes, not a 'counterinsurgent'. He was fighting *against* a formed and relatively well-trained army.

There is, even here at Shrivenham, a certain degree of inter-service rivalry. This is evident in the joint exercises that dominate a good deal of most curricula.[2] But far more unites these officers – from the outsider's perspective – than divides them. Notions of leadership, integrity, service and patriotism are not simply empty phrases for the majority sitting there at dinner: they are generally believed and regularly practised.

All services are represented here. The Royal Navy is trained in the maritime division. This is the oldest fighting service in the world, and probably the most consistently victorious. Its officers are dressed the same, with the occasional flyer or submariner bearing a discreet identifier – wings or crossed dolphins. The 'junior service', the Royal Air Force, in its light blue uniforms, is largely homogeneous – the aircrew are slightly more obvious than their naval comrades, sporting as they do 'wings' on the chests of their uniforms.

On land, there is no *Royal* Army – only the British army, filled with a tribal panoply of regiments and corps – many of them sporting the 'royal' sobriquet. Each has its strong heritage derived from traditions dating back almost as far as the navy's. Every army officer's regimental affiliation is clearly evident, with a truly arcane (to the outsider) system of belts, badges, berets, differently coloured shirts or trousers. As the long-serving former military chaplain Dr Peter Lee put it to me, 'Never has the word "uniform" been more abused than when applied to the British army. The only time they dress the same is when they are in civilian clothes!' Flippant perhaps, but with more than a hint of truth. Unlike in the other two services, an army officer is, for the first and longest phase of his life, first and foremost a member of his regiment, and only then of the army as a whole. More than any other British institution, the British army – with its regiments and their rituals and nuances of dress, behaviour and even language – is a tribal organization. Loyalty to regiment is lifelong and goes, all too often, well beyond the rational.

Beyond the loyalty due to regiment there is, for all services, the all-consuming and exclusive loyalty to service – army, navy or air force. Indoctrination starts early and is highly effective. We saw in Chapter 3 how the survival of regiments and the necessity to prove the utility of kit may have been the real driving force behind the deployment to Helmand. We have also seen how inter-service rivalry produces (and, just as importantly, sustains) the vastly over-bloated cadre of general officers.

Almost all the officers here speak with the sure tone of the British officer, delivered in middle-class Received Pronunciation, although there is the occasional regional accent. All are clearly fit and healthy; overweight officers are almost unknown, except perhaps in the more sedentary reaches of the navy or air force. Few black or brown faces are in evidence, and most of those are visiting officers – either from countries that are paying for the privilege of sending their more promising future leaders, or from nations with which the UK feels it might benefit from improving relations. When I did my course at the college – a highly condensed 'reserve' equivalent of the year-long flagship Advanced Command and Staff course – I was intrigued to meet and speak with the same Serbian officers whom my colleagues and I had been trying assiduously to kill only a few years previously. Officers from the former Soviet Union and China are now relatively common at Shrivenham.

The three services have their initial officer training in their own academies: Dartmouth for the navy, Sandhurst for the army and Cranwell for the air force. These are not academic institutions along the lines of the American service academies, but rather training establishments to equip the young officers with a foundation knowledge of their respective services. Most of the entrants to these initial training establishments are graduates (about 85 per cent) and entry is governed by the service 'selection boards'.

There are no figures issued for the success rate at these boards. About 50 per cent of those who pass the Army Officer Selection Board (AOSB) and go on to Sandhurst, whether or not they are graduates, will have gone to independent schools.[3] The proportion of privately educated young people is far lower in the less socially elite air force and navy (notwithstanding the presence of Prince William in the RAF) or indeed the more technically capable reaches of the army. The implication here is either that independently educated boys and girls are inherently better military leaders, or that their officer potential – for it is potential that the AOSB states to be its primary criterion – is greater than among state-educated candidates.[4] If so, one might wonder why this should be. The alternative would be that state-school pupils, who comprise 93 per cent of the British population, do not apply to be army officers. While this book is not a discourse on the social problems of British society or the army, it is instructive that the US army recruits almost no officers from the few private schools that exist in the USA. It is important, however, that the preponderance of public schoolboys in the army is not an excuse for caricature. There was a time when the languid amateurism of the English upper classes, with an attendant contempt for professionalism, was common, if not prevalent. The British army's brutal encounter with the German army in the First World War temporarily halted that approach; its savaging at the hands of the Wehrmacht in the Second World War put paid to it. Stagnant relics of this attitude exist in certain regiments; but they no longer prosper.[5]

When an officer leaves Sandhurst, he or she will be able to command a platoon of about thirty soldiers in combat. A naval graduate of Dartmouth will be familiar with the procedures on Her Majesty's ships, and an RAF officer, while generally unable yet to pilot his own aircraft, will be acquainted with every aspect of the workings of the Royal Air Force. The courses they do, in other words, are essentially trade courses. There is very little time available for what, in other environments, would be thought of as reflective education. Education is very much secondary to the often tough and vital business of training. For those officers destined (or with ambitions) for senior command, there will be very little time for anything outside the fast stream of promotion to the highest ranks. As we saw in the previous chapter, relative to the armed services of other countries, they have a fairly good chance of reaching those exalted ranks.

For most of these officers, Shrivenham is likely to be the first time they have been brought together with colleagues from the other services for professional training. The Advanced Command and Staff course, its sister the Initial Command and Staff course for junior officers, and indeed the Higher Command and Staff course for those tipped for the rank of general (or equivalent) are intended to ensure that all are trained in the arts of 'staff work'. Staff officers – who comprise the bulk of all officers over the rank of army captain (or equivalent) – exist to form the 'staff'. This is the body of officers who conduct the administration and function of the armed forces. Outside the day-to-day running of the services, on operations staff officers exist to plan, plan and plan some more. For if one learns nothing else at the Advanced Command and Staff course, it is, to borrow the aphorism of the legendary Prussian General von Moltke, 'plans are nothing, planning is everything'.[6] Planning must always be conducted with contingencies constantly in mind, so that when the initial plan does not (as the well-worn phrase has it) 'survive first contact with the enemy', there is sufficient preparation and flexibility to adjust.

The JSCSC exists to unify officers around a single common doctrine – the established common practices, routines and ideas required to plan and execute military operations of all sizes. The college essentially exists to create an officer corps capable of conducting operations in which the three services act in unison. JSCSC seeks uniquely, therefore, to bond the British officer corps: as its motto declares, 'Unity is Strength'.[7] The doctrine that its students are required to internalize reflects strongly the approaches, and indeed the culture, common to all British military services. We turn to that now.

'Cracking on'

Anyone well acquainted with armed forces personnel – a dwindling number in an increasingly demilitarized society – will appreciate the 'military approach', which might be defined as a relentlessly forward-looking, positive, indeed aggressive approach. For the army, this might be summarized as the 'cracking on' approach. This has been described by Professor Anthony King as involving 'the centrality of activity, of tempo and offensive action'.[8] For the navy, it is characterized by the central ideal, inculcated 200 years ago by Nelson, of 'engage the enemy more closely'.

There are, of course, exceptionally good reasons for this aggressive approach. Chief among them is the reality of war and the kind of war the British armed forces are equipped both intellectually and physically to fight. For anyone trained in the armed forces prior to 1992, when the wars in the Balkans began to loom in the consciousness of the army, the armed forces existed for one overriding reason – to defend the United Kingdom and its possessions against attack by numerically far superior forces. The threat to the UK was clear and came from only one quarter (with the significant exception of the IRA, with which we will deal in due course). The posture of all the armed forces was directed to the single aim of resisting an attack from the Soviet Union. The key front in the envisaged defence was the North German plain, where the Soviet 3rd Shock Army faced the British Army of the Rhine throughout the Cold War period.

The Soviet army was a truly fearsome potential opponent: with its thousands of tanks, armoured vehicles and ground attack aircraft, it had developed a doctrine of 'deep battle' – in short, using its vastly greater numbers to overwhelm and envelop NATO, should the order be given to do so. Few British soldiers doubted that the front lines would be overrun in hours. 'As a platoon commander in what was called the "main defensive force" the role of my battalion was to die gloriously,' as one former Cold War officer, now a retired general, put it.[9] Another officer, a friend of mine from an engineer regiment, on joining his unit in Germany asked his senior NCO why his troop was issued with only three days' worth of ammunition: 'Don't you worry about that, Sir,' his sergeant major told him. 'We won't be needing any more than that.' The only question was whether the lines could be held while the US army's reinforcements could be brought across the Atlantic to save the day. To assist in that process, it was planned and expected that tactical nuclear weapons would be considered. No one was in any doubt that the fighting would be savage, merciless, and quite possibly conducted in the literal fog of an environment soaked with chemical and biological weapons. All arms of the land and air forces would be engaged in holding back the tide of Soviet armour, with the RAF flying raids deep into enemy territory in a desperate attempt to staunch the flow of enemy tanks and men to the front.

Salvation in the form of the US army's reserves could only arrive via convoys across the Atlantic. Unfortunately, lurking in their path were dozens of submarines and the formidable Soviet Northern Fleet air forces. The Royal Navy was equipped, and was expected to give its life, for the purpose of getting those precious convoys to Germany – much as had happened in the early 1940s; this time, few sailors anticipated surviving the experience, in what most expected would be something of a nautical *Götterdämmerung*.

The United Kingdom's armed forces were specifically and consciously structured for that Third World War. The signs are with us still. Every serviceman is trained on the SA80 rifle, or weapons system, as it is more properly called. This rifle, until every operational example was modified by a German weapons company, was notoriously unreliable. It is designed to equip 'fire teams', which would travel the chemically soaked, bullet-ridden battlefield in Warrior armoured fighting vehicles. This, inciden-tally, is why the SA80 rifle is so short: that way it can fit inside these vehicles without seriously encumbering its owner, who has to fire it right-handed. Supported by tanks, artillery and engineering and other assets, a battalion of 600 such men and its Warriors would form a 'battle group'. These were the lowest-level 'manoeuvre units' – the basic components of the army built to resist the Soviets. They remain the basic unit of the army, even in the painfully different environment of Afghanistan. Air support would come from Harrier jump jet aircraft based near the front lines, thereby allowing them quickly to assist army units under pressure without having to worry about the defence of airfields. Assistance would also be available in the form of the army's attack helicopters – the supreme anti-tank weapon, the Apache, with its fearsome gun and missiles capable of shredding Soviet armour. Overhead, Eurofighter Typhoon superjets would defend British and NATO airspace and air transport against assault by Russian fighters.

The weapons, ships, aircraft and equipment of the British armed forces today are, almost in their entirety, the same as those which were required to defend the North German plains and the Atlantic wastes against mass Soviet attack.[10] So are the attitudes and structures.

This defence system was predicated on an innovative doctrine, developed by General Nigel Bagnall: 'manoeuvre warfare'.[11] Until the 1980s there was a (tacit) assumption that the NATO forces would need to 'go nuclear' early if they were to have a hope of victory – whatever that might mean in the circumstances of a devastated, chemically polluted Europe. They simply would not otherwise be able to hold back the Soviet tide. Bagnall, with his acolytes collectively known as the 'Ginger Group', reintroduced to the army a 'theory of victory'.[12] Manoeuvre warfare, based, in essence, on similar American ideas developed in the wake of the Vietnam War – 'AirLand battle' – emphasized fighting large units, such as divisions, on a large canvas at the 'operational' level, rather than having larger number of smaller battles at the lower, or tactical, level of the battle group.[13] The 'manoeuvrist' approach to operations applies strength against identified vulnerabilities, involving predominantly indirect ways and means of targeting the conceptual and moral component of an opponent's fighting power. Significant features are momentum, tempo and agility, which in combination aim to achieve shock and surprise.[14] The idea was to 'find, fix and finish': locate the enemy, corner it at a place of your choosing, and kill it. In other words, Bagnall's aim was not to die gloriously, but to defeat the enemy and drive him back.

There was a great stress on seizing and maintaining the initiative, 'mission command' – meaning that lower-level commanders are familiar with the higher commander's intent, but largely free to choose the method for carrying it out. There was to be close cooperation between land forces and air support, and the focus was to be on the application of mass at critical points. The age of 'battle lines' was over. Movement, aggression and speed were the new keynotes. There was, of course, little that was new in this idea. It was essentially a reframing of Napoleonic methods of warfare (and, to a lesser extent, those of the Wehrmacht in the early years of the Second World War). It chimed perfectly with British military attitudes, giving new force to the traditional motto 'Doing nothing is never an option'. When a platoon is under fire in the hedgerows of Normandy in 1944, the streets of Belfast in 1985 or a wadi in Iraq or Afghanistan in 2007, it is unarguable that something must be done. The only question being asked by the platoon of its officer is *what* should be done.

This approach was (and continues to be) inculcated in every young officer. The reasoning goes that, even if you make the wrong move, you are likely to force the hand of your opponent, who, being forced to act, is likely to make an even worse blunder that you can exploit.

> Officers must be decisive. They must constantly seek to seize the initiative through offensive action since it is more likely that a technically incorrect but aggressively pursued course of action on the battlefield will succeed over passivity and indecision.[15]

This doctrine coexists happily with the positive approach of the military to all forms of business – that, with enough vim, anything is possible. 'Cracking on' – a term which might be defined as 'getting on with whatever is at hand with enthusiasm' – is a theme that runs through the approach of the army to almost everything it undertakes.[16] Alongside the manoeuvrist approach is the 'warfighting ethos'. British military doctrine states boldly: 'A warfighting ethos, as distinct from a purely professional one, is absolutely fundamental to all those in the British Armed Forces.'[17] The problem with this attitude, as we will see, is that motion is often confused with progress. In fighting 'wars among the people', doing nothing is often precisely the best option and the one that is most likely to result, at the very least, in doing no harm.

However, unlike those 'wars among the people', conventional warfare – though certainly chaotic – has the advantage of having well-defined aims. It also has winners and losers. Everyone is clear about what he has to do and is trained to do it as part of a very large machine.

Manoeuvre warfare is not so much a question of hardware, as of attitude. It has had its critics, who regard it as 'based [on] the selective use of examples, altered definitions, and some deliberate misrepresentation'.[18] While their views no doubt hold water, the fact is that this ideal has formed the basis of British military practice and theory (together known as doctrine) in all services for over two decades. Its essential tenets form the core of the curriculum at Shrivenham, and the student officers are required to imbibe and digest them. The apotheosis of the principles of manoeuvre warfare was the Gulf War of 1991, during which General Rupert Smith commanded several of his former students to a victory (over admittedly second- or third-rate opposition) using tactics remarkably faithful to essential manoeuvre principles. He proved that, in full-on military armoured conflict, there is no substitute for resolute action and a relentlessly positive approach.[19] These qualities are very much in evidence among almost all ambitious, middle-ranking officers. The practices, language, approach, equipment, training and ethos are all still, and arguably rightly so, directed towards the destruction of the enemy. Towards, in other words, classical warfighting in its highest-intensity form. After all, is that not the essence of any defence force?

These ideas of warfare were (and are) expressed in relatively systematic terms. The environments for which servicemen train are, by definition, chaotic, so there is an understandable (indeed essential) instinct to try to apply order to this chaos – to overlay the nightmarish violence with a template of notional organization. Two highly successful senior special forces officers, General Graeme Lamb and Lieutenant Colonel Richard Williams, explained in a paper published in 2010 that: 'This is partly due to the way that industrial-age war has been described in military staff colleges, all events happen in neat distinct phases and are drilled to order.'[20] Even at my own, relatively junior, level of command, missions would be expressed in this way. For a very simple mission – to go to speak to someone in Iraq, for example – training would dictate that full orders would comprise the following elements at the very least:

The objective is to obtain intelligence on this or that. Enemy forces are here, friendly ones there. I am in command, X is second in command. Communications are as follows . . . Execution will take place like this: phase one, leave the base; phase two, proceed to target; phase three, secure at target; phase four, obtain the required intelligence; phase five, return to base. If this, then that . . . [so called 'actions on' certain eventualities]. Our rules of engagement are as follows . . .[21]

Each phase would be broken down into ever smaller components. There are objectives to be attained within each phase, and indicators and 'decision points' provide guidance for progress. This approach, repeated with ever more complexity at each level of operation, is eminently sensible and effective in conventional warfare, but it breaks down badly in the kind of wars we have recently been fighting. As we will see, this is highly evident in the supposedly innovative ideas of 'clear, hold, build'. This form of sequential (rather than concurrent or holistic) thinking has been very damaging. As Colonel Richard Williams and General Graeme Lamb, both former SAS commanding officers, put it in a 2010 report, this type of approach 'creates a pattern of over-simplification that is hard to break and does not work in complex interventions as it separates in time the mutually supporting military and civilian activity'.[22]

A damaging instance of this kind of approach seeping into the Helmand campaign occurred in the much-touted Operation Moshtarak, launched to retake a group of farms and hamlets known as Marjah in early 2010. Once the soldiers, almost unopposed, had taken the area, a 'stabilization plan' was developed. The plan, developed after extensive consideration by experienced civilian and military planners within the PRT, had envisaged a 'conditions-based', rather than a time-dictated, flow of activities. This approach recognizes that, in Afghanistan as in much of the rest of the world, it is not always possible to dictate planning by reference to time. For example, it may well not be practicable, for dozens of reasons, to build a school and get it up and running, complete with pupils and staff, within six weeks. The military command, rejecting firm, well-founded and hard-earned advice that there was simply no point in attempting to force activities beyond the bounds of practicality, insisted upon a 'time-based' plan. Indeed the responsible brigadier simply bypassed the civilian planners, who would have to implement these projects long after the brigadier's tour was finished, and imported a group of soldiers – the HQ company of the Duke of Lancaster's Regiment, who were the theatre stand-by reserve – to provide a new time-based 'stabilization plan', complete with deadlines. Needless to say, that plan, written by a group of infantry soldiers with no experience or knowledge of civilian development, remains unfulfilled.

The outstanding military historian of the late twentieth century, Michael Howard, himself a veteran of the later battles of the Second World War, once wrote:

> I am tempted to declare dogmatically that whatever the doctrine the Armed Forces are working on now they have got it wrong. What matters is their capacity to get it right quickly when the moment arrives.[23]

The moment has indeed arrived. Unfortunately, we have not got it right. The conflicts in Iraq and Afghanistan have come as something of an existential shock – particularly to the army.

For centuries there has been a natural conflict between the army as a major warfighting service and as a 'counterinsurgency army'. One senior serving army officer, Colonel Richard Iron, a keenly perceptive commentator, has said that the British army has had a post-war existence 'as almost two separate armies: the army in Germany to face the Soviets, and the post-colonial army that fought our small wars'.[24] This is an effective image, although in the absence of true colonial wars after the 1960s it would be more precise to talk of the army in Germany and the army stationed in Northern Ireland. Of course, there wese not two armies at all; almost all British soldiers rotated in and out of Germany and their British bases and Northern Ireland. The image is nonetheless valid.

Since 1918 – and then after four years of the harshest possible evolution – the army has never really been first rate in terms of size or global impact. Once the Northern Ireland campaign sputtered to a (thankfully) largely peaceful conclusion in the 1990s, the military establishment entered something of a state of drift, despite the distractions of the Balkans. With no enemy in sight, it seemed that destiny was leading it to irrelevance. Then in 1998 came the Strategic Defence Review (SDR), which seemed to answer that supreme Clausewitzian question – 'What kind of war will we fight?'

The kind of war envisaged by the 1998 SDR was different from the all-out war for which the UK armed forces were structured and equipped. It would be 'expeditionary' and 'limited' in nature, like the Falklands War or the Sierra Leone intervention, both of which at least achieved their limited aims. Quick in and quick out was the ideal. That ideal was, of course, backed by a realistically sized application of force, and often by a level of local command initiative which enabled the force to obviate the dangers of 'remote control' from a headquarters or a number of headquarters far away.[25] That some interventions *did not* take place is also of significance. Sensible and well-informed strategic analysis 'on the spot' prevented UK forces from becoming heavily involved in a quagmire in the Congo in 1996: a reconnaissance mission by (then) Brigadier Graeme Lamb concluded, surely correctly, that there was little that UK forces could usefully contribute at that time, having regard to British strategic interests.[26] This was the kind of realistic analysis that was very sorely lacking in later years.

The two recent wars in which Britain became involved (or assisted in starting) have been neither 'quick in and quick out' nor limited in nature – although both were intended to be. They were of a totally different size, nature and intensity from anything the UK had been involved in since the early 1950s. Equally, they were not 'manoeuvre' campaigns, for which the British army was equipped, structured and trained.

These were the kind of conflicts that soldiers are wont to call 'counterinsurgencies' of an unusually large scale. As every student at Shrivenham is taught, if the Germans were, until 1945, the masters of the conduct of great field armies, until 2003 the British were considered to be *sans pareil* when it came to counterinsurgency and the fighting of 'small wars' 'among the people'.

As the British army stood before the gates of Basra in 2003, every member of the armed forces who had given the matter any thought would have agreed. Unfortunately, at that stage few senior officers had given any thought to the fact that the results of their actions would be 'insurgency'. The planning had been for classic 'manoeuvre warfare', and the army's efforts had been gifted with apparent success. As we have seen, there had been no realistic contingency planning for any follow-up, let alone ' counterinsurgency'. The same applied three years later in Helmand. Only in 1945 had the British engaged in an operation of the kind they were to undertake in Iraq, toppling a regime and occupying a country. This was a common enough task in the nineteenth century, when it was all part and parcel of the burden of imperialism. The British army believed that this heritage had endowed it with an excellent – indeed unique – insight into the form of warfare it believed it was fighting. If, as the anthropologist Clifford Geertz has it, culture is 'the ensemble of stories we tell ourselves about ourselves', very many of those stories have involved small wars of the kind we now call 'insurgency'.

CHAPTER 7

'Tactics without Strategy?': The Counterinsurgency Conundrum[1]

The experience of numerous 'small wars' has provided the British army with a unique insight into this demanding form of conflict.
Army Field Manual, Vol. 1, Part 10, *Countering Insurgency*, p. B-2-1

'It was not the techniques per se that won the campaign, but the strategy.'
Commodore Steven Jermy, referring to Malaya[2]

Old stories

In Iraq and Afghanistan, the UK and US found themselves deep in 'the fog of war'. Clausewitz, the doyen of strategists and thinkers of war, calls this 'friction'. In Chapter Seven of Book One of *On War* Clausewitz describes how war is essentially a 'wicked problem'. With every apparent solution, new problems are thrown up: 'Everything in war is very simple, but the simplest thing is very difficult ... Friction, as we choose to call it, is the force that makes the apparently easy so difficult.'[3] As ever, Clausewitz goes on to prescribe countermeasures. He identifies experience as the only true 'lubricant' for the friction; if that is not available, then 'habit' and 'exertion' must come into play.[4] In this chapter we will examine the relevance of the experience of the British army, as well as the training and doctrine. How useful has the army's much-vaunted 'unique insight' been in lubricating Clausewitz's 'friction' in Iraq and Afghanistan?

Prior to 2003, and indeed for a short time afterwards, the British, and especially their army, presented themselves as having particular success in the practice of fighting rebellions and small wars. They had, we were told, a distinct approach, founded on decades of colonial experience, and a unique perspective that was derived from the lessons supposedly learned over those decades: '[The British army] has much to teach a world increasingly challenged by the problem of internal war.'[5]

In Iraq and Afghanistan, the wars being fought were, initially at least, presented as being 'right up the British street'. They were 'counterinsurgencies' – allegedly our strong suit. Certainly British officers were much given to lecturing the Americans on supposedly relevant experiences. These 'theatres' were ideal, one might suppose, for showing our mettle in 'counterinsurgency'. Yet when matters really came to a crisis in 2007 in Iraq, it was not the British who led the way with a pragmatic set of tactics – it was the Americans. Not only that, but the British became increasingly sidelined, to the point where American officers would 'roll their eyes' and switch off when a British officer mentioned Malaya or Northern Ireland. The situation became so bad, I am told, that British officers were forbidden even to mention either of these campaigns in US headquarters. In Afghanistan, the lessons of the long war on the North West Frontier – the need for a realistic approach, deep knowledge and, above all, a coherent policy backed by workable strategy – have been entirely forgotten. As one retired senior British officer, Rear Admiral Chris Parry has put it: 'We had an immature attitude to what is now called counterinsurgency . . . I think at the time there was considerable senior resistance to ditching the lessons from the past and moving on to more radical and progressive ideas . . . The old doctrine, the thinking about how we conduct that sort of campaign still prevailed.'[6]

Imperial vistas

From the accession of Queen Victoria in 1837 to her death in 1901, the British army fought no fewer than 250 campaigns, large and small.[7] Many of these struggles were rebellions by people (or rulers) who did not wish to be ruled by the Empire. 'So perverse is mankind that every nation prefers to be misgoverned by its own people than to be well ruled by another', as one of the Empire's leading generals, Charles James Napier, put it.[8]

In the early twentieth century, the British fought dozens of small campaigns, with greater or lesser degrees of success. They developed techniques which, although sporadically applied, were to become the keynote of a 'British way' of 'counterinsurgency'. These ideas revolved around a strong degree of civil–military cooperation and respect for a basic level of rule of law. Their aim was 'not the annihilation of an enemy but the suppression of a temporary disorder, and therefore the degree of force to be employed must be directed to that which is necessary to restore order and must never exceed it'.[9] In essence this was 'minimum force'.[10] These ideas were developed further in the 1930s, with the publication of a range of books on suppression of rebellion, notably Charles Gwynn's *Imperial Policing*. Most important of all was the hundred-year campaign on the Indian imperial borders with Afghanistan – the area the British knew as the 'North West Frontier'.

Rebellions in Iraq, Palestine, India and a dozen other places demonstrated, however, that while principles were easily articulated, the British army was not averse to using a very great level of coercion, and was indeed not averse to the occasional atrocity. Indeed, it was this kind of behaviour that characterized the British approach in Ireland during the 'War of Independence' (1919–21) – along with an extraordinary degree of chaos in command and control arrangements. The brutality of the 'Black and Tans' irregular military force is still remembered today. Their activities heavily contributed to British failure in Ireland. In Palestine, between 1936 and 1939, the appalling way in which the first *intifada* – otherwise known as the Arab Insurgency – was put down by the British, complete with punitive village clearances and massacres, is also still recalled.[11]

There has been much scholarly debate as to the extent to which there was, in fact, a coherent British approach to the set of tactics known now as 'counterinsurgency', and in colonial days as 'imperial policing'.[12] Although the British army (as opposed to the more hardened Indian regiments) often found itself outclassed by its Pathan adversaries during the hundred-year North West Frontier campaign, it is clear that soldiers were not 'making it up as they were going along'.[13] Aside from the invaluable assistance of the expert 'politicals' – of whom more anon – there was plenty of tradition. The trouble was that the army was a dispersed force, essentially an administrative gathering of regiments rather than a cohesive unit with common doctrine. Indeed, it was very difficult to ensure a common approach, or even to develop a common doctrine, let alone implement it. Equally, there were constant disagreements within the army as to what exactly it was for. Was it a colonial army – intended to fight 'limited war' – what might now be termed 'expeditionary warfare'? Or was the army a force for major warfare against 'conventional' enemies who threatened the home islands? It was the form of conflict for which the army had been primarily equipped and trained for over a hundred years. After the maelstrom of the Second World War, the threat to Britain itself was still perceived to be significant, only this time it came from the Soviet Union. While the priority had to be direct home defence, it was clear that the Empire still needed defending. Equally, those two strategic imperatives were not necessarily inconsistent, as many of Britain's possessions 'East of Suez' – indeed Suez itself at the time – were perceived as vital to national security. As the age of empires drew to a close, British imperial forces were engaged in a series of what amounted to fighting retreats.

Choosing your battles

It was in the 1950s that the British reinforced their reputation in fighting the wars that were to become known as 'insurgencies'. One author has referred to this (somewhat poetically) as the 'high period of British counterinsurgency'.[14] The French were fighting their doomed attempt to keep the core of their empire in Vietnam and North Africa through military force, an effort the British had elected not to make, with the peaceful transition of India to independence (peaceful, that is, from the British perspective – millions were killed in the awful ethnic cleansings that followed independence). India was the great independence war that never happened. This was just as well, as it would certainly have been a catastrophic defeat. It is often forgotten that a significant party within Britain felt that independence for India was not, and should not be, a foregone conclusion. That party was led, of course, by Winston Churchill. Had Churchill been returned to power in the 1945 elections, there might have been a bloodbath to rival anything the French faced in Vietnam or Algeria.

Unlike the French, however, the British political nation was astute enough to realize that an Indian war of independence was not a war it was going to win, and so avoided it. It was clear that the political and grand strategic interests of Britain were better served by controlled withdrawal from colonial imperialism rather than by attempting to hold on. The treasury was empty and the country was tired of conflict. Neither the financial, the military nor the moral resources were present to engage in large wars of imperial defence. On a grand scale, the means were matched to the ends – in other words, there was a coherent policy backed by a workable grand strategy that might be termed 'retreat with honour'. None of the wars that were fought approached the scale of Algeria or Vietnam in terms of suffering or international consequence. Almost all of them were fought within the framework of that grand strategy. As we will see, the tactics employed, particularly in Malaya, fitted well within it.

Since the Second World War, Britain has fought a great many wars. At least one credible study has suggested that Britain has fought more conflicts than any other country in the world.[15] As for the results, the British army (like most professions) loves keeping score: in the post-war period, the British have been involved in no fewer than seventy military campaigns (by no means all of them wars) of varying sizes, eighteen of which may be classified as 'counter-insurgency' actions. In true military style, the Army Staff College official handbook on counter-revolutionary warfare lists the score as seven successes, three partial successes, five failures, one draw and two ongoing.[16] While naming Kenya as a success is rather questionable, there is no real question that the British army has had a great deal of experience in this kind of warfare.

How can we characterize this experience? Should it be seen as a series of wars punctuated by blunders, massacres, concentration camps, defeat and collective punishment, reframed only with the assistance of rose-tinted historical spectacles? Or an enlightened series of well-thought-out and humanely conducted campaigns, breaking a trail for governments everywhere in their struggle against subversion? Both versions are, of course, caricatures of the British army approach (insofar as there is one) to rebellion – 'quite its favourite occupation', as one recent commentator put it, harking back to the days of pig-sticking and tiffin.[17] Both versions have a certain degree of validity. Most of the conflicts upon which these judgements are based took place well over fifty years ago; they relied on a thorough familiarity with country and people and a clear understanding of the overall strategic context of imperial withdrawal; and they were ended by realistic, pragmatic negotiators who understood the need for compromise.

'Inkspots and all that . . .'

Above all, the British and their admirers look to what they see as two campaigns they consider to be successes: Malaya and Northern Ireland. Of all Britain's end-of-empire wars, it is that in Malaya, fought between 1948 and 1960, that has developed the most resonance for Britain's military reputation. If any war has attained mythical status, it is surely this one: even now it is seen as the exemplar of what has become known as the 'classic period' of counterinsurgency. No visitor to military headquarters in Iraq or, especially, Afghanistan could miss the almost compulsory mentions in presentations to guests (and indeed serving soldiers) of this jungle war, a long time ago, far away, and in the most different environment imaginable.[18]

The crucial aspects of the Malaya campaign as presented today are 'inkspots' (the practice of allowing development to spread from areas of concentrated security force presence – originally a French counterinsurgency innovation known as *tâches d'huile*)[19] and 'hearts and minds'. These and other ideas involving 'separating the guerrilla from the people' were rolled out for the benefit of visitors by British army officers, seeking through PowerPoint presentations to explain what they were doing in Iraq and especially Afghanistan. Sir Suma Chakrabati, a veteran British aid official and until 2007 civil service head of DfID, felt that it was becoming a little tedious: '[The] number of times Malaya was mentioned . . . it didn't seem to me to be terribly relevant; ink spots and all that.'[20]

In one sense, Sir Suma was wrong: these old campaigns do matter. The army thought they did and believed it could translate the techniques used in both Malaya and Northern Ireland to their current operations. Malaya and Northern Ireland do point up some vital lessons that are highly applicable to the situation today. The problem is that the relevant lessons, insofar as they are understood at all, have been ignored.

The Malayan Emergency[21]

The first four years of the Malayan 'Emergency' were marked by what now seem blundering attempts by the British to get to grips with an enemy that was rarely willing to engage in direct combat. Their enemy was the Malay Races Liberation Army (MRLA). This group was the direct descendant of the

Malayan People's Anti-Japanese Army, which had fought alongside British commandos (such as Spencer Chapman) against the occupying Japanese forces during the Second World War. Its aim was the expulsion of the British presence from Malaya and the installation of communist government.

After the failure of an extended campaign of industrial unrest and limited sabotage, the guerrillas fled to the jungle where they had conducted their war against the Japanese, and now began a fight against another, albeit less ruthless, colonial power. They were led by a wartime commander, Chin Peng OBE, whose Order of the British Empire, awarded for services in resisting the Japanese, rendered him one of two royally decorated insurgent leaders to have fought against British rule. (The other was Ibn Saud, founder of Saudi Arabia, who took the British protectorate of Hejaz in 1928.)[22] Support, though, remained overwhelmingly ethnic Chinese (about 40 per cent of the total population)[23] – a critical factor.

For the first four years of the war, British army battalions conducted 'sweeps' throughout jungle areas, essentially involving large groups of ill-trained conscripts blundering about the jungle. Thousands were arrested and dozens shot 'trying to escape'. There was at least one major massacre at Batang Kali, where twenty-four men were taken from the village, separated into four groups and shot.[24]

A plan and a man

'I need a plan and I need a man,' declared Chief of the Imperial General Staff Montgomery. He got both. The man was General Gerald Templer, who was appointed in late 1951 and took up his post in 1952. The 'plan' was the Briggs Plan, developed by, and named after, the director of operations in Malaya in the very early 1950s. The permanent secretary of defence for the colony at the time was Sir Robert Thompson. With deep experience in the area, Thompson, a Chinese speaker and former Special Operations Executive (SOE) officer, as well as a long-time member of the civil service in Malaya, was the ideal man for the job of implementing the Briggs Plan alongside the dynamic Templer. The plan was based around the idea of separating the guerrillas from their potential support.

The country was divided up into zones of 'black' (areas under guerrilla control), 'grey' (areas being cleared) and 'white' (secure areas, clear of guerrillas). These clearances were initially conducted in a simple south–north sequence. Malaya being a peninsula, with its northern border with Thailand sealed and its shores patrolled by the Royal Navy, the guerrillas were very much on their own; unlike the Taliban of today, they had no 'big brother' across a porous border. The appointment of General Gerald Templer as high commissioner galvanized the campaign. He received plenary powers and used them brilliantly. It is important to realize that, although he was a general, his appointment was emphatically a *civilian* one. Templer was not in Malaya to command the military campaign. This was a joint effort led not by the army, but by the government.

Military success

Once Templer had ensured that the administration of the fifteen provinces was in good hands (using the simple expedient of firing those he felt were not up to the job), he got out among the soldiers and ensured their morale was high. Any officer not meeting his standards was sent home immediately. The SAS Regiment was revived for service in Malaya, and it achieved some success, though it was in no way decisive, being credited with only 108 of the 6,300 MRLA guerrillas killed. More significantly for the long-term viability of that remarkable regiment, Major John Woodhouse, who had helped re-found the SAS, introduced for Malaya the selection procedures that were to establish it as arguably the pre-eminent fighting unit in the Western world. The most effective units in the imperial forces were generally thought to be the Fijian and Gurkha units, with the East African infantry battalions not far behind. In the later years of the Emergency, the indigenous Sakai tribes, using their local awareness and tracking skills, killed more MRLA than all other elements combined.

The resources devoted to putting down the guerrillas should not be underestimated. Over 100,000 police and special police were supported by a 'home guard' and auxiliary police force of nearly 300,000, all commanded by former Commissioner of Metropolitan Police Sir Arthur Young. At the height of the Emergency there were 40,000 regular troops from Britain, East Africa, Fiji and Australia, the Gurkhas and, of course, the nascent Malayan army. British soldiers did a tour of a year. Against these forces was ranged an MRLA of – at the height of its power – 10,000. Unlike the

Vietnamese, with whom facile comparisons have been made, no support could be expected from outside the country, as Thailand, fearful of the potential for communist rebellion there, was assisting the British. Units of the Royal Navy ranged the coasts. Even food was a constant problem for the guerrillas. Looked at in these terms, it is a testament to the resilience and courage of these fighters that they lasted so long against such an unremitting and large effort. Their story has not yet fully been told.

The guerrillas were separated from the people primarily via the rounding up about 500,000 ethnic Chinese 'squatters' – relatively recent immigrants – who were placed in so-called 'temporary villages'. These 'villages' were surrounded by barbed wire, and movement in and out of them was tightly controlled. The importance of food supply to the rebels was fully realized and exploited. The chief of staff to General Templer explained, in a lecture in 1954, that 'the most successful operations have been those launched against the terrorists' lines for food supply'.[25] In a master stroke, a rule was enforced that no uncooked rice could be taken out of the settlements. Cooked rice lasts less than a day in tropical weather, and that rule cut off a major source of food for the jungle-dwelling guerrillas. Indeed, in the latter part of the conflict, some soldiers reported that MRLA men and women were captured with large sums of money but starving, being unable to get hold of any food.

Templer took the view that the Emergency 'will be won by our intelligence system'. The planners ensured that intelligence was properly organized and that the turf wars that so often plague intelligence officers were simply not tolerated. A highly effective network of agents began to dismantle the communists' support networks in the towns. Many of these were run with the assistance of young ethnic Chinese women, who tended, said Thompson, to attract less suspicion in their work of surveillance and contacting agents.[26] A system was set up whereby Chinese villagers could divulge information about guerrillas – Operation Letterbox.

Effective interrogation methods were used, involving no element of torture or mistreatment. The idea was explicit and intensely pragmatic: no one would willingly surrender if they believed there was the prospect of torture. Indeed there was a programme – the 'Surrendered Enemy Personnel Programme' – for those who did. The effect of the close cooperation between a consummate civil servant and one of the finest British generals ever to serve was decisive. It is vital to remember that Templer, although a retired general, was a *civilian* official. This was not perceived to be, and was not primarily, a *military* campaign.

Hearts and minds?

The techniques used by the British in Malaya are often described through historical soft focus, with the phrase 'hearts and minds' very prominent. But coercion in Malaya was much in evidence.[27] As David Benest has put it in his fine study of British small wars from 1966 to 1976, 'coercion was the reality, hearts and minds the myth'.[28] Over 10,000 people were deported. During the period of the Malayan Emergency about 226 men were executed – more than the French judicially killed in Algeria. In none of the reports written for the army's in-house journal, the *British Army Review*,[29] during the Malaya years is there any mention of the 'hearts and minds' ideal that has since come to define the campaign.[30] In any event, this ideal carried very different connotations from those that it bears today. As one British veteran put it, 'the severity with which the civilian population had to be controlled and restricted depended on how desperate or favourable was the military situation, a fact that served as a strong incentive to the people to help the legitimate forces'.[31]

Sir Hew Strachan, Chichele Professor of the History of War at Oxford University, has commented: 'When we speak about "hearts and minds", we are not talking about being nice to the natives, but about giving them the firm smack of government. "Hearts and minds" denoted authority not appeasement.'[32] As Templer himself put it: 'You can only win the people over in my opinion – to use that nauseating phrase I think I invented – by capturing their hearts and minds.'[33] There was nothing soft-hearted, vague or woolly about that process in Malaya.

A realistic political strategy: removing the 'cause'

Separating the guerrilla from his support entailed more, of course, than simple physical measures of control. The cause motivating the rebels needed to be addressed. Politics was a major concern of Templer's. For the Chinese Malayans, real and 'acceptable' alternatives to the MRLA were encouraged in the form of 'moderate' political groupings, regarded as critical to the British success. The effort was assisted greatly by the fact that prices for tin and rubber – both of them major Malayan exports – were at an all-time high, due to the demands of the Korean War and post-Second World War reconstruction worldwide. The government had money to spend from the taxes paid by a relatively prosperous population, and the economy as a whole was thriving.

Perhaps most of all, what Templer brought was a real strategy, combining a road map for independence, with full citizenship for ethnic Chinese. All these initiatives swept any credible political legitimacy from the MRLA. Its chief *casus belli* – liberation – for any non-communist was removed at a stroke. Meanwhile, Thompson gradually engineered a handover of power to the Malayan authorities. Templer only stayed in post for two years (though twice as long as any British general in post today, two years then was considered a short tour), but by the end of his time the MRLA was finished as a potential threat to Malayan stability (though the insurgency stumbled on until 1960, three years after independence).

Some commentators have agreed with the view that Malaya 'was in many respects ideally suited for an insurgency based on the Maoist model'.[34] In retrospect, however, the British held all the cards: the MRLA was almost entirely ethnic Chinese in a majority Malay country; the guerrillas were confined to the jungles, with no external source of support and very limited weaponry; the only land border with Thailand was sealed and patrolled by Thai forces; and the ports and coastline were efficiently covered by the Royal Navy.

Most importantly, from the perspective of the 'target' population for the MRLA – essentially the ethnic Chinese – it had nothing to offer in the way of public goods, such as justice or the provision of real security that would outperform what the state already offered. Besides, sympathy for a communist grouping was limited among the ethnic Chinese community, which was essentially aspirant and commercially minded. This was especially true of the growing urban Chinese population – curiously the MRLA never began a concerted urban campaign – which stood to lose a great deal in the event of a communist victory.

In other words, with the priceless advantage of hindsight, it looks very much as though the British held all the cards. One can be sure, however, that the situation did not appear like that at the start of the Emergency. It is fair to say that, had the British played their cards differently, matters could have gone very badly wrong. There is also no doubt whatsoever that there is significance in the fact that, alone of all colonial powers, the British managed to draw apparent success from a prolonged counterinsurgent fight.[35] Some commentators have asserted that the success of this campaign rested with ideas of 'divide and rule'. Thompson himself, intimately familiar as he was with how the campaign was planned and executed, was firmly of the view that to have gone down that road would have been 'catastrophic', in that it could well have resulted in a race war, in which the British would have been caught in the middle.[36]

Of course, there was not simply one 'Malayan campaign'. This was a conflict with several phases. There was the initial 'armed sweeps' phase, then the initial elements of the Briggs Plan. Templer's arrival galvanized that process. Only in the later stages were the 'softer' elements of 'counterinsurgency' and the successful political instruments applied.[37]

The 80:20 ratio

David Galula, a French officer with experience in Vietnam and Algeria and a guru of COIN (COunterINsurgency), took the view that political/ civilian to military efforts should be in the proportion of 80:20.[38] Templer agreed (though his ratio was 85:15). This is a ratio often mentioned, but almost never implemented. In both Iraq and Afghanistan, political or civilian efforts were never the priority (except rhetorically) until late in each campaign, by which time the initiative had passed away from the occupiers and their client governments.

By 1960, the Emergency was over and British involvement in Malaya had ended. There was no Malay Union hiding the interests of Britain behind those of a notionally independent dependency – Malaysia, as it was now called, had said goodbye to British involvement for good. Once again, withdrawal was the answer to an intractable problem. As Professor Hew Strachan put it in 2009, 'The campaigns of the 1950s and 60s were actually predicated on the presumption of Britain's military defeat. Britain was getting out.'[39] The real skill was getting out in a way that looked credibly like victory. If it was victory, it was Field Marshal Templer (as he became) – the Tiger of Malaya – who was responsible for it.

Essentially, the British had neutered the cause on which the MRLA could expect to recruit – independence – in an emphatically political move. Indeed, the hallmark of the British response to resistance in this form – whether on the North West Frontier, in India, in Malaya or later in Northern Ireland – was a combination of political realism and tactical and military experience, shot through with advice given by tough and highly experienced administrators with decades of experience in the relevant regions. This was as true of Malaya as it was true on the Afghan frontier in the 1940s and the preceding century. As Hew Strachan points out, 'as an agent of an imperial power, the army had regularly practised colonial warfare, and were considerably more experienced in it than "major" or "continental" war'.[40] The army was also used to dealing closely with joint political and military authority. None of these conditions applies now – a fact not yet internalized by the British army and its leaders.

Are there lessons for today?

Yes, there are – plenty. Not the ones often rolled out, involving 'hearts and minds' and 'separating the guerrilla from the people' – what has become known as 'population-centred counterinsurgency'.[41] The huge schemes of social engineering carried out by the British and Malaya governments to win 'hearts and minds' and isolate the guerrillas physically are simply not practically possible today: the levels of coercion required are unacceptable to Western liberal democracies. Even if the political and legal circumstances permitted this form of 'population-centred' activity, the huge manpower needed to effect the policies is simply not available. Similarly, the investment required to initiate, secure and sustain economies in the 'new villages' was huge. As one senior serving army officer said to me, 'You need ink to put in inkspots.' Today, that 'ink' is not available from British sources. Similarly, the extensive use of indigenous forces in Malaya, not often remarked upon, was itself built upon decades of continuous development and involvement by British officials, who both personally and professionally invested heavily in the colony.

There is one absolutely central element that is missing from any comparison between Malaya and today's campaigns: legitimate government. Malaya and the Mau Mau conflict in Kenya (and indeed the French wars in

Algeria and Vietnam) were post-colonial struggles. The British, and particularly the Malay government (which increasingly took primacy as the campaign went on) were the legitimate, popularly supported (in the case of the ethnic Malays) government. Listening to Sir Robert Thompson describe his work during the 'emergency', in his extended interview for the Imperial War Museum sound archives, one is struck by how closely the British elements of government worked seamlessly with (and later in the campaign *under*) Malay political leaders.[42] This was no case of colonial domination: the idea of independence and transfer to local control was treated with the utmost seriousness.

Like their colleagues on the North West Frontier, some Malayan colonial administrators stayed after independence to become Malay citizens. Most of all, and partly because of these factors, they understood the limits of what they might be able to achieve and what would be tolerated (and indeed wanted) by the people, or peoples, of the country. The techniques used in Malaya were not themselves a strategy. They were components of a wider strategy of favourable disengagement, the planning of which was aligned closely to the resources available – military, political and indeed legal.

Closer to home – the 'Province'

Even more than Malaya, Northern Ireland became a symbol of the British army's proficiency in 'counterinsurgency'. This latest phase in a centuries-long struggle started with the civil rights movement of the late 1960s, which sought to ensure the equal treatment of the Catholic community, most of whom favoured British withdrawal. In 1969, soldiers were sent in to protect that nationalist community from loyalist predation. Over two years the situation deteriorated, until the army was seen by the 'target' population, as so often before and since, as the agents of a deeply unpopular government that had no interest in protecting or assisting the minority community. This perception was aided by several public relations disasters born of military primacy. Internment – known as Operation Demetrius – began in August 1971. Serious ill-treatment of prisoners during interrogation amounted to torture.[43] 'Bloody Sunday', in April 1972, which saw the death of thirteen unarmed civilians at the hands of the British army, still has acute resonance. These incidents, along with other smaller but heavily exploited military massacres, constituted an excellent recruitment opportunity for the IRA, which exploited it to the full.

A veteran of those early days of that long Northern Ireland campaign, General John Kiszely writes highly critically of the British army in those years:

[It] nevertheless appears surprising in retrospect that the British Army's wide experience in counterinsurgency campaigns in the 1950s and 60s in such places as Malaya, Cyprus, Kenya, Borneo and Aden, did not prepare it better for the challenges it faced in Northern Ireland at this time. This is all the more surprising since these campaigns had been well documented, and a process existed for feeding 'lessons learned' into British military doctrine, with such publications as *Keeping the Peace* (1963) and *Counter-Revolutionary Warfare* (1969).[44]

Colonel David Benest, another scholar and expert on British counter-insurgency history, takes the view that:

Participation by officers in one or more I[nternal] S[ecurity] operation in other parts of the world does NOT mean that they know all about things in the new theatre. A liberal dose of humility is essential, while making use of previous experience, to learn from the experience of others.[45]

Eventually they did learn. Techniques evolved which served, if not to neutralize the IRA, then at least to contain it. A framework of intelligence, particularly human intelligence (agent-running, in other words), local awareness and, eventually, good interagency cooperation developed against a background of superb training and continuity, with a mixture of six-month and two-year deployments of battalions. Another veteran of Northern Ireland, Colonel Richard Iron, has rightly described the British as having become 'experts' in fighting that conflict. He states that the army serving in Northern Ireland was by the late 1980s 'one of the best armies Britain has ever fielded'. Above all, the skills developed were practised against the background of a sound and clear political and strategic direction and leadership, resulting in political settlement after lengthy and expert negotiation over a period of many years.

Success and expertise in fighting an insurgency in north-west Europe does not imply such prowess elsewhere. Iron puts the problem this way: 'something had gone terribly wrong. What seem to have been institutional lessons from Northern Ireland were not applied in Iraq and Afghanistan or, if they were, only after great expenditure of time, money and blood.'[46]

When questions of reconciliation and political settlement came to be considered in Basra province in 2007, there were facile comparisons with the long-drawn-out negotiations carried out by negotiators in Northern Ireland. Those who conducted the talks with Sinn Fein,and indeed the IRA, were intimately familiar with the issues at stake and, thanks to the pervasive media and excellent intelligence on both sides, with each other. As Hew Strachan has written (echoing Iron): 'if we apply models from one war to another we are in danger of being guided solely by operational and tactical concerns'.[47] This is exactly what happened in Basra in 2007–8, with highly destructive results.

One element is luminously clear from all the successfully concluded conflicts in which the British have been involved. A senior retired British officer and leading expert on British counterinsurgency, Colonel David Benest, identifies it as 'the inherent danger of applying any counterinsurgency strategy which does not include an end-state that is achievable within a finite period'.[48] Even in the mishandled Mau Mau operations in Kenya in 1948–60, there came a point when practical concerns ensured a reasonably smooth handover of power – although in that case not without a great deal of residual bitterness and continuing controversy. In simple terms, the British knew when they were beaten, or, in the cases of Malaya and Northern Ireland, understood the limits of their powers. From that realization they attempted to produce the best possible deal, using the considerable local knowledge and expertise available to them. This, in turn, derived – whether we consider Malaya, Kenya or Northern Ireland – from the fact that the British essentially constituted the government in all these places. In consequence, there was no requirement whatsoever for the army to concern itself with such matters as state-building. Other people, rightly, did that.

In neither Iraq nor Afghanistan was there a government in place that could facilitate success, and the UK and US militaries were simply not equipped to compensate for this huge absence. This gaping void – governance – was not appreciated by the British, who persisted well into both campaigns in believing that they had the knowledge, the military capability and the skills to overcome it. In fact, they did not possess such skills. It is forty years since Britain fought any meaningful rebellion abroad. That was the highly successful campaign in the Dhofar region of Oman, fought strictly not by the British army but by Arabic-speaking SAS and other officers on detachment to the sultan's forces. 'Experience of small wars' does not run in the blood. Even in terms of living memory, as Colonel Iron points out, the average battalion commander deploying to Afghanistan today would have been twenty-three years old when the Provisional IRA declared its ceasefire. So if he had served in Northern Ireland at all during the conflict, it would have been as a platoon commander at the tail end of the conflict.[49] The upshot is that the entire framework of intelligence, doctrine and structure, painfully developed over thirty years (and in any event specific to Northern Ireland), was already in place. It could, as it were, be taken for granted. This was absolutely not the case in Basra or Helmand, where the British came in as an occupying force. Perhaps it was not to Malaya, or even Northern Ireland, that they should have looked, but to the hard but ultimately triumphant successes of occupation in post-war Germany.

New doctrine

The other of Clausewitz's antidotes to the friction of war is training. This must be informed by 'doctrine'. Doctrine in this sense means a commonly understood method or technique of fighting – a common standardizing frame of reference, often (but not always) expressed in manuals. In 2002, the American army officer and scholar John Nagl published *Learning to Eat Soup with a Knife*, comparing Malaya with the US army's experience in Vietnam. His central argument was that the British army had a more flexible learning culture and was better able to assimilate experience than its US counterpart. 'Official doctrine', he said, 'remains secondary to the substantial experience of many British officers in counterinsurgency.'[50] As we have seen, while that was once the case, this assertion is now questionable. Malaya is well beyond the memory of any serving officer, the campaigns of the 1960s to the 1980s are remote, and even the violence of Northern Ireland – to the extent that it is at all relevant – ended in the 1990s. The experience that Clausewitz saw as so central to overcoming the friction of war is somewhat lacking.

In the absence of deep experience, the solution to the wars in which the British and Americans found themselves was new 'doctrine'. In the US, this came in the form of the US army and Marine Corps *Counterinsurgency* field manual – better known as 'FM 3–24' – released in 2006.[51] Counter-insurgency doctrine is replete with precepts and slogans. Colonel I.A. Rigden has identified sixteen.[52] General David Petraeus in Iraq had about twenty-three (different ones) for Iraq. That same general produced twenty-five following his appointment to Afghanistan.[53] FM 3–24 itself contains seven primary precepts and a raft of secondary tenets.[54] David Kilcullen, an Australian academic and former soldier, has produced twenty-eight 'Articles', in conscious homage to T.E. Lawrence, whose '27 Articles' was issued in 1917.[55] Some of Kilcullen's articles – 'be prepared for setbacks' (number 17), 'have a game plan' (number 9), 'be there' (number 10) and 'rank is nothing: talent is everything' (number 8) may read as if extracted from a commonplace self-help guide. Nonetheless, it is always instructive to see the musings of the young Arabist Lawrence (he was twenty-nine at the time he published these reflections) referred to, imitated or contained in military reading lists. British, and indeed American, officers fighting for invading non-Muslim armies might have done well to remember Lawrence's eleventh precept: 'The foreigner and Christian is not a popular person in Arabia. However friendly and informal the treatment of yourself may be, remember always that your foundations are very sandy ones.'

In 2009, the British army weighed in with volume 1, part 10 of the *Army Field Manual*, entitled *Countering Insurgency*. That glossy book reflects upon ten 'principles of counterinsurgency'.[56] Partly as a result of the proliferation of sources, what has become known as 'population-centred' counterinsurgency has become the province of the PowerPoint presenters and diagram makers of the various armed forces; academics have not been slow to follow with their input.

As we have seen, what the sainted example of Malaya had was government, which, as Templer said, must do 85 per cent of the task of defeating rebellion to the military's 15 per cent. These elements comprise the 'ink' that should, in theory, be filling out those 'inkspots' created by military force bringing 'security'. Unfortunately, such ink has been sadly lacking in our recent interventions. The new term for the provision of such govern-ance is 'stabilization' – a concept helpfully summarized in four words by General McChrystal, former commander of the International Security Assistance Force for Afghanistan: 'government in a box'. 'Stabilization' is expressed and projected by means of the 'comprehensive approach', through the medium of 'co-ordination, consultation and interaction between all actors'.[57] The British armed forces have attempted to clarify these not entirely helpful definitions by producing a long exposition of how stabilization is done. Rather confusingly, this is supplemental to the army's counterinsurgency doctrine referred to above. Joint Doctrine Publication 3–40 – *Security and Stabilisation: The military contribution* – essentially sets out the process of building government. At 600 pages, this behemoth is unlikely to be part of any officer's deployment kit. Indeed, as one officer told me: 'If it isn't laminated and can fit in my pocket, it isn't going to get read.' Whether or not it is widely read (and personally I hope it is, since my own thoughts[58] are given half a page in the document), its prescriptions for 'state-building', richly illustrated with flow charts and diagrams, require the kind of resources no country today can possibly commit. As we have seen in the foregoing chapters, this is most especially the case for the United Kingdom.

Critiques of 'counterinsurgency'

Criticism of counterinsurgency and its offshoots such as 'stabilization' is nothing new. A commentator writing in the early 1960s complained, 'There is a muddy verbosity and pompous profundity that are beginning to mark the whole subject of counterterrorism and guerrilla war.'[59]

The eminent Israeli historian Martin van Crefeld asserted: 'The first, and absolutely indispensable, thing to do is throw overboard 99 percent of the literature on counterinsurgency, counterguerrilla, counterterrorism, and the like. Since most of it was written by the losing side, it is of little value.'[60] Expanding on those opinions, a view has developed within the vibrant (relative to the UK's) United States military intellectual world that the theory is nothing more than 'a strategy of tactics'. A serving professor at the West Point US Military Academy, Gian Gentile, takes the view that population-centred counterinsurgency:

> has become the only operational tool in the Army's repertoire to deal with problems of insurgency and instability throughout the world . . . It has reduced rather than promoted flexibility . . . it is a method and no more, merely a set of tactics. To elevate it, as has been done, to a strategy is to confine the options of the armed forces whose role, in essence, is the application of extreme force . . . It should not be viewed as strategy, or even policy for that matter.[61]

All wars are different and it is a serious error to characterize all 'small wars' as insurgencies, requiring similar countermeasures. As Gentile says, this limits the options and results in the remedy defining the illness, rather than the other way round.

Furthermore, he says, there are serious historical misconceptions at work. In a debate conducted in the leading US military journal *Joint Force Quarterly*, Gentile made this compelling point:

> [Our] Army has been steamrollered by a counterinsurgency doctrine that was developed by Western military officers to deal with insurgencies and national wars of independence from the mountains of northern Algeria in the 1950s to the swamps of Indochina in the 1960s. The simple truth is that we have bought into a doctrine for countering insurgencies that did not work in the past, as proven by history, and whose efficacy and utility remain highly problematic today.[62]

Another highly regarded American former soldier and academic, Andrew Bacevich, is even more unequivocal. He has compared the current enthusiasm for counterinsurgency and its relations with the disastrous financial constructs which brought the banking world to its knees. He says counterinsurgency:

is the military's equivalent of the financial sector's relationship with collateralized debt obligation, or CDOs. In the past few years, financial and military leaders have embraced complexity and believed that uncertainty and complexity if properly managed and monitored could be controlled. Both COIN and CDOs have proponents who believe in taking giant risks in endeavors because of their belief in the triumph of intelligence and motivation over chaos and uncertainty.[63]

All 'counterinsurgency' is hard-edged and exceedingly resource-intensive. It is almost always accompanied by a significant degree of repression. As we have seen, this was amply present in conflicts such as Malaya, as well as many other British 'small wars'. The only readily identifiable recent success against an effective guerilla war of the kind being fought in Afghanistan today was the savage and utterly ruthless campaign conducted by the Russians in Chechnya in the 1990s.[64] The strategic theorist Colin Gray bluntly but effectively suggests why this might be: 'the proposition that repression never succeeds is, unfortunately a myth. Half-hearted repression conducted by self-doubting persons of liberal conscience certainly does not work. That will be as true in the future as it was in the past.'[65] The strong implication here is that an invader is an invader, and he will be fought however many schools, courts and health centres are built.

To a very great degree, the proponents and opponents of 'population-centred counterinsurgency' have been talking past each other. In certain environments, it is obvious that tactics derived from British (and indeed other countries') successes in population-centred counterinsurgency can work. Iraq and Afghanistan, being more in the nature of occupations and complicated by significant civil wars, were not those environments. Even on the terms of COIN there was little attempt to 'protect the people' in either theatre. Indeed, in Afghanistan, given that NATO is perceived to be less than careful about the delivery of its lethal ordnance, it was not entirely clear to the 'people' from whom they needed to be protected, NATO forces or the Taliban.

Do no harm

As we have seen, successful counterinsurgency, in its 'traditional' form, may sometimes involve the use of ruthless force. Such force must be applied within a highly coherent and solid strategic framework, against the background of a clear realistic political context and firmly understood end-state. As we saw, the SAS took part in such well-directed extreme violence with a clear strategic objective alongside its US colleagues, as they effectively, if temporarily, eliminated Al Qaeda in Iraq from Baghdad.

While British military leaders in Basra and Helmand have deployed extensive force to support their declared aim to 'protect the people', that force has been applied in a disparate and un-coordinated way. In trying to 'do' population-centred counterinsurgency, they failed to look at matters from the realistic perspective of the 'people'. In Basra, they failed to secure the city from the key threat to both themselves and the Basrawis. In Helmand, the British are all too often seen as a threat themselves. To that degree, they have added to, rather than controlled, the chaos and uncertainty contingent to any war – they have, in Clausewitzian terms, increased the level of friction.

One overriding principle – familiar to anyone in any field of international assistance, or indeed any doctor – is (or should be) 'do no harm'. For aid workers, this precept is absolutely central. That 'doing no harm' is a lesson to be drawn from history is explicitly stated in a short but excellent history of British counterinsurgency practice, written to supplement JDP 3–40 for the Ministry of Defence by retired Colonel Michael Crawshaw. The very first paragraph summarizes all the history and theory of population-centred (as opposed to Russian-style) counterinsurgency in this chapter highly effectively:

> At the heart of any counter-insurgency (COIN) campaign lies one basic requirement – the population of the territory concerned should form the perception that the government offers a better deal than do the insurgents. In this perception, security of the person and of property, and the establishment of the rule of law, are paramount considerations. It follows that whatever else the government may do, it should start from that edict in the Hippocratic Oath which states: 'do no harm'.[66]

The phrase 'do no harm' appears only once in the main text of the vast JDP 3–40, and then only in connection with 'quick impact projects'. One might wonder why the phrase should not be the title and guiding thread running through the entire document. It does not appear in the Army Field Manual, *Countering Insurgency*, at all.

CHAPTER 8

Doing No Harm? The Question of Force

Guided missiles and misguided men . . .

Martin Luther King

I would not give my son for all the wealth these foreigners have. Every day they are killing innocent people. When NATO say they are killing less civilians, it is a lie. I hate them, especially when I see them. I hate them every time, as I remember my family.

Father of a civilian victim of British forces[1]

In January 2006, Zulu Company, 45 Commando – about 120 men – deployed to Garmsir, a village in the desolate and sparsely populated south of Helmand province. The parapets overlooked a road controlled by checkpoints. On the other side of the road was a large area of scrubland. Knowing that the British would certainly engage them, the Taliban would send their new fighters there to be blooded, and the British would oblige. 'It was just like boys meeting for a fight after school,' one soldier who was there at the time told me. The bizarre nature of the place was enhanced by the installation of loudspeakers, from which, at dawn every day, one of the interpreters would call in Pashtu: 'Good morning, Taalibaaan! Today your blood will soak the sacred soil of Afghanistan.' The interpreter's nickname was 'Robin', after Robin Williams, who starred in the film *Good Morning, Vietnam*. The marines called this place 'Garmsirland'. The fun stopped one day when a mortar shell fired at some Taliban went astray, killing a woman and seriously injuring her daughter. The girl's father brought her into the camp and she was evacuated to hospital by helicopter. She was followed shortly afterwards by the man who had aimed the mortar, who was evacuated from the base 'mentally destroyed' by what he had done.

Collateral damage

In 2009, the Ministry of Defence paid compensation for the deaths of 105 civilians in Helmand.[2] Of course, such figures are likely to be the tip of the iceberg, reflecting only those who were willing to brave the ordeal of coming to one of the intimidating bases of the forces who killed their relatives and enduring the humiliation of repetitive questioning by MoD civil servants. The majority of relatives will not have claimed at all. In one case, of which I was made aware by journalists in 2007, many dozens of people were killed in an American air strike in northern Helmand. The British, within whose 'AOR' this incident took place, acknowledged only seventeen fatal casualties – those whose names could be recalled by the few people who both made it to Lashkar Gah hospital 200 kilometres away and were willing to speak to the British authorities.

It is certain that the numbers actually killed are generally a large multiple of those reported. No real effort is made on a systematic basis to count or record civilian casualties. Clearly, in Taliban-controlled areas, claims for money from UK forces will be very few. The Taliban has an unforgiving attitude to those who are perceived to be involved in any way with the security forces. No mention at all is made in such reports of the injured – the blind and permanently disabled, the living 'collateral damage' – and there are, as yet, no records of compensation for those shattered lives. Given the absence of any adequate records, the fact that only a small proportion report their relatives' deaths, and the security situation, it is reasonable to assume that thousands of Afghans have been killed or injured by UK forces in Helmand since 2006.

Unfortunately it is only an assumption. NATO as a whole, and the British in particular, are more than coy when it comes to civilian casualties. Indeed, one officer, Lieutenant Colonel Owen McNally, whose responsibility it was to liaise with human rights organizations and others, was sent home in disgrace and threatened with prosecution for breach of the

Official Secrets Act.[3] In initial uncritical reports, by a press relying on military cooperation, it was alleged that he had told an official of Human Rights Watch that there had been, supposedly, 7,000 civilian casualties in Afghanistan in 2007. Why this figure should anyway be secret is not clear. The question 'why is this secret?' is rarely asked in the UK and never answered, beyond nebulous, puerile and vapid assertions of national security. That notwithstanding, no jury in England would convict an officer for relating the numbers of civilians slaughtered by NATO. In reality, there never was any question of prosecution – a statement easy to make for the informed observer, but of little comfort to anyone on the receiving end of the attention of UK government lawyers. It was not only lawyers who were mobilized against Colonel McNally. Journalists from 'friendly' tabloids were briefed by press officers that his relationship with the Human Rights Watch official was 'close'.[4] Unfortunately for the hapless press officers, the woman concerned – one Rachel Reid – had worked as a BBC journalist and was more than capable of successfully rebutting this libellous and false innuendo. Colonel McNally and Ms Reid had, in fact, met only twice, and then in connection with their duties. Her contacts with the BBC and her skills in handling the media are, of course, not available to everyone who embarrasses the Ministry of Defence.

Openness in recording civilian casualties is not simply a moral question. An article in the summer 2010 edition of the *British Army Review*[5] outlines three ancillary benefits. First, there is the impression of a 'shared humanity' – all casualties have validity, demonstrating that an occupying army respects locals enough to deal with them honestly. Second, recording might provide an evidentiary basis for substantiating claims, for example, about the effectiveness of measures taken to reduce casualties. Third, accurate recording of civilian casualties might be used as a measure of effectiveness of operations to 'protect' civilians from violence on the part of insurgents, as well as on the part of the occupying army. Unfortunately, we are a long way from such an approach: civilian casualties have to be calculated on the basis of information released by UK military sources only under duress. Very importantly, if notions of 'protecting the people' are to be taken seriously by those people, the same degree of care and focus that 'friendly fire' casualties attract – full inquiry and investigation conducted in a diligent fashion – must be applied to the many more civilians killed by UK and other forces. As matters stand, the attention given to such investigation is peremptory at best.

A 'minimum force' philosophy has long been a feature of British military culture.[6] It has been said that this is attributable to the values of humanitarianism and civilization – the 'good chap' ethos, as it were, that faintly subsists in the unconscious of the British officer class.[7] There is undoubtedly some truth in this, although it may well be that the perspective of Afghan villagers or Basrawis today is rather different. Indeed, as we have seen, even during the Malayan campaign, the British killed well over 6,000 guerrillas, there were atrocities, and there are assertions that many indigenous civilian tribesmen died from disease in the 'model villages'. Some highly credible scholars have suggested that the 'minimum force' ideal has been somewhat exaggerated.[8]

The ideals of minimum force are, in essence, an expression of the international law of the use of force. Every British serviceman is required, as part of his mandatory annual training, to receive a lecture on this apparently relatively simple aspect of humanitarian law.[9] It is considered as essential as his weapons training and basic medical drills. The soldier is taught that force may only be used if four conditions are satisfied: necessity, humanity, distinction (ensuring that civilians are not targeted) and proportionality. Some soldiers might understandably agree with the British Second World War combat infantry veteran who said: 'the Geneva Convention is a dangerous piece of stupidity because it leads people to believe that war can be civilised. It can't.'[10]

Whatever the views of soldiers, or indeed wherever the truth lies in academic arguments over its provenance, the truth is that the 'minimum force' approach works. It was a sensible and rational approach that lived necessarily with the most famous term associated with the legendary British adroitness in small wars – 'hearts and minds'. It is fair to say that the taking of Basra in April 2003 does stand as a lasting example of how to take a city with minimum damage and casualties to all concerned, with the Geneva Convention rules largely observed. The very early days of Basra showed the ethos of minimum force at its best.

The tension between a culture of law and the military's cavilling against it is nothing new. In 1837, the legendary General Napier had put the officer's dilemma with black humour. Confronted by a mob, 'his thoughts dwell on the (to him) most interesting question; "Shall I be *shot* for my forbearance by a court martial, or *hanged* for over zeal by a jury?" '[11] More recently, it was put with slightly less humour in the House of Lords by Admiral Boyce, a former chief of the defence staff, when he complained that the armed forces were under 'legal siege':

> They are being pushed in the direction in which an order could be seen as improper or legally unsound . . . They are being pushed by people not schooled in operations but only in political correctness.[12]

Up to a point, the admiral is entirely correct. Lawyers and legislators are, by and large, unschooled in operations. They are not, however, *only* educated in political correctness. Lawyers are generally 'unschooled' in crime or the conduct of business, but most make their living from advising on criminal or company law. It is worth mentioning here, perhaps, that Admiral Boyce was, until the very last years of his career, a submariner; he is therefore unschooled, except possibly for the occasional short course, in high-intensity 'manoeuvre' warfare. He was nonetheless responsible for exactly such an operation, the Iraq War, as he was chief of the defence staff between 2001 and 2003. It might also be added that he was quick to fly to lawyers – specifically the attorney general and his team – for assistance in determining whether he was lining himself up for a war-crimes indictment in commanding such a legally dubious operation.[13] Any lawyer involved in any way with today's military operations will have heard complaints similar to Napier's and Boyce's from servicemen every day.

Military concerns were echoed by a British government whose attachment to international law could be distinctly selective. The defence secretary in 2006, John Reid, is more famous for his expressed desire to leave Helmand 'without firing a shot'. In an address to the Royal United Services Institute, he spoke of the change in the nature of conflict, and went on: 'In the light of those changes I believe we must ask serious questions about whether or not further developments in international law in this area are necessary.'[14]

The idea of 'legal siege' is, of course, nothing new. The restraint of civilian political officers – many of whom were former senior army officers – was said to stand between soldiers and their medals in the old imperial days of the North West Frontier. Those who stand between soldiers and glory these days are lawyers. For good or ill, the law is as much part of the environment in which soldiers work as the hot weather. It was ever so, but this has never stopped any serviceman from griping about it.

Some of the subtlety of the 'minimum force' ethos seems to have faded. As one development worker with considerable experience of Afghanistan, and particularly Helmand, told me:

> They [British soldiers] come down the road with grenades hanging off them, tattoos up and down their arms, daggers and machine guns slung all over them, covered in ammunition. 'We come in peace,' they say, and expect people to talk to them. Do they imagine how it would be in their own home towns if foreign soldiers turned up like that?

One senior officer put it to me this way:

> The British Army's formative experience in the late twentieth century was Northern Ireland, and by 1990 we were masters at what we did, including minimum force. We carried this ethos/habit with us to the Balkans, where we were equally restrained. We opened up in the 2003 invasion of Iraq, but very soon returned back to where we had been (beret wearing, etc.). The rest of the Basra campaign was a schizophrenic experience, veering between use of 'exemplary' violence and minimum force. The point about Afghanistan is that the level of violence we use is mainly a result of our own experience there. We did not bring a culture of violence with us from the Cold War or anywhere else. Partly it was the result of the Paras' experience in the platoon houses; but mostly I think it was a psychological response to our own perceived failure in Basra and the damage to our reputation (in particular with the US army) that led us to be extra-macho in the use of violence.[15]

Judgement training and the law

The army is not at all blind to the need to try to ensure adequate awareness of the legal and presentational difficulties of the use of lethal force. Surrounded by twenty miles of Wiltshire countryside in every direction is the military town of Warminster. The town itself is ringed by army bases, in one of which is the centre of military thinking on training in tactics and deployment. On this base there is a very large-scale, deadly serious video game, known as the 'judgement trainer'. A screen taking up an entire wall faces the audience of soldiers who are to be deployed to an operational zone. The soldiers are given a half-hour lecture on the law of the use of force: it is to be necessary, proportionate and used only against those who are 'active' combatants.

When the lecture is over, each soldier is given the chance to try out his understanding. In front of the screen lie four SA80 rifles, similar to the ones the soldiers will take on operations. These rifles are rigged up to project beams at the screen. The soldiers take up their stations behind the rifles and are given a briefing outlining the scenario they will face. Perhaps it is a simple drive through a village; perhaps duty at a checkpoint. One thing they know is that something will happen. As the scenario proceeds, projected on the large screen in front of them, the dilemmas facing them become very stark indeed. It might be gunmen using human shields. Maybe there is simply a great deal of running around, shooting and shouting, and a serious difficulty in identifying targets that are actually armed *and* presenting an immediate threat. If they are running away, do they present an immediate threat? After each scenario the scene is replayed in slow time and the screen displays where each shot 'fired' has struck. The instructing sergeant asks the shooters why they fired each of those shots. He asks how they would justify each shot by reference to the law they have been taught.

There is one particular scenario that in one sense is very simple, but that crystallizes the impossible questions soldiers have to answer every day. The soldier is told that he is at a checkpoint, doing 'top cover' on a Land Rover as his colleagues search people seventy metres or so ahead of him. He sees some scuffling at the search point and a woman emerges, walking towards the Land Rover. She is wearing a burka and carrying a baby. Shouting is heard: 'She has not been searched!' The woman walks on calmly. Every metre she advances without him firing increases the chance of death or maiming – *if* she is a suicide bomber. She may, of course, simply be a woman in a hurry to get her child to a doctor. There is no way of knowing.

It is the ultimate dilemma. When I went through this exercise several years ago, the sergeant overseeing our instruction told me that the previous week a soldier had broken down in tears after 'opening fire' on that particular scene. The awful subtext of this exercise is that there is no right answer. Very few soldiers complete the judgement training in anything other than the spirit in which it is intended. At every stage, the reality is impressed upon them that they are responsible for their actions, and not only in the moral sense: wanton disregard will result in criminal liability.

In critiquing, or even discussing, this hugely difficult matter, one elementary factor must be borne in mind. Of all the writers and critics who discuss aspects of the use of military force and casualties, not one in a hundred has the slightest experience of battle at the sharpest end. It is the soldier who closes with and kills the enemy, and who faces the kind of dilemma that is never encountered or even considered in civilian life.

The reality of the kind of war labelled by soldiers and their academic cohorts as 'insurgency' is squalid and terrifying for all involved. It is rarely leavened or relieved by the consolations of camaraderie or perceived heroism, or even, really, by the ideals of fighting for a cause – at least for the foreign soldiers, who often have only the haziest idea of what they are doing and why. For the soldiers, any time spent outside the fort is a time of constant fear and suspicion of every local, each of whom may harbour hostile intent. I was told by one soldier that it was not uncommon for soldiers to vomit in fear before a patrol, knowing there was a significant chance that they might not return the same way they left. Knowing that and then going out and completing the patrol is raw courage of a quite remarkable kind.

As General Richards reminds us,[16] criticizing from a distance is easy. Indeed, unlike comment on a court case, or a medical operation, not only do the critics have no experience of personal involvement, but so horrendous is the reality for everyone involved that, in a society where minor road accidents can result in post-traumatic stress, they *cannot even imagine* how it might be to engage in the fury and chaos of close combat. Furthermore, the decisions that result either in the death of civilians in combat – perhaps through some mistake or inappropriate force – or in the horrific reality that we call 'collateral damage' are often being made by eighteen-year-old boys.

Those giving the orders know that wrong decisions can result in the death or injury of friends and comrades. Faced with the choice of risking having a friend lose his life, his sight or his testicles, for example, or risking civilian strangers, the decision crystallizes – if not easily, then often all too clearly. Very many soldiers now are directly aware of the consequences to their own men of making the wrong decisions in combat. Every soldier who has served on the front line has attended 'ramp ceremonies' for those who did not make it. Most know someone personally who has been seriously injured, often with what the MoD calls 'life-changing injuries' (inability to walk, to clean or feed oneself, to see, to reproduce, to excrete in a socially acceptable manner, and so on). Given the direct and immediate consequences of the choices facing these men, it is far harder to level distant criticism at them than at the generals who command them.

Overwhelming force

Traditionally, a palliative to the risk of being killed in a shoot-out was to apply overwhelming firepower. Every infantryman is trained, and has been for many decades, to identify the threat and apply controlled, effective but overwhelming firepower to it. This is the approach engendered by the Cold War mentality. A tornado of lethal projectiles will at least have the benefit of making the attacker think again; at best, it will kill him. Unfortunately, it may also kill others who had no choice or interest in being targets – civilians. Legal notions of 'necessity, humanity, distinction and proportionality' have little force when your life is at risk. Nonetheless, before any mission where weapons are to be carried, it is the duty of the commander, as part of the orders process, to remind his troops of the 'rules of engagement', which regularly differ from theatre to theatre (so those in operation in Iraq differed from those in Northern Ireland, for example). These are generally written on a laminated card and are to be carried by each soldier. In Northern Ireland, they were known as 'yellow cards'; in Iraq 'white cards'.

Practically speaking, what happens generally, in a typical confrontation, is that once they are 'contacted' – which is to say 'come under effective enemy fire' – the entire unit fires in the direction from where the enemy's fire appears to come, ideally having identified a target first. This immediate return of fire has the ancillary advantage of allowing the unit commander time to decide what to do. The tactical reality is that he has to decide how to get his men out of a seriously dangerous situation. Having to make such decisions, while complying strictly with the laws of war (or, at a more basic level, with the often confusing directions on the laminated card), is no easy task. After such a 'contact' (all occasions where gunfire is exchanged are 'contacts'), reports are written, which are scrutinized by the legal advisers usually attached to the brigade headquarters. These lawyers (who are, by any standards, of extremely high quality) are generally overworked and underappreciated. Assessment of contact reports is treated as a priority. Soldiers are made fully aware that they will be held accountable for mistakes, although extensive allowance is made, in practice, for the heat of battle.

For the British infantry, however, the default overall tactical approach in circumstances such as these – contact – is to close with and destroy the enemy, using overwhelming violence. That is as it should be, if the troops find themselves fighting battles as traditionally practised. In theatres such as Helmand, traditional responses can be exceedingly counterproductive. Here, it might be said, is where the problems really begin.

There is also a more rarely mentioned cultural issue: soldiers want to fight. This is in no way palatable for the cosseted civilian, but the bare reality is that fighting and killing is what infantrymen do. Young men join the army for action and, as in any other contentious profession, generally speaking they feel a great desire to test themselves against opponents. It is their job, and every infantryman wants action. As one infantry officer told me: 'It takes between three and five contacts to get this out of their system.' This is, after all, the ultimate adrenaline rush, and those who never undergo it are forced to experience it at second hand, through the medium of 'herographies'. Such books sell well, even among civilians. On one occasion, Tony Blair visited Camp Bastion and was talking with some soldiers. One of them was an enthusiastic supporter: 'I am going to keep voting for you, Sir,' he said, 'as long as you keep sending me to places where I can blow things up and kill people.'[17] This is certainly a minority view, and needs to be taken in the context of a soldier having a laugh with his friends. However, there is some truth in it. A senior police officer, a thirty-year veteran of the Royal Ulster Constabulary, hit the mark:

The thing that has not been understood is that where soldiers go, trouble generally follows. This is entirely normal as soldiers by their nature are looking for trouble. The other young fighters are doing much the same. Trouble finds its friends. When we had incidents in Northern Ireland I was never that keen to see the army. The IRA would far rather have a go at them than us, they would get a fight from them.[18]

It is instructive that one of the options not covered in at least the scenarios I saw at the judgement trainer, is the option of reversing from a village in which you are attacked and not engaging at all. As one senior officer, a veteran of Northern Ireland, pointed out, an officer proudly reporting that he had refused contact would not attract the approval of standard-issue senior officers. There can be no question that this is a serious cultural problem.

The question of medals, and their underlying cultural function of displaying courage and (contingent to that) professional competence, comes up time and again in discussion with officers and men. If culture is 'the stories we tell ourselves about ourselves' then the physical manifestation of such a culture is medals. A serving infantry officer put it this way: 'The objective of the institution is to get more gongs and promotions . . . if you didn't get a medal it's not that you weren't exceptional, it's that you weren't adequate.'[19] And medals are won by demonstrating decisive aggressive action. Clearly that is a notion that does not sit happily with any idea of 'courageous restraint'. As another officer put it to me starkly: 'I've yet to see a medal citation for courageous restraint. We won't get anywhere until that changes.'[20] In one form or another, this has been a sentiment expressed by very many thoughtful young officers.

It is not only at the relatively simple level of the section (eight men) or even the platoon (thirty men) that the problems of fighting and of operating among the people exist. In none of the counterinsurgency campaigns of the 'classic' period were heavy weapons used to anything like the extent they have been in Iraq or Helmand. To the extent that they were used in Malaya and Kenya, they were a byword for ineffective waste.

In Helmand, however, every patrol has a vast panoply of weaponry on call. It carries with it Javelin rockets (designed originally as anti-tank weapons, they have proved invaluable in 'taking out' single snipers or machine-gun positions), and each unit will have mortars attached. Then there will be artillery, ten miles or so away, perhaps. This may take the form of conventional guns, or the immensely destructive 'multi-launch rocket system', designed to drench entire Soviet armoured formations in splinters and high explosive.

Then, of course, there is 'air'. The Apache helicopters have proved particularly useful, with their automatic cannon and guided rockets. Then come 'fighter-bombers', sometimes British Tornados (the fantastically expensive Eurofighter Typhoons could not be made to drop bombs) and sometimes aircraft from other NATO countries. Even higher up are 'strategic bombers'. A friend of mine spent a tour in Afghanistan, in his own words, 'seeing how low he could get B1 bombers to fly'. The B1 is an American aircraft that was specifically designed to breach the air defences of the Soviet Union and obliterate its bases and cities with nuclear weapons. Fortunately (if that is the right word), these dinosaurs have now been re-armed with 'precision' weapons. This officer was acting as a 'forward observation officer' (FOO) – deployed with army units, he had the task of guiding aircraft in to destroy targets designated by the ground commander, usually small groups of peasant farmers armed with rifles.

A former senior artillery officer set this job in context:

In the old days, for example, the FOO was directed by his tactical commander. It was a relatively simple job, just reporting and observation on behalf of the [artillery] guns he was controlling. He did not need to think too deeply about what he was firing at. Now the thing he does least is control his own guns; he has air, aviation (attack helicopters), lots of observation devices and communications equipment. But most critically he is required to exercise moral judgement in addition to the technical knowledge required for collateral damage assessment. This represents a greater stress than so-called 'modern' wars, such as the First Gulf War and the early stages of the current Iraq War. We think of that kind of 'general war' as bloodier. Actually, recently, that has not been the case. We lost eight men to enemy action in the First Gulf War – an almost purely 'conventional' action.[21]

Needless to say, even with the hugely expensive suites of communications and reconnaissance equipment, there can never be certainty as to what exactly has been achieved. A junior intelligence officer describes an incident one night in 2007:

> The UAV [unmanned aerial vehicle] spotted a group of men coming down off the hills. They were armed with rifles and it was reported to the senior officer on duty. We counted fourteen men as they entered a building in a small village. It was determined that they were likely to be Taliban. An air strike was authorized, and a bomb dropped on the building. After the blast, we observed the building to try to assess damage. On the viewer, in green light as it was still dark, I saw one man crawling out of the wreckage. He seemed to be hauling something with him by his side. It took me a minute or so to see that he was pulling what remained of his intestines . . . I realized then that this was no video game. Were they Taliban? I don't know. Every man in Helmand has a rifle.[22]

It is not the responsibility of small unit tactical commanders to get this kind of matter right: this is a question for those setting policy. If a force of highly trained fighters is given huge quantities of highly expensive ordnance[23] designed for a high-intensity European armoured war, it is highly likely to use them. Once again, it falls to competent generals to plan well and set the conditions for appropriate action. This, in turn, needless to say, requires a crystal-clear idea of what the operation is intended to achieve. One might be given to ask, for example, as a commander at the theatre level, why units in a supposed 'counterinsurgency' have been armed with heavy artillery and equipped with strategic bombers.

Courageous restraint

In true British style, the grandly titled Land Warfare Development Centre is housed largely in a series of Portakabins and tired-looking 1960s build-ings. It lies just across the road from the Army Judgement Trainer. One of the temporary buildings contains the office of the *British Army Review*, whose editor is a retired colonel, John Wilson. Colonel Wilson had exten-sive experience of operations undertaken from the 1960s to the 1990s, including in Northern Ireland. He believes the time has come for a funda-mental shift in the way the army conducts itself on operations:

Big-war fighting is the most demanding of tasks; the conventional wisdom has been that if you train for big mobile battle it is easier to step 'down' to lower-intensity conflict. It is accepted now that demands of current ops are such that, in some ways, they are *more* demanding than general war at the individual unit level.

At Brecon [the Infantry Battle School] they are still teaching conventional war, low-level-fire team skills. This is an incomplete preparation for war in the new sectors – they are taught the kinetic way. But maybe we should ask 'did you really need to have that engagement at all?' . . . Responsibilities of junior officers have increased and deepened. The reality for junior officers is that it could be difficult to report that you avoided contact [combat] at any possible time. The wrong construction could be put on that, Lieutenant Bloggs is avoiding combat and that sort of thing; at best the response might be 'show more aggression'.

But we do have a tradition of this. To ask an army deliberately *not* to fight happened in Northern Ireland. The battalion commanding officer would or might be pleased to report that 'we came back from our tour without having fired a shot'. The ethos was that it wasn't bad not to have fired a shot. This may not have been pleasing to individual soldiers. It is an attitude you can develop at the organizational level.[24]

This is demonstrably true. Wilson summarizes the situation:

It is remarkable how restrained most units and soldiers were [in Northern Ireland] . . . patrols were ambushed and did not return fire despite taking casualties because there were no identifiable targets. The P[rovisional] IRA killed six soldiers for every IRA volunteer killed in combat. This ratio is probably reversed in Iraq and Afghanistan. It was not because the army in NI [Northern Ireland] was poor; it was the nature of the conflict.[25]

Of course, if you are denied the ability to respond to an attack with massive force, matters are out of the hands of the soldiers.[26]

In Northern Ireland the practice of effective use of 'minimum force' was ensured partly by the simple expedient of issuing only light weapons, the heaviest being the general-purpose machine gun. 'This was a deliberate decision,' Colonel John Wilson told me:

even the Saxon armoured vehicle was an uncomfortable addition, big, intrusive and cumbersome, it was presentationally difficult. Very occasionally for specific ops in specific places, we were issued with claymores [anti-personnel mines carried with patrols and used for defending fixed positions or ambushes] to secure temporary positions.[27]

Thus no temptation existed to respond to small arms attacks with the use of rocket, artillery or even strike aircraft. There was also little incentive to embark on hopeless or futile endeavours – such as many of the patrols conduct in Helmand today – merely to prove 'authority' or 'presence'. Almost all the transport of soldiers in areas with significant IRA presence was by helicopter. In areas that were recognized to be effectively controlled by the IRA – South Armagh, for example – little effort was made militarily to challenge this by sending patrols down roads to be shot at or attacked with IEDs. It would have been regarded as nothing short of stupidity to have done otherwise. Legal provisions relating to the use of force were, generally, rigorously applied. Soldiers who transgressed could expect to be prosecuted. At the height of the Troubles, 28,000 British soldiers were deployed to the six counties, in addition to the tens of thousands of well-trained police and military reserves. There were few complaints of too few soldiers.

What happened to the ethos that seemed to work so well in Northern Ireland for most of the thirty years of involvement? In Ireland, every shot needed to be strictly accounted for. Now the response to a sniper (an AK-47 costs between $50 and $300, depending on the market) is to suppress him with thousands of rounds of machine-gun fire and, if that fails (as it often does), to fire a Javelin rocket (cost £70,000) at his firing position. Until early 2010 it was common to call in an air strike and drop 1,000 kilogramme bombs (cost £250,000 plus £35,000 an hour fuel for the constantly patrolling jets) on the position. A senior officer I spoke to was at a slight loss:

I don't know, maybe it is seen to be easier to kill dark-skinned persons. My worry is the effect it is having on our capability to do this sort of operation. What would happen now if those guys were posted to Northern Ireland or anywhere else and responded in the way they do now in Afghanistan? Would the attitude be: 'We killed a couple of kids, so what?'

Iraq and Afghanistan are different, and it may well be that there is another explanation: Northern Ireland is part of the United Kingdom. Even during the Troubles it was, with the exception of very small areas of inner cities, under the 'rule of law'. Soldiers who killed a child would know that there were legal repercussions, in the form of, at the very least, an investigation. Indeed, the consequences of such actions could be very severe indeed, and not just for the soldier who fired the shot. Situations in which a child was killed by a soldier – even, as was invariably the case, clearly inadvertently – sparked riots and political point-scoring by the opposition, which was very quick to attach the 'child-killer' epithet. In Afghanistan, as matters stand, there is little oversight, and the practical likelihood of any form of real redress is vanishingly small – unpalatable, but nonetheless true. Not a single prosecution has resulted from the many dozens of civilian casualties inflicted by British forces.

There is also the somewhat painful fact that the Taliban are rather good fighters. Over the period during which the British have been involved in Helmand, the tactics of their opponents have evolved to the point where they are capable of what the army calls 'complex ambushes', of the kind it took the IRA, for example, many more years to perfect. When a unit is ambushed it can find itself in very serious difficulties very quickly; this is obviously even more of a problem when casualties are taken, as the Taliban is perfectly capable of determining where casualty evacuation helicopters will touch down.

If you only have a hammer, every problem is a nail

This returns us to the problem of approach. What are British infantrymen doing patrolling highly dangerous roads and villages in the first place – the sorts of places they would not have considered entering in Northern Ireland? In Ulster, roads were avoided as a matter of course, for the simple reason that they were easy targets for roadside bombs. No sensible army commander would consider sending a patrol several kilometres down a road in South Armagh during most of the 1980s. It would have been considered a reckless invitation to the IRA to inflict pointless casualties – an invitation the IRA would have been keen to take up. The answer to this question is 'presence'. Rather than securing their base areas in the major towns, the fiction of control of areas that are clearly *not* under control is maintained. Why such presence was not considered necessary in the United Kingdom is not clear. In the absence of sufficient force, the only substitute is heavy weaponry, from supersonic bombers to anti-tank rockets. There is an old military saying that tactical action can have strategic effect. The substitution of heavy and indiscriminate weaponry for adequate forces is an instance of strategic blunders having direct tactical consequences.

The problem of overuse of weaponry might be summarized by a well-known saying first coined by Abraham Maslow: 'If you only have a hammer, you tend to see every problem as a nail.' This particular 'hammer and nail' problem arises, of course, not primarily from a desire on the part of soldiers to use their toys: they have a real dilemma, foisted upon them by the decisions made early in the campaign disastrously to overstretch what few forces the British could apply to the problem of Helmand. The lack of 'boots on the ground' is being compensated for by heavy weaponry and also (until early 2010, when the American commander in Afghanistan, Stanley McChrystal, applied the brakes to its cavalier use) by air power. (The brakes may subsequently have been eased somewhat after his replacement by General David Petraeus.) It is from this rather basic fact that the importance of numbers – identified by James Quinlivan[28] and discussed above in Chapter 5 – stems in the contemporary context. In order to secure an area in conflict, there is an inescapably constant proportion – a 'painful arithmetic', Quinlivan calls it – of men with guns to the civilian population. Clearly, Quinlivan's ratios shift according to how secure the environment is, but in the world's most intense combat environment (paradoxically created by the *lack* of such an adequate proportion in 2006–7), that proportion may need to be about 1:10 or 1:20. In Helmand alone, that would approximate to something in the region of at least 50,000 troops, a number that would have denuded the UK of all its deployable infantry several times over. In order simply to *secure themselves*, the British needed to deploy a great deal of 'heavy metal' to make up for that critical lack of boots on the ground.

This ruthless arithmetic must be placed alongside a deeper cultural problem. One officer who served as a company commander in Helmand believed that 'insufficient value, indeed no value, was placed upon what some have called "courageous restraint"'.[29]

Outrageous restraint?

In June 2010, a potentially groundbreaking meeting took place in the library of the Royal United Services Institute in London. An eclectic and impressive group of experts was assembled: military staff officers from the (almost) next door MoD, every one of them a combat veteran; officials from NGOs such as Oxfam and Save the Children; academics; and police experts on the use of lethal force.

The meeting, which took the form of a seminar, was convened by one of the newest institutions in the army, its Counterinsurgency Centre. Only six months previously, it had produced the field manual on counterinsurgency.[30]

The peace of this Victorian centre of study, the world's oldest centre of strategic expertise, with the Whitehall traffic whispering outside, was in stark contrast to the bloody topic being discussed – civilian casualties. The purpose of the meeting was to advise on immediate steps to reduce the casualties caused by British military action. Much of what has been discussed here was covered. As with so much else, only time will tell whether there will be any real change in culture as a result of this and many other similar meetings.

It was not, though, the size or the level of expertise of the gathering that was remarkable; it was the tone. Chaired by one of the more intellectually impressive retired generals, Sir John Kiszely, the atmosphere of the meeting was very much of the army in what appeared to be genuine listening mode – a mode not often encountered in recent years. There was perhaps even, for those inclined to seek it, something of a sense of humility. These were men – and the military contingent was entirely male – who were willing to listen. There was intense discussion of the problems raised in this chapter: of the conflict between an army trained to fight a high-intensity war with high-intensity manoeuvre doctrine and the culture that goes with it, in an environment that requires quite a different approach. The terrible dilemmas facing young men under pressure and the ideal of courageous restraint taxed all the participants. One former senior police officer caught what is perhaps the central problem: 'This kind of meeting is fine. We all basically agree. The key will be to change the conversations in the canteens and officers' messes. We are a long way from that.'

As if in confirmation of this, two weeks later, once the directives issued by the theatre commander, General McChrystal, had 'bedded in', the cavilling began from those embedded in the old military culture. One NCO put it this way in a report in the *Daily Telegraph*: 'Our hands are tied the way we are asked to do courageous restraint. I agree with it to the extent that previously too many civilians were killed but we have got people shooting us and we are not allowed to shoot back. Outrageous [*sic*] restraint is a lot easier to say than to implement.'[31] This highlights the acute difficulty of changing a deeply embedded culture – those 'stories we tell ourselves about ourselves' – in the face of deadly threat. Having generals announce new rules is one thing; gaining compliance from a profoundly conservative and sceptical soldiery, faced with a highly skilful enemy that has absolutely no compunction about applying maximum force, whatever the circumstances, is altogether different.

Confirming this difficulty, an officer spoke of the solution hit upon in his own area of operations: 'It's a major bugbear for the British Army, it [courageous restraint] affects us massively. Thank God we have the ANA [Afghan National Army] here because they have different rules of engagement to us and can smash the enemy.'[32] Rather more encouragingly, Lieutenant Colonel Paul James, commanding officer of 40 Commando, Royal Marines, ruled out launching an air strike on fifteen locals digging in an IED: 'I chose not to strike them because that would have been fifteen fathers of fifteen sons who would almost certainly have been driven into the insurgents' arms. You could also not rule out who was foe or who was curious onlooker.'[33] Courageous restraint in action. From the perspective of the overall mission, this approach works far better. Indeed, it is the only way that the mission can get anywhere near being achieved. As General Michael Flynn put it in a report he wrote on intelligence in Afghanistan: '[Merely] killing insurgents usually serves to multiply enemies rather than subtract them. This counterintuitive dynamic is common in many guerrilla conflicts and is especially relevant in the revenge-prone Pashtun communities whose cooperation military forces seek to earn and maintain.'[34]

Flynn is no soft-hearted armchair general. It was he who commanded the vital intelligence component of General Stanley McChrystal's lethally effective anti-terrorist operations in Baghdad. He reinforces David Kilcullen's insight that the arithmetic of 'counterinsurgency' can be strange: if you have twenty and you kill five, you might end up with fifteen; none – if the others go home; or sixty-five, as ten from each family join the insurgency for revenge.

There is another, harsher formula for this approach:

> Put crudely, if the only way to save soldiers' lives is to kill civilians then the men in uniform may just have to get killed. This is a horrible calculus – especially when laid out by civilian writers ensconced in comfy London offices – but it goes beyond ivory tower strategist navel gazing.[35]

It does indeed. For if soldiers are not in Helmand, Basra or any other theatre to achieve the 'mission', then one might be forgiven for asking why they are there. The mission is certainly not assisted by the regular killing of civilians. Indeed, in the medium and longer terms, the military effort is not assisted thereby, indeed it is very much damaged. A consequence of this approach is that greater thought might be given to what soldiers are going to be doing in any given area that might place them, or anyone else, in the position where that fearful choice has to be made.

Collocating talk and action

Even more difficult would be collocating the words of UK senior officers concerning civilian casualties with actions against soldiers. If a soldier is killed or seriously injured by a 'blue on blue' – otherwise known as 'friendly fire' – investigations are detailed, intense and lengthy. Civilians killed in their own country by foreign forces are accorded the briefest of glances by comparison. A 'contact report' is scrutinized by a frantically busy brigade lawyer. If there are no factors indicating wrongdoing, no further action is taken. At the time of writing, in Afghanistan, not a single soldier has been disciplined, let alone brought before any form of military or civilian tribunal, for the unlawful killing of civilians. In Iraq, of course, the results of such inquiries are lamentably inconclusive. So what? The reality is that, over the next decade, as stories emerge and cases are fought, the failure to take account of the basic human reality that an Afghan life is, in fact, worth as much as a British one will impact severely on the reputation of UK forces.

For civilians, these civil wars we call 'insurgencies' are unremitting combinations of fear, insecurity, lawlessness and daily petty inconvenience at best. In every civil war the real terrors of the night are the knock on the door, the note slipped under the door, the whispered threat. It does not go away. If life is lost, it is lost for ever. And then there are the missing, who never return and are never found. Unmarked graves, kidnap in the night, torture and the other unimaginable horrors of civil war or wars of resistance ... The state is not interested; there is no National Health Service. The shattered human beings left behind must rely on their families, or very scarce charity. One of the better known of the old 'new' wars, the war we refer to as the 'Peninsular War', featured a religious Spanish peasantry up against the most formidable war machine of the day, Napoleon's army. Goya's series *The Disasters of War* provides some idea of what such conflicts are really like.

In an environment that requires finesse and judgement, and sometimes where 'doing nothing' is, in every possible sense of the word, the most courageous option, the prevailing ethos of the army remains one of combat, and the prevailing culture remains aggressive and 'decisive', with the concept of 'cracking on' at its core. Whatever the declared mission, it is understandably driven by an ethos of 'force protection' rather than a mission-centred one. One very positive result, and unquestionably the objective of the new 'counterinsurgency' doctrine, is that emphasis has started to shift away from 'kinetic' operations. This approach has a very long way to travel before it beds in. Yet even if the ethos changes, might there be an even more fundamental difficulty in placing these men from a totally alien culture among a foreign people?

Civvies

Consider something for a moment. If there is a patrol walking down your street in Britain or the USA, it is likely to be made up of policemen. Well trained, English-speaking, in Britain unarmed. There are still barriers, of course – the uniform primarily. These are men, though, who are probably relatively local, and they speak your language.

Now imagine another patrol, this one hypothetical. These men are heavily armed, dressed in the uniform of a foreign army – let's say the Chinese army. They have been 'invited' in by a government they have themselves installed, and for which they occasionally ask you to vote. Anything you say to them is met with blank looks – or the summons of a young, nervous, local boy. He may be wearing a balaclava, as it would not be good for certain people to learn that he was working for the foreigners. His Chinese is not particularly good, and he clearly has little idea what these soldiers are saying. He is the interpreter.

The other night, without the benefit of interpreters, these soldiers smashed their way into the house of a neighbour three doors down – you have yet to discover why, but the man of the house has not been seen since, and his wife is clearly not dealing with this well. Two weeks ago, these soldiers, or their friends, flattened a farmhouse not too far away with a bomb or rocket. You heard the massive bang of the explosion, but it was the shockwave of the bomb that really frightened you. A Chinese officer, who stopped you on the street to 'talk', told you that intelligence had indicated there had been terrorists hiding there. You saw the family every week at church and had heard nothing of any links to criminals or gunmen. The five people killed there did not even make the inside pages of the paper in the foreigners' capital.

These heavily armed foreign invaders say they come in peace. They are here in your country, on your street, to help. To this end, they have installed a group of well-known gangster oligarchs in your capital. There is a resistance group in your area, composed of former criminals. They, too, occasionally 'patrol' your street and ask you when it was you last saw an 'enemy' military unit and where they were. The officer who stopped you is later interviewed by Chinese TV: 'My biggest gripe,' he says, 'is convincing the locals to help themselves and in getting them to appreciate that this is their country. We really are here to help . . .'

Having considered this vignette, I ask you this question: what is it about these putative Chinese soldiers that is frightening? Is it that they are Chinese and do not speak your language? Or is it that they are heavily armed men who have an apparent propensity to kill? Something of both, perhaps?

Cultural awareness

With failure in both wars has come, as we have seen, a great deal of intelligent analysis. It has not escaped the notice of innovators that Iraq and Afghanistan are very different cultures from our own. A problem of 'cultural knowledge' has been identified. In the US, the response has been decisive and quick. But is it appropriate? One of the cardinal virtues proclaimed by and on behalf of the British has been their supposed cultural awareness.

Yet this inheritance was spent long ago. This issue has penetrated even the more populist reaches of literature. In the book *Bravo Two Zero*, the first of many recent 'herographies' of fighting men, an SAS patrol is dropped into Iraq in 1991 to join the hunt for Scud missiles.[1] The story goes that, shortly after its members land in Iraq, they are spotted by an Iraqi shepherd. One of the soldiers, affecting nonchalance, waves to him – but with his *left hand*, which (as every supposed expert on Arab culture knows) is used only for toilet ablutions. The shepherd realizes that these men must be foreign, and reports their presence to the authorities. And so begins the ordeal of Bravo Two Zero patrol. If only they had been taught to wave with the right hand before they left! The point here is that Iraq is perceived not only as a hostile place, but also as a strange one, where people do not wave as you or I would. In fact, one will see men waving with both hands in every Muslim country, including Iraq. The real reason this patrol was compromised is probably that it was a heavily armed group of men who seemed out of place in the area.

In the United States there is an awareness that cultural knowledge has been ignored. This school of thought perceives this to have been a crucial factor in the failure of the American military establishment to understand and deal successfully with irregular warfare. There has been a focus on 'winning on the battlefield', where cultural knowledge most certainly takes second place to obliteration of the enemy. The FM 3–24 counterinsurgency manual has led the charge in reframing the debate on 'culture', which it mentions on no fewer than 178 occasions in its 228 pages.[2]

As Patrick Porter has pointed out in his book *Military Orientalism*, a distressed US military was drawn to culture as a potential solution.[3] General Robert Scales argued for 'cultural-centric warfare' before Congress:

> [Success is] going to require a real transformation in how the Department of Defense views war, that we move from a technocentric view of warfare to a cultural-centric view of warfare, and that the human, behavioral, cognitive, and cultural aspects of warfare become as much a part of our lexicon, our research and development, our training and education, as learning how to operate machines is today.[4]

Scales goes on to say that the potential 'cultural counter-revolution'[5] would ideally provide the 'conceptual lessons required to return fire'.[6]

The turning point in this approach was reached with a seminal article in the US *Military Review* in April 2005, as things were going very badly wrong in Iraq. The author was a young anthropologist called Montgomery McFate, who pointed out what was beginning to become clear to many inside and outside the military: that there had been a serious misunderstanding of what occupation of a country required:

Countering the insurgency in Iraq requires cultural and social knowledge of the adversary. Yet, none of the elements of US national power – diplomatic, military, intelligence, or economic – explicitly take adversary culture into account in the formation or execution of policy. This cultural knowledge gap has a simple cause – the almost total absence of anthropology within the national-security establishment.[7]

She took a rosy view of British capability in this respect:

The alternative approach to fighting insurgency, such as the British eventually adopted through trial and error in Northern Ireland, involves the following: A comprehensive plan to alleviate the political conditions behind the insurgency; civil-military cooperation; the application of minimum force; deep intelligence; and an acceptance of the protracted nature of the conflict. Deep cultural knowledge of the adversary is inherent to the British approach.[8]

The holder of a PhD in the insurgency in Northern Ireland, Dr McFate will have known that Ulster culture is not significantly different in most significant respects from mainland British culture, and is very similar to that found in certain English and Scottish cities, such as Liverpool or Glasgow, from where very many British soldiers hailed. Indeed, a disproportionately large proportion of British soldiers (including the author of this book) were – and indeed are – citizens of the Irish Republic or British/Irish dual nationals. At the time she was writing, in early 2005, the shine had yet to come off the 'British approach' to insurgency. It still appeared to many, despite the raging Shi'a insurgency in the south, that the situation was at least better than the carnage in Baghdad and central Iraq – as indeed it was.

Dr McFate correctly pointed out that anthropology had its roots in the need – particularly for the British – to understand those whose lands they colonized. Indeed, it had at one time been called 'the handmaiden of colonialism'. While circumstances had undoubtedly changed, it was one thing figuratively to stand on the sidelines and criticize, as, she said, the anthropological establishment was doing, and quite another to attempt to assist the US in getting out of the quagmire into which it had got itself: 'In a counterinsurgency operation against a non-Western adversary, however, culture matters.'[9]

The reception of her article illustrates a typical American willingness to act upon recognition of a problem. It galvanized the American military to create the famous 'Human Terrain System' teams. These were set up by Dr McFate herself, who was approached by the US army after she had published the article, and have been extensively deployed in Iraq and Afghanistan. Originally they were intended to be composed of specialists in local culture and 'designed to address cultural awareness shortcomings by giving brigade commanders an organic capability to help understand and deal with "human terrain" – the social, ethnographic, cultural, economic and political elements of the people among whom a force is operating'.[10] Five cultural and regional studies experts were intended to be deployed to every brigade combat team[11] deployed in Iraq and Afghanistan.

Language and culture

The British have begun the process of instituting similar teams. The inaugural training course, run by the Defence Cultural Specialist Unit, based at RAF Henlow in Bedfordshire, was held in February 2010. Unfortunately, its organizers did not trouble to involve – or even to contact – several genuine experts on Afghan history or culture (who are anyway very few and far between).[12] As with any organization that operates a 'course mentality', there are certain obvious attendant risks, not least that those who graduate from a three-week course may begin to act and believe that they are in some way qualified to be cultural experts. These groups, whenever and in whatever form they are deployed, and with whatever degree of real expertise, will certainly have a job to do.

This unit is supported, as all such units must be, by military doctrine. In early 2009, the Development, Concepts and Doctrine Centre produced a Joint Doctrine Note on culture: *The Significance of Culture to the Military*.[13]

This is a positive move, undoubtedly, although on examination it has the distinct appearance of a primer on sociology, culture and identity, with a strong (and welcome) stress on avoiding a 'them and us approach'. Understandably, much of it is pretty basic material – understanding that gunfire can be celebratory as well as hostile, and that various different interpretations attach to body language or time. As with any mention of Afghan culture, one wonders when the ubiquitous 'you have the watches but we have the time' saying – often attributed to Afghans, but only ever used by foreigners – will appear (on page 2–10, as it happens), missing the point that this saying is not about attitudes to timekeeping, but about who has that time and its importance to a campaign. Most importantly, the note encourages its readers to attempt self-analysis. It is here that the note begins to falter.

As matters stand, with very little in the way of local knowledge or deep expertise, let alone language proficiency, interpreters are absolutely vital. Without good interpreters, an occupying force is essentially nothing (or little) more than an armed presence, whose interaction with the community is extremely limited at best. Indeed, even with interpreters, an army with an inadequate attitude will be little better placed. Clearly, in a 'war among the people' such as that in Iraq, where 'influence' and intelligence were paramount considerations, this was not acceptable.

The army had immediate access to a large number of Basrawi English speakers recruited locally. In normal circumstances, where the main duties of the army were confined to peacekeeping or basic policing these locally employed interpreters (LEIs) would have been adequate for the needs of regular line troops. But these were not normal circumstances, and Iraqi LEIs worked under constant threat to themselves and their families. Over sixty Iraqi interpreters who had worked for the British are alleged to have been killed.[14] Exactly the same situation prevailed in Helmand. For intelligence or liaison work of any degree of sensitivity, military interpreters were required – that is to say military (or occasionally contract hire civilian) personnel with the required security clearances. Good military interpreters take at least three years to train properly. They are 'mission critical' in a way that helicopters or body armour rarely are. Even with good, well-trained interpreters, there is always the problem of what might charitably be termed 'limited perspectives' on the part of those who do not speak the language.

This limitation could produce some difficult situations. One interpreter, an Arabic-speaking intelligence officer with several years' experience of living in the Middle East, told me:

> I had to interpret for one of the army handlers in a meeting with a Shi'a cleric, a mullah. The handler wanted to know what was said at Friday prayers – what the 'atmospherics' were.
>
> 'Ah,' said the mullah, 'there was a very holy atmosphere . . . it was as if the Imam Ali himself was there.' Now, the Imam Ali is a seriously important figure for Shi'as, roughly comparable to St Peter or even Jesus. So when the handler asked in English: 'Give me a full description of the Imam Ali', I did not translate it, but told the handler who the Imam Ali was. He was not sympathetic: 'I ask the fucking questions; you translate.'
>
> So I did.
>
> The mullah replied: 'He died thirteen hundred years ago, so I don't know. Tell your friend I think he had a beard.'
>
> I had many frankly embarrassing experiences like that, and they did us no good at all.[15]

In another case, an intelligence officer and his interpreter met a very well-connected businessman who was initially disposed to work with the British – a rare and potentially rich source of contacts and information. After the meeting, the officer, with years of experience in Northern Ireland, wanted to offer the businessman a few pounds by way of expenses for his trouble. This had been normal practice for the usual 'customers' of the officer, who were almost always poor. Besides, it was standard operating procedure to offer expenses, as it is in any sensibly run business.

The interpreter warned the intelligence operator that in this case his offer would be perceived as insulting, on levels far beyond anything to be found in the rather informal environment of the United Kingdom. It implied not only poverty, but dishonesty, in that the 'source' had implicitly claimed wealth and influence. The interpreter was told to offer the money; he did and the businessman got up and walked out, never to be seen again. There is a saying that it is more effective to find a good intelligence operator and teach him to speak Arabic than to find an interpreter and teach him to be an operator. Even if this facile aphorism was correct, which it self-evidently is not, virtually none of these supposedly hard-to-find military or civilian intelligence officers were prepared to put in the effort to learn Arabic or any other language.

Throughout its imperial involvement, Britain's soldiers and civilians regarded knowledge of the language of those among whom they worked as an irreducible minimum qualification. In the British Indian army it was a prerequisite for promotion to captain for officers to learn an Indian language to a level roughly equivalent to A level today. There is a relic of this attitude in the requirement for the 60 per cent of Gurkha officers who are British to learn Nepali. Political officers during the British imperial presence in Pashtun lands had to be able to speak Pashto to a level enabling them to intervene in a running argument. Knowledge of a language enables soldiers to lay down what one scholar has called 'a sediment of knowledge of the human environment within which he works'.[16] The ability to exist and exercise influence upon those with whom they interacted, using charm and, where necessary, applying judicious threats, was also a crucial quality required of 'politicals'. Clearly, a basic sense of 'situational awareness' or 'emotional intelligence' was essential, so that boundaries were pushed but not crossed.

Dan Jarman worked for DfID and spent two years in Iraq and a year working alongside the British army in Helmand in 2006–7:

> Soldiers tend to view Afghan people like pictures in a book. There needs
> to be a lot more learning at all levels instead of running around pretend
> Afghan villages on Salisbury plain.

In his book *Military Orientalism*, Patrick Porter points out the acute danger in ready-made solutions, such as the Human Terrain System or its British cousin – that they have the tendency to remove the host population even further from an already distant and segregated military occupying force:

> As the new [US counterinsurgency] Field Manual [FM 3–24] warns we
> must guard against the mistake of viewing others only on our own terms.

But in the rush to the different, the exotic and the bizarre, Westerners may embrace the opposite error. Instead of assuming sameness, they can regard foreigners as eternally separate and primordial, an alien species with their 'ancient hatreds' or 'primal urges'.[17]

The only experience most soldiers have of foreign civilians is gleaned from TV or, at best, holidays. The background or 'culture' of the contemporary British (or for that matter American) soldier could not be further removed from that of an Afghan countryman. In circumstances like this, how can a British soldier be expected to understand who, for example, is the real power broker in some village in the deserts of Helmand? How would our putative Chinese officer occupying Britain or the US determine who in the underworld of a town is the man to deal with in any attempt to separate the 'guerrilla from the people'? The answer is of course 'from their intelligence system' and we will examine that in the next chapter.

There is no doubt that questions of culture present acute problems to occupying forces. The British military system is beginning to recognize this and act upon it. The development of the Defence Cultural Specialist Unit certainly represents a step forward. There is at least a recognition now that the societies in which British soldiers work are very different from that at home. So much for 'them'. However, is there a rather more fundamental misunderstanding at work? Is the problem, perhaps, not so much British or 'Western' culture as military culture itself?

The real cultural problem

I took part in a raid one warm evening in southern Iraq: a 'strike operation' intended to arrest some men alleged to be part of a 'terrorist' group. It was to be a so-called 'hard knock', a term from Northern Ireland meaning forced entry.

The raid went well, as far as these things go, although there was a short bout of shooting as the men in the 'target' house feared initially that the raiding soldiers were 'Ali Babas' – thieves. My job was to gain as much information as I could from these men and assess whether I would recommend that they should be detained for longer than a few hours. Once the house had been secured, I was brought forward to begin the process of assessment. The first thing I did was try to confirm identity. There was no point in asking men, who, we presumed, might be trained guerrillas. And so I asked one of the women of the house. But being culturally aware, I knew that it would be insulting to everyone, not least the women, if I were to say anything without first asking permission of her husband, who happened to be one of the prisoners. I did this as politely as I could, the man said he had no objection – not that it would have made any difference – and the woman told me the names of the men we had captured, as they sat on the floor of their house surrounded by armed foreign soldiers.

Proud of my cultural sensitivity, I spent the next few hours at the local base, questioning the men and confirming that they were of not the slightest risk to any of us. Our intelligence, as so often, had been not only flawed, but just plain wrong. Now, as I look back on that incident, my own 'cultural sensitivity' seems but a poor joke. When matters were reduced to their essentials, foreign soldiers had broken into a house and taken its male occupants away into a military base for questioning. Whether one of the foreign soldiers had displayed a modicum of 'cultural sensitivity' would hardly matter to those whose home had been violated for, in their eyes, no good reason.

There is another requirement for a cultural 'paradigm shift' in the UK military. This lies not just in awareness of local manners and customs, reinforced by the eternal military salve of a 'course'. Rather, this shift lies in the appreciation that the culture the military needs to internalize is not Afghan or Iraqi (or, for that matter, the culture of Libya, Somalia or Yemen – often regarded as the next destinations for US and UK military intervention). The necessary shift lies in the basic realization that the people among whom they fight are civilian, like any others, including British, and that treating or conceiving of them as 'the other' is actively destructive. The key cultural aspect of 'wars among the people' is explicitly indicated in the descriptor. They are fought among civilians. The 'self-analysis' urged upon soldiers in the Joint Doctrine Note *The Significance of Culture to the Military* we saw above only goes so far.

It is very difficult for soldiers to understand what it is like to be on the other side of their weapons. At the most basic level of day-to-day interaction, soldiers are conditioned by their own way of life not to consider the perspective of 'the other' beyond looking at them through the 'cultural' or anthropological lens. It does not strike us as strange to patrol other countries, to threaten their property. Officers find it almost affronting that Afghans do not understand that the violence occasioned by their presence is blamed on them. After all, the reasoning goes, we are here for their benefit, why don't they understand this?

Indeed, the 'culture' and experience of the modern British soldier is far removed from that of the British civilians he is said to serve. For there are few more insular societies than the British military universe, and within that the army is a world unto itself. The regiment provides yet another stage of removal. Furthermore, the training, which in any other environment would be regarded as brainwashing – breaking characters down and rebuilding them – conditions soldiers to believe they are an elite, a group apart.

This problem is, of course, a two-way street. To the civilians, both British and foreign, alongside whom they are, in theory, supposed to work, the soldiers constitute a different world. Any civilian who has worked with or for the UK military in development will have found him or herself in an almost entirely unfamiliar culture, with, literally, its own language and very different worldview. Many military officers would say exactly the same, of course, about civilian aid workers, most of whom have vastly greater experience than soldiers, who are essentially temporary, cocooned residents of crisis areas. The term 'tree-hugger' is commonly applied to civilian assistance workers, especially anyone who deals with development or is in any of the areas touched on by human rights. This problem has been blamed, rightly, on what has been described by Cedric Thornberry, former Assistant Secretary-General of the United Nations, as a 'two-way lack of familiarity . . . [because of] the attitudinal abyss which separates aid workers from the military. Aid workers are often suspicious of the military, and the military is similarly incredulous of aid workers.'[18]

Colonel (now Brigadier General) H.R. McMaster has argued that rapid, highly mobile action has 'artificially divorced war from its political, human and psychological dimensions . . . we were behind at [the war's] outset'.[19] Until commanders understand the real terrain in which they fight, the day-to-day problems of justice, disputes, security, commerce and, not least, the natural dislike of any or all communities for any invader, failure is inevitable. These concerns are far more universal than manuals of culture might indicate. They do not require graduates of the Defence Cultural Specialist Unit to give advice about them. They are common to all civilian societies. One solution intended to offset this divorce of war, and indeed soldiers, from its essentially civilian dimension is the so-called 'comprehensive approach'.

The comprehensive approach

The dominant approach to 'wars among the people' on the part of the British government as a whole is the so-called 'comprehensive approach'. Although hedged about with jargon and governmental newspeak, the central idea is that the military should work together with civilian authorities. This is a reasonable and appropriate aspiration, though born more in the halls of Whitehall than on the battlefields of the Middle East. Stabilization during conflict is a Sisyphean task, akin to attempting to put a tent up in a storm. Until 2009 the cross-departmental 'Stabilisation Unit' of the UK government, set up in order to oversee the so-called 'comprehensive approach', was known as the 'Post-conflict Reconstruction Unit'. That title reflected the entirely sensible aspiration of assisting countries recovering from conflict, rather than while deeply mired in it.

The idea of the 'comprehensive approach' was born within the rather lavishly manned offices of the Ministry of Defence Main Building. As Professor Hew Strachan has said: 'The problem was that it came with the MoD stamped all over it.'[20] In practice, it amounts to little more than a rhetorical 'Potemkin village': while planning of operations is often carried out 'jointly', the reality has been that the civilians are considered at best an irritant. General Andrew Mackay, arguably the most successful of the many brigade commanders to have rotated through Helmand, agrees:

the allure of the comprehensive approach – what it promises – has not been matched by an effective outcome. Indeed its ability to create competitive tensions across OGDs [other governmental departments] rather than creative tensions has resulted in levels of bureaucracy being attached to it that actively inhibits [sic] adaptation rather than encourages it.[21]

This is entirely true, and it is not the fault of the British army that this is the case. However, while there is no question that there were and are commanders such as Mackay, open and receptive to new ideas and concepts, they have by no means been in the majority.

One major problem – indeed critical problem – is that no one is quite sure which government department is in charge of this 'comprehensive approach'. This is a truly astonishing lacuna, as there is no clear line of command, coordination or responsibility. General Andrew Salmon, the last British commanding general in Basra, certainly had no idea: 'but who is in charge? I mean that still hasn't been decided.'[22] Mark Etherington, a former army officer and one of the UK's most experienced and thoughtful post-conflict development experts, was a leading member of the team that produced the initial, possibly workable, Helmand Plan in 2006. Later he headed the UK civilian effort in Basra in 2008. In evidence to the Iraq Inquiry he expressed very similar sentiments: 'Departments generally lack ... the substantive experience required jointly to plan, engineer, execute and measure stabilisation operations.'[23] He was not optimistic that this would be developed.

The problem was addressed again, but in no way solved, in a parliamentary report by the House of Commons Defence Committee, *The Comprehensive Approach: The point of war is not just to win but to make a better peace*. It concluded: 'The MoD, the FCO and DFID all stated that it would not be appropriate for one departmental Minister to be designated for a conflict situation such as Afghanistan as it would lead to other Ministers giving it a lower priority.'[24] To an outsider, the situation as it stands sounds like a recipe for bureaucratic confusion on the ground. As one witness, Stephen Grey, stated in evidence to the committee, the comprehensive approach is 'more in words than reality'.[25] According to one civilian aid worker who had served for years alongside soldiers: 'The military coming up with a plan and asking what are we going to do to help is not the comprehensive approach.'[26] Daniel Korski, speaking to the UK Parliamentary Defence Select Committee, summed the situation up well:

the institutions that we created 60 years ago to undertake national security assignments are simply not structured for this task: they do not incentivise people, we do not train them the right way, we do not resource appropriately.[27]

Civil–military rivalry – nothing new

One of the institutions that was trained and manned more than appropriately was the Political Service of the Indian Civil Service. Its members – political officers or 'politicals' – in the restive North West Frontier region of India implemented and largely controlled national strategy during the Empire's hundred-year war there to control and contain the often rebellious and difficult tribes. These politicals were an extremely impressive group of men. They were very carefully selected for their toughness, intellect and aptitude from the ranks of the army and the elite Indian Civil Service, whose members were also frequently ex-military. They were also required to develop an exceedingly close familiarity with the tribes and peoples of their areas of responsibility.[28]

They were trained to provide government to the tribes and settlements in the zones, from the organization and command of police to arranging the maintenance of the roads. Much time was spent in hearing legal cases and delivering sound court judgments. This required them to go 'on tour' regularly through their areas, journeys which often took weeks, as they held court in the villages and towns of their areas. When the tribes rose in rebellion, as often happened, they called in military help and advised the military commanders on how the operations should be conducted. In the last resort, the authority to use force or refrain from doing so lay with them, and this regularly resulted in friction between the military and civilian elements.[29] Politicals, many of whom were Pashtun themselves, provided a quite extraordinary capability. They were able to advise on how exactly and when to apply force – what we might now call 'kinetic' pressure – and how and when to use softer measures, usually involving the payment of money (what we might now call 'bribes', but what then were termed 'subsidies'). They were able to gauge and exploit the extraordinarily complex relationships within and between the tribes on the frontier. Most importantly, identification of the true power brokers was critical. Familiarity with their work and area was assisted by the fact that they had to serve for *sixteen years* before they were permitted one year's leave.[30]

A 'political' was, as a leading scholar on this aspect of history, Christian Tripodi, has put it:

the living embodiment of cultural understanding. He provided his government with the perfect vehicle for such understanding to be transmitted from the wilds of the Frontier to the offices of central government policy-makers and he was well-placed, in return to help implement any tribal policy that made best use of such understanding.[31]

In contemporary terms, the political officer served as a combination of the intelligence officer and 'human terrain' adviser. Yet even here, largely because of cultural understanding problems – not between British and Pathan tribesman but between military and civilian personnel – this expertise benefited them 'no great deal'.[32] There was often a high degree of mistrust, with political officers sometimes being accused of standing 'between the soldiers and their medals',[33] and even, on occasion, of 'going native'. A military officer described a 'political' – one Major D.A. Barnes – as having supported 'his' tribe a little too much. As a result, Barnes had 'lost the confidence of the higher military'.[34] Barnes' colleague, 'Lotus' Lowis, took the more robustly expressed view that the military officer concerned was 'an entirely ignorant little tyke'.[35] This rivalry shows that, as Christian Tripodi puts it: 'one can possess a vast degree of cultural understanding and awareness and still fail to create truly effective policy'.[36]

The form and degree of expertise offered by the 'politicals' is, with a very few exceptions, not available now. There is literally no comparison to be made with any expertise available now to the UK military in any theatre outside Europe. In the UK's main effort of Afghanistan none of those who have a deep knowledge of the frontier and the Pashtuns is working now or is likely to work with or directly for the UK military, although from time to time they may assist. The nearest thing the UK military has to such experts are those provided by DfID, who very regularly have tens of years' experience working in societies very similar to the ones in which the British army finds itself.

The son of a Royal Marine and brought up around soldiers, Dan Jarman, whom we met earlier, is a man whose directness, professionalism and extensive experience in difficult areas of the world does not immediately conjure up the term 'tree-hugger'. During his three years working as a civilian adviser alongside the British army in Iraq and Helmand, he formed strong impressions of the way in which his work was perceived.

The benefit which experience like his brings is well illustrated by a proposal brought forward by an army team, confronted with the problem of unexploded ordnance and old weaponry:

> It took a long time to get across the 'do no harm' principle [the self-explanatory central idea of development]. These guys had the idea that we should pay people to bring in their UXO [unexploded ordnance]. It was difficult to know where to begin. For a start, who was going to pick the stuff up? Were we going to pay for the inevitable injuries sustained by kids looking to make a buck or two? All this was in addition to the fact that in Liberia this sort of idea went ahead. It resulted in a regional mini-arms race.[37]

General Rupert Smith, who has a great deal of experience in working in dysfunctional places, put the 'do no harm' principle into military terms:

> It is crucial that the military objectives should be chosen for their value in achieving the political purpose, not just because they are militarily possible, one should not confuse activity with outcome, as is so often the case with the 'something must be done' school. Doing something because a reaction, any reaction, is apparently needed to an undesirable situation will rarely achieve a desirable outcome and very probably incur a considerable cost, in human lives and materiel.[38]

The 'something must be done' school is, of course, born directly of the 'cracking on/manoeuvre warfare' world in which most soldiers are steeped.

'Local' culture

Jarman and very many other civilians with whom I have spoken are scathing about ignorance of local matters. This is not, it should be stressed, an entirely Afghan–British culture issue. It is a more fundamental failure to appreciate that ordinary people – civilians – have ordinary concerns. Everywhere. Indeed, when I was serving as a civilian in Helmand, I had the strong impression that not only was there very limited appreciation of local priorities, but there was also almost no desire to engage with anyone who might wish to express interest in such parochial concerns. Very little of this was due to a failure of 'cultural awareness', save in the broadest possible sense that there was a very limited desire to form such acquaintance. One officer, interviewed for a short film on the *Guardian* website during yet another six-monthly operation – this one called 'Black Prince', supposedly to 'retake' a village – said Afghan villagers 'are not interested in the bigger picture. They're only interested in their little crop of land and their children . . .'[39] One of the officer's men seems to have an equally firm grasp of their attitude: 'They just seem to want to be left alone and left to their own devices.'[40]

Dan Jarman looks at it from a different angle:

> I was asked – you have been here three months now, what progress have you made in governance in [the town I cover]? I said 'none'. This is not Croydon we are dealing with. Having said that, most soldiers wouldn't have a clue how Croydon is run. They live in bases where everything is done for them and they then come out here and are instant experts in how to run a town full of civilians. They think that because some local worthy has the title 'Chief of the District Council' he is the same sort of man you'd find in Croydon or Bolton. That is just absolutely not the case. This guy has a whole shed full of family he needs to set up. And after that, he needs to be looking after his friends.[41]

In a complex environment such as Helmand, failure to engage actively with the civilian effort can be damaging. I served in Helmand as justice adviser to the PRT and indeed the task force. It was part of my job to assess the situation with respect to justice in its widest sense. It was important, as it would be anywhere, to have an idea of how judges and prosecutors were seen by the people they were supposed to serve. I had heard particularly disturbing accounts of the situation in a certain town in Helmand. Each area had its battle group, and each battle group had an officer whose job it was to liaise with civilian experts such as me.

The procedure for this was simple enough: I would speak to the liaison officer in Lashkar Gah, the capital, where I was based. A message would be sent, and the requested information would be collected and forwarded to me. That was the idea. The reply I received on that occasion set the tone for what I was to find day in and day out: 'The prosecutor is a good man and the judge is fine' (or words to that effect). This might be an adequate reply in some circumstances, but not here. The prosecutor and judge in the particular town with which I was concerned were at the time engaging state personnel and facilities to run a private kidnapping and property extortion racket. This was very well known in the district, and indeed throughout the province. So what? The importance of this story is twofold. First, there are the obvious connotations of a slapdash approach. Second, even from the army's perspective this was dangerous. Every day soldiers were on patrol with the Afghan police – the same police that the prosecutor and judge were using to enforce their abuse of power within their domain. How would local Afghans feel when they saw British soldiers supporting this form of rule? It does not take a human terrain team to assess the view among local people. None of these problems are 'cultural', save in the widest sense of the term – that the army is incapable of seeing (or unwilling to see) how its actions might be viewed by anyone, not simply 'the Afghan'.

Some of these problems were, admittedly, procedural and, in fairness, it may well be that the officers with whom I dealt were insufficiently briefed. More likely the officer in question was overworked and simply saw no value in putting effort into a blatantly civilian (and therefore at best secondary) priority. In a war that is supposedly being fought with a 'comprehensive approach', this is clearly not good enough. We saw in Iraq how no one grasped, until far too late, the immense potential of inoculating the Marsh Arabs' cattle. This reflects not so much a lack of specialist cultural knowledge, as a failure to think sensibly, and ask intelligent questions about what people's needs might be.

In the very few remaining areas of British military control in Helmand, I have little doubt that matters are changing and several of the problems touched upon in this chapter are being addressed. Certainly there is an increasing awareness of the civilian nature of the environment within which the army work. As we will see in the next chapter, there needs to be more than a 'realization'. One very senior and experienced government development worker, with extensive close acquaintance with the UK military, told me that the army needs to become far more 'outward-facing'. That, in two words, is the cultural shift that is required if the British are once again to be effective in 'wars among the people'. Making such a fundamental shift in culture effective in military terms is the subject of the next chapter.

CHAPTER 10

Bad Influences

We need to start being explorers rather than conquerors.
Interview with Stephen Grey, June 2010

I doubt if anyone would listen to us in Southern Afghanistan if we were unarmed.
Captain Emile Simpson, 'Gaining the influence initiative'

An entirely new field of military activity, as well as a fruitful source of jargon and military chatter, has grown up to try to cope with working and succeeding in that harsh environment of foreign, hostile civilian populations. It is called 'Influence'. In essence, like 'effects', another fashionable military buzzword, 'influence' can be made to cover the results of almost any warlike activity. It has been defined as 'the power or ability to affect someone's beliefs or actions'. Indeed, war itself is, it is often argued, merely the exercise of armed influence. As with so much contemporary military jargon, this term is a new way of reframing very old concepts.

In the context of warlike activities today, the term usually refers to what soldiers call 'soft activities'. However, soldiers are not shy of discussing the application of force as a 'kinetic' application of 'influence' – a euphemism for violence.[1] Influence by force can be effective, and in the right circumstances there is nothing wrong with it. As Captain Simpson says, 'every action sends a message – and actions are our strongest messages'. That is certainly true, but those messages need to be saying the right thing.

It is usually in the context of the 'information war' that the term 'influence' is used. In the conceptual discussions of 'influence', the words of one of the current gurus of 'counterinsurgency' David Kilcullen are regularly quoted:

> We typically design physical operations first then craft supporting information operations to explain our actions. This is the reverse of al Qaeda's approach. For all our supposed professionalism, compared to the enemy's our public information effort is an afterthought. In military terms, for al Qaeda the 'main effort' is information: For us information is 'supporting effort.'[2]

This indeed remains the case. David Galula, the COIN guru, writing in the 1950s, said: 'If there was a field in which we are definitely and infinitely more stupid than our opponents, it was propaganda.'[3] Galula, of course, appreciates that, when an occupying power is operating in a foreign, entirely alien and – more importantly – hostile country, that power is at an initial disadvantage. 'Influence' operations are designed to overcome this deficit of credibility.

The British manual of counterinsurgency (AFM 1–10) places a great deal of stress on influence, unlike its larger American cousin, FM 3–24, which barely uses the term at all. Influence is stated to be one of the three major components (along with intelligence and sound operational planning) of a successful 'counterinsurgency' campaign, and has an entire section devoted to it. Tools and techniques for the application of influence are said to include deception, psychological operations (which used to be called 'propaganda', black or otherwise), presence, key leader engagement, computer operations, electronic warfare and finally, of course, destruction or 'kinetic' influence.[4]

'The direct application of force through physical destruction has significant psychological impact,' states the manual correctly. Without irony it goes on: 'it can play a major role in persuasion, coercion and deterrence'.[5] There is little new about any of these techniques in limited war. Interestingly, in the Afghanistan war of the 1980s, the Soviets used 'air strike diplomacy' – they were also masters of euphemism. If Soviet prisoners were known to be held in a certain village, an air strike would be conducted on an area near the village. This would be followed up by a leaflet drop on the village that supposedly contained the captured Soviet soldiers, 'leaving the villagers in no doubt that they would soon receive a similar visit unless the prisoners were released'.[6] In colonial days, the British were masters of this sort of application of threat, particularly on the North West Frontier.

The manual goes on to advise how teams of soldiers might act to 'deliver' influence. The stress on the more 'kinetic' use of influence is consciously revealed by the fact that, until recently, the officer responsible for these matters within a brigade was titled 'SO1 Fires and Influence'.[7] In army parlance, 'fires' is a term used for the projection of explosive force. Accordingly, this officer was usually, indeed almost always, drawn from the Royal Artillery. After all, went the reasoning, what is artillery if not the projection of one form of influence? A cynic might point out that, at a time when artillery might have seemed to be losing its relevance (the role to some extent being taken by jet planes and helicopters), this post often provided useful employment for senior artillerymen.

In a battle for the vital ground of 'the people' it is surely imperative not to ignore the enemy. It supposedly does not use influence as 'we' do. It uses 'armed propaganda' and 'a subtle blend of force through terror and intimidation'. Its tools include 'disinformation', 'misinformation' and 'opposing information'. The effects of failing to counter these activities will include 'losing consent as a result of the local people being uncertain about our intentions'.[8] Given, as we have seen, that the British are uncertain of their own intentions (strategy) in both Iraq and Helmand, one might ponder the likelihood of this. Counter-influence activities 'should ensure the population that they will be protected'. A counter-propaganda campaign should be credible and be 'first with the truth'.[9] It is important to say here that 'influence', like missiles, is ideally directed at particular targets. One day it might be the civilian population of a town. The next it might be a group of fighters in the hills.

It all sounds very impressive. Yet, as I was told by the journalist Stephen Grey, who has had extensive experience in Helmand: 'Influence has got to be a two-way street. The people have to influence us. Influence should be a way of bringing the voice of the local population into the planning process.'[10] In Iraq, Major General Andy Salmon, uniquely among general officers commanding, had the revolutionary idea of consulting Iraqis as part of his planning and preparation before deployment: 'It was one of the themes of our campaign. First of all, put Iraqis first, listen to them, respect them, connect with them right and be patient. Never tell an Iraqi what to do.'[11]

In neither Iraq nor Afghanistan did this happen. This is because 'influence' has very much been (and continues to be) a 'one-way street'. The reality of 'influence operations' (and indeed a great deal of the rhetoric too) has been that it is 'us talking to you' – and generally 'we' have very little idea indeed of who 'you' are. This is akin to a large company deciding to embark on a public-relations strategy without having troubled to assess the market in advance.

When I served in the military, I attended a short course on 'psyops', where two different leaflets were compared. Leaflets had proved a successful way of communicating in the Kosovo and both Iraq wars, and particularly in convincing enemy soldiers to surrender. In a somewhat unfortunate example of what now would be called 'influence', one was phrased in the Pashto grammatical conditional mood: 'If British soldiers enter your village on this operation, please stay indoors . . .' The other was a direct warning: 'ISAF [British] soldiers will be coming to your village. Stay indoors.' This might have had some effect, were it not for the fact that the overwhelming majority (some estimates place the literacy rate at around 5 per cent) of Helmandis cannot read, let alone parse the subtle implications buried in Pashtu grammar. Is this a cultural matter? No. It is a simple factual mistake, the sort of fundamental error that, in any other field, would probably have been picked up. However, in fighting wars, knowledge of literacy rates is not seen as a priority.

Similarly, perhaps because Afghans are seen as religious and 'this is the sort of thing they like', there is an emphasis on giving loudspeakers and carpets as gifts to local mullahs. Indeed, it is true that Afghans are religious. They are not stupid, however, and are as capable of seeing when people are trying to buy them off as any Irish parish priest would have been during the Troubles (or indeed since) had the army decided to adopt a policy of buying bells and altar cloths. One man, a former UN political officer with many years experience in Afghanistan, told me that very often Afghans regarded their mullahs in much the same way as Irish farmers (or British ones for that matter) regarded priests: with sometimes saintly exceptions, they are generally seen as an unfortunate necessity (and in the Afghan case they have an additional propensity to be an economic drain, for it is the mullah who receives the *zakat* or tithe). Then again, what are Afghan farmers or peasants to do with the medical packs that are liberally distributed, filled as they are with devices such as syringes that few British civilians would be able to use, let alone an Afghan.

Winning consent

Such activities, of course, would be called in military terms 'consent-winning' – part of 'influence ops'. From the perspective of an experienced development worker, such projects, if they are to have any real effect, generally need some serious consideration before approval – looking at second-order effects and consequences. Jarman puts it this way:

> The military complained that we never approved projects. This is because the projects they suggested were not good value and might achieve little if anything and it would be a waste of taxpayers' money to have approved them.

The kind of awareness required for this sort of (admittedly cack-handed) attempt to buy some form of loyalty is not necessarily cultural. It requires an understanding of what real people want, and then for that knowledge to be used to manipulate them to your own ends. This was not lost on Brigadier Andrew Mackay, who conducted intensive and, as we have seen, innovative studies into how social sciences might assist in winning 'influence'. One key element of this is – and must be – to take a far more circumspect approach to intelligence and the cultures surrounding it. The aim, of course, is to establish in what form and to whom you should address your 'soft' influence. This may well take the unpalatable form of money. As was mentioned above, what you or I would call 'bribes' were used extensively by political officers on the North West Frontier to ensure tribal compliance with British-Indian interests. These so-called 'subsidies' could have very far-reaching effects: the formidable Afridi tribe, which straddled the Khyber Pass, was persuaded to refrain from attacking British interests in the First World War, allowing many thousands of British and

Indian soldiers to be released to other fronts. In previous times, though it was never on the cards that such tribes could be maintained as allies, it had been just as important to keep them on side whenever Russia threatened the frontier.[12]

Generally speaking, subsidies were almost surgically applied, and always on the advice of the political officer on the spot, who knew exactly who was pulling the local strings of power. We have no such expertise nowadays within the military complex; however, there are ways of applying what we do have, in order to learn who really has power and what might influence them. We may very well not like what we learn, and may regard it as unsavoury. As we saw in Chapter 3 it was Western metropolitan distaste towards Sher Muhammed Akhundzada that may have resulted in 3,000 of his men becoming recruits for the Taliban and enemies of the British. We nonetheless need to know these things as a key element of the environment in which we work. Andrew Mackay and Stephen Tatham quote R.V. Jones, a leading British scientist of the Second World War: 'Do not believe what you want to believe until you know what it is you want to know.'[13] In military terms, knowing what it is you want to know is a rather important component of the military discipline of 'intelligence'. Knowing what you want to know is one thing – it is an essential predicate for good intelligence; hearing what you want to hear is another matter.

Talking to yourself . . . and liking what you hear

So what are the British telling themselves? There is, of course, 'steady progress'. Operations are launched to 'liberate' various areas under Taliban control. One of these well-publicized operations – Moshtarak ('Together') – resulted in British presence in the district of Nad Ali, complete with a 'government in a box'.

This was a typical military operation, with 'shaping', intelligence gathering and 'influence' followed by a straightforward military assault, complete with a real 'D-Day'. The results were presented as something of an exemplar of the genre – the new counterinsurgency plan of the overall ISAF commander of the day, Stanley McChrystal, in action. A report supported by the Ministry of Defence and issued by the Royal United Services Institute, 'Appraising Moshtarak', stated: 'The message that ISAF and the GIRoA [Government of the Islamic Republic of Afghanistan] are "coming to stay", and that things would be better under the Afghan government, was critical to ensuring local support for the operation.'[14]

The civilian aspect was not ignored:

COMRC(S) [Commander of NATO forces in Regional Command South] is clear that governance is his main effort, and hence the metrics of campaign progress most important to him concern district governance. Here too, things look most positive in Helmand. There is effective and representative district governance in Nad-e-Ali, Nawa and Garmsir. The success of *Moshtarak* also empowered [provincial governor] Mangal, enabling him to replace the corrupt district governors of Sangin and Musa Qala.[15]

All very positive. One thing in the report (or rather not in the report) is particularly interesting. In all the footnotes, and indeed throughout the text, some twenty-eight individuals are quoted or referred to – although, as is normal practice, never by name. There are about twenty-six MoD officials, British soldiers, members of the PRT and US marines; two Afghans are among them – one army officer and one government official. The reader will have identified the odd category out: ordinary Afghans. This was for the simple but very telling reason that it was not safe to go about chatting to ordinary Afghans. The report is, as it must be, essentially the British talking to themselves, and liking what they hear.

Time will tell whether ISAF and the Afghan government are in fact 'here to stay' in Nad Ali or anywhere else. Unfortunately, the fact remains that, even if Nad Ali were to become the Welwyn Garden City of Helmand, there remain the other (at least) fourteen districts of Helmand. Helmand is is itself but one of thirty-four provinces. Nad Ali would be one district out of over 430 (no one is quite sure exactly how many there are) in this most difficult country.

It is intelligence, if conducted properly, that may tell us how to apply those 'soft' influences. It is intelligence that could be one of several conduits for 'influence' running, as Grey suggests, both ways. He gives the example of how, without good intelligence, the deployment of the 'soft weapon' of money can backfire: 'if you have not got any intelligence, if you walk into a village

with a suitcase of cash you probably hand the money to the drug lord – I
would say the biggest source of finance for the insurgency is actually NATO
and its contracts, not any money coming from Al Qaeda or the Gulf.'[16]

'Intelligence preparation of the battlefield'

Before every military campaign, the land forces undertake a process that
is intended to help them begin to understand where they will be fighting.[17]
This process is termed 'intelligence preparation of the battlefield', and is
known, of course, by its three-letter acronym 'IPB'. This is a crucial
element in 'manoeuvre warfare', for which the army was so well trained
and equipped, as we saw in Chapter 6. IPB seeks to ensure that all relevant
personnel are brought 'up to speed' with the ground, the enemy forces and
the options available to the commander for him to achieve his aim.

IPB is a rigorous and efficient way of 'knowing your enemy' – provided,
that is, the information at hand is accurate. For military intelligence
officers, 'information' differs from 'intelligence', in that it has not been
analysed as part of what is called the 'intelligence cycle', which consists of
direction (orders to collect), collection (the gathering of the information),
processing (editing the information gathered), analysis (studying and
determining the reliability of the information and its relevance), dissemi-
nation (putting the intelligence out to interested parties who require it)
and feedback. This then informs the commander as he sets new requirements for collection – direction again. This is a thoroughly tried and tested
process. When all the components are working even remotely well, this
simple and logical system returns the required results. If one of the
components is out of kilter, the system will break down.

In relatively successful operations, such as Malaya and Northern Ireland,
intelligence was recognized as the single most important element. This
was constantly appreciated by those who had fought and reflected on their
experiences – men such as Frank Kitson, a veteran of Kenya, Malaya and
Cyprus. He was an early commander of British forces in Northern Ireland,
where his ideas of civil–military cooperation had a difficult gestation. He
advocated a firm foundation of collection assets, including, for example,
what would now be called databases of such information as vehicle regis-
tration numbers. More importantly, such cooperation required a deep

understanding of the environment – what might be called the 'conflict ecosystem', which consists of far more than simple 'cultural knowledge'. In places such as Iraq and Afghanistan, this is exceedingly difficult. Is it impossible? Absolutely not. It simply takes a great deal of time and, far more importantly, an approach that is open to new and radical ideas. This attitude to intelligence has not been evident in the British army.

It is understandable that, in a conventional army, intelligence and the techniques related to it should be 'enemy focused'. Unfortunately, in a war fought among ordinary people, where the enemy is not readily identifiable – let's call it an insurgency – this is not the case. The classic 'counterinsurgency' – separating the people from the guerrillas – which has been a mantra of that form of war, takes on very subtle meanings. The problem is that, as in Afghanistan (though less so in Basra), the enemy might well *be* the people – an unpleasant reality that is very rarely addressed. With admirable openness, the British counterinsurgency manual touches on this, quoting an officer with operational experience in Afghanistan:

Among the locals some had a degree of education and training but most were someone's son, brother, father in that village and the coalition had killed them for being in, what amounted to them, a neighbourhood watch scheme. Just because they fought does not mean to say they were the enemy we should have fought. It takes a sophisticated, patient and disciplined counterinsurgent force with the full backing of its population to play that kind of game. This took me about four months to establish, so who knows how much damage we did to the campaign before I stopped picking fights with the playground weaklings and focussed my attention on the bullies. I will have no doubt created more insurgents and IED emplacers for our successors in Garmsir to deal with. Our ability to do anything about this on the ground recedes as we cower behind armoured firepower.[18]

Unfortunately, with some very notable exceptions, we are not currently in possession of 'a sophisticated, patient and disciplined counterinsurgent force with the full backing of its population'.

In another key town, Sangin – like Garmsir, handed over to US forces after British withdrawal due to overextension – four years of constant presence produced majority support for the insurgents. One farmer is quoted as saying: 'The Taliban do not even have a bakery that they can give bread to the people, but still most people support the Taliban – that's because people are sick of night raids and being treated badly by the foreigners.'[19]

How, then, should intelligence begin to deal with this, so that it can inform not only armed action, but 'influence'? Unfortunately, the army counterinsurgency manual's enlightened approach shifts grindingly into reverse when it begins an extensive discussion of intelligence – along with 'influence' and 'planning', the key element, by its own account, of 'counterinsurgency'.

There are advances. No longer is IPB called that: now it is termed 'Intelligence Preparation of the Environment'. Little else has changed, however, as the function of intelligence is to assist in the 'intelligence/ operations cycle', which consists of 'find, fix, finish, exploit, analyse' and goes under the alphanumeric acronym F3EA. The intention is to produce a collection plan, which aims to 'dominate' the 'Area of Intelligence Interest' (a straightforward three-letter acronym, AII) with the assistance of a 'target list'. The 'finish' element generally means 'kill or capture'.

The tools to be used in producing this target list are said in the British counterinsurgency manual to include signals intelligence (SIGINT – phone-tapping to the layman), imagery (IMINT – usually photographic), documents (DOCEX), technical information (TECHINT – usually relating to weapons) and more recondite methods, such as the analysis of border regions through 'measurement and signatures intelligence' (MASINT – the art of looking at the tracks people and objects leave). The combination of these and other techniques has now been given the acronym ISTAR – Intelligence Surveillance Target Acquisition and Reconnaissance – yet another technique that promises much but delivers little more than an increased body count.

'Humint' and the ghosts of Northern Ireland

The early days of the Northern Ireland campaign brought disasters that were the result of heavy-handed and ill-thought-out operations.[20] These included 'Bloody Sunday', as well as the propaganda gift to the IRA and other organizations of internment without trial. Despite these, over the years the British army developed a deep, instinctive awareness of the cultural, political, social, religious, criminal and even sporting environments of their opponent. After all, those environments were largely the same as the soldiers'. Needless to say, the language in which everything was conducted was always idiomatic English. Many of the soldiers were from exactly the same urban, Western European milieu from which their opponents in the various Republican, and indeed loyalist, guerrilla groups were drawn. They spoke the same language (in more ways than one), followed the same football teams, and, in the case of those soldiers from cities such as Liverpool and Glasgow, had often been exposed to the same political/religious rivalry or indeed, on occasion, hostility.

The natural familiarity of 'home ground' was vitally reinforced by the presence of a highly effective police service (albeit one that took several years properly to develop) – indeed the police became, in practice as well as in theory, the leading force in the province. A highly effective system of intelligence collection and collation developed on home ground in Northern Ireland over a thirty-year period. The systems ranged from surveillance, collection of vehicle data, human intelligence tactics, down to the nuts and bolts of how best to plan and configure patrols. Working closely with the police, the British got the measure of urban warfare in north-west Europe in an internal security context. Clearly this is a rather narrow area of expertise and hardly transferable to other theatres.

When these techniques were transplanted in the 1990s to the relatively benign (for the UK armed forces) operations in Bosnia and Kosovo, they proved useful but not dominant. The simple fact that the soldiers were operating in another country was enough to render many Northern Ireland techniques irrelevant. Tracking vehicles using number plates is difficult in a country where there is no central database. Human intelligence collection, the jewel in the crown of counterterrorist weapons, was a very different beast when conducted in a language not one word of which its operators spoke. In this respect, as in so many others, Bosnia (to say nothing of Basra) was to prove very different from Belfast.

The experience of the British army in Northern Ireland, and indeed the Balkans, was potentially useful, so long as its limitations in non-UK/ European environments were appreciated. In Northern Ireland, the work of intelligence was considered to be that of the entire force: from patrolling through to checkpoints, every opportunity was taken to increase the background knowledge base of the force and to use that to direct operations. This was a key element in the 'Kitson model' of counterinsurgency, proposed by the veteran counterinsurgent officer Frank Kitson in two landmark books.[21] His was an all-encompassing framework that, in the context of Northern Ireland, could at least be approached with some hope of success.

A rather obvious fact that was missed in the British occupation of southern Iraq was that it *was* an occupation. The facilities of surveillance, record keeping and access to a working government (or indeed any government at all), as well as the even more fundamental elements of local knowledge, language and general awareness, were all denied to the British, as they are to every occupying army by virtue of their status as occupiers. There were far, far fewer soldiers on the streets than at any time during the Ulster crisis. Such soldiers as were on patrol were seeing the city through several layers of cultural, social and linguistic ignorance. Furthermore, there was little time for units to gain any real familiarity with their areas. In Northern Ireland, many regiments did two-year tours. Any comparison of Iraq with the campaign in 'the Province' (Northern Ireland) was lazy indeed.

During the occupation of Iraq, there had been a distinct tendency to rely on previous, mostly personally derived, experience. Most officers had little or no experience or knowledge of real counterinsurgency practice or theory applicable to Basra in 2003. As we have seen, there was precious little effective institutional knowledge either. The Allies lacked deep knowledge of the country in which they were fighting, a clear strategy about what they were fighting for, and – most importantly at that stage – the necessary legitimate government. The Coalition Provisional Authority, essentially a chaotically assembled, rapidly recruited group of assorted former diplomats, aid workers and ex-soldiers, projected no effective authority. Nonetheless, until late 2004, there was a distinct sense that the British were, if not comfortable, then at least capable of dealing with what they found in Basra. There was a 'soft footprint', few checkpoints and very little contact with the local population. There was the assumption that the people of Basra would 'sort it out'. Little emphasis was put on local politics. Awareness of local events was passed on through the medium of interpreters, as no resources were devoted to reading, watching or listening to the local media. It was exactly the same in Helmand.

The inadequacy of the civilian Secret Intelligence Service (SIS) with respect to Iraq, and specifically its role in the WMD fiasco, is a matter of public record.[22] The failure of military intelligence, although less well known, was equally profound. In Malaya and Northern Ireland, intelligence was, as we have seen, considered to be absolutely central to success. As we saw in Chapter 7, Templer and Thompson ensured that rivalry between agencies was reduced to almost zero in Malaya. The profile of the force encouraged those willing to give information to the security forces to do so.

It took many years to do in Northern Ireland what Templer had achieved in two. That said, the Malayan intelligence structure was founded on many years of close familiarity with the country and on a strong staff of operators. The problem in Malaya, as indeed in Northern Ireland, was to get them to work together. The UK has the same intelligence service rivalries as any other regime, and this was a major problem until late in the Irish campaign. The Royal Ulster Constabulary's Special Branch, the Security Service (better known as MI5) and military intelligence did eventually work effectively together. In due course they got the measure of the IRA – and, of course, the loyalist gangs, with whom they had in the past worked all too closely. This intelligence success came about after twenty years of bitter experience, not untainted by controversy. By the end of the 1990s, the human intelligence operators of the British army and the other services had evolved, in a savage world, into highly effective, highly aware collectors of intelligence and manipulators of people. Very often they were drawn from the same sort of social milieux as their opponents in the IRA – poor, tough, urban environments. A large number were from those poorer areas of Newcastle, Liverpool or Glasgow, where sectarianism was still very much alive. They were profoundly 'streetwise'. Of course, they spoke English – an obvious but vital fact – and were steeped in the lore of the Northern Irish housing estates and farms. In Ulster they could walk the walk and talk the talk.

But Ulster was not Iraq and, as the British army was beginning to realize, Basra was not Belfast, any more than rugby is soccer merely by virtue of the fact that both are ball games. If anything, Helmand resembles Northern Ireland even less than Iraq does. At the operational and tactical levels, in both southern Iraq and Helmand, intelligence was all too often poor to the point of uselessness.

Holistic intelligence

The importance of taking a 'holistic' view of intelligence has yet to be realized by an ossified intelligence architecture focused on enemy intentions and capabilities and hemmed in by pointless bureaucracy; former senior special forces officers Graeme Lamb and Richard Williams suggest that: 'We need to adjust and flatten the way that information is shared between departments . . . with less focus on the tanks of the Third Shock Army and more on understanding the networks that make up an insurgency or popular movement.'[23]

As justice adviser in Helmand, I was denied information that I was told the army might have had on Taliban judges, on the grounds that I could not prove I had a high enough security clearance. The information had been classified at a high level by a junior officer – probably the 'originator' or person who had collected the information by talking to an Afghan. Having the classification reduced to 'my' level was beyond the powers of anyone present. I was not willing to become involved in an unseemly row with the military authorities about who else would be the user of this somewhat specialist information, so I found out what I needed to discover through the simple expedient of talking to a local journalist who was personally familiar with several Taliban judges – something I should probably have done in the first place. I have little doubt that his perspective represented a more accurate account than anything military intelligence could have offered anyway.

Talking to journalists, however, is most certainly something intelligence officers are not encouraged to do. Yet there are very strong reasons for believing that it was precisely what might be called a 'holistic' view of intelligence that backed up the successful hundred-year containment of the North West Frontier. Rob Johnson, in his fine study of intelligence and 'Great Game Playing' on the frontier writes: 'It is important to widen the definition of intelligence beyond the realm of tactical information to include a range of political, diplomatic and geographical criteria.'[24] He goes on, talking about intelligence in the days of the 'Great Game': 'intelligence gathering was concerned with far more than the acquisition of tactical information'.[25] Intelligence in that successful series of campaigns was based very much on the idea that any information was potentially useful to the mission.

Outside the 'sexy' realms of high-tech gadgetry or the 'special duties' glamour of 'humint' is open source intelligence (OSINT). Open source intelligence is information that is available to anyone. Though fairly obvious, it is rarely realized that it comprises 99.9 per cent of the information that is relevant to almost any mission. The *Countering Insurgency* handbook enjoins its readers to remember to monitor local media and to develop a formal relationship between media operations and intelligence staffs. Media operations are, essentially, the spokesmen who handle and speak to media outlets. There is the well-known story of the KGB director of operations, who said that, given a choice between a subscription to the *New York Times* and an agent deep in the CIA, he would choose the newspaper. This was not a facetious statement: journalists have, or should have, excellent sources – far better than those of any intelligence agency. Indeed, a former senior diplomat has reported that, on occasion, MI6 copies foreign newspaper reports and presents them as its own.[26] Open source intelligence is, in fact, the single most useful source of non-target-related information there is.

I never served in Afghanistan as a military intelligence officer, though I did in Bosnia and Iraq. In both theatres, the tactical importance of 'open source' media was made abundantly clear to me by events. In Bosnia, one of the tasks of the team to which I belonged was to find war criminals indicted by the International Criminal Tribunal for former Yugoslavia (Persons Indicted for War Crimes – PIFWCs, or Piffwicks, as we called them). I had been well trained in collection techniques that had been tried and tested in Northern Ireland. We were encouraged not to speak to journalists and to avoid NGOs, as they had 'agendas'.

On the face of it, this was apparently sensible advice, by and large. There was very little, if any, monitoring of media in Bosnia conducted by intelligence officers – and I include myself in that omission. My team was seeking one particular war criminal. The key task was to find out where he lived, so that 'special forces' could go and arrest him. To that end, I was speaking to a local police officer, trying to determine whether he had any sources that might assist our efforts. He asked me whether I read a particular popular Serbian newspaper. I did not, and nor did anyone I knew. He handed me a copy of the most recent issue: 'Have a look at page seven', he said. 'Bottom left.' There on the page was a picture of our Piffwick, with a short article bemoaning the fact that this hero had been reduced to penury, living in a particular small town. There was also a helpful photo of his hut. He was arrested shortly afterwards, taken to The Hague, and tried and convicted for murder and torture.

In Basra, the capability for analysing local media was very limited, from an intelligence perspective – although it certainly improved towards the end of the mission there in 2007–8. It may well have assisted those charged with reporting political intelligence to have read the many newspapers in Basra, or to have had them translated. Every single diplomatic mission in the world monitors local media so that it is properly informed. This is not the case for military missions, which are far more set on 'clandestine' means of discovering their 'int'. Clearly, in Afghanistan, the low levels of literacy mean that there is very little print media. There are, however, a great many radio stations.

Similarly, in Bosnia, I found the best-informed military groups to be the civil affairs officers and engineers. Why was this? Because they had something to offer and the people amongst whom they worked were keen that any threat to them should be dealt with. Also, generally speaking, they were trusted and capable of relating to the local people – far more so than most intelligence collectors. That the great majority of them were, in fact, reservists, and therefore essentially civilians, may have been incidental. Clearly, they reported any matters that touched on the ever vital 'force protection'. However, the depth of background knowledge they possessed was very regularly lost. It was, in intelligence terms, not 'captured'.

'Open source' intelligence comes in an unlimited variety of forms. When I moved from being a military officer to a civilian human-rights worker for the Organization for Security and Co-operation in Europe, I lived for nearly two years in a Kosovo town beset by an insurgent war. Within three months, I was far more intimately aware of what was really happening than any soldier could have been in a two-year military intelligence deployment to such a place. Since I had been a military intelligence officer in such a place two years previously, that is a comparison that is particularly telling. The kind of information I had, on power networks, relationships, disputes and politics, was exactly the sort of material that, while non-lethal in nature, might, in an environment such as Iraq or Afghanistan, be 'mission critical'. Moreover, there is no reason whatsoever why such information should be considered confidential or even sensitive, any more than political information available in any human environment.

And what of journalists? They have a professional obligation to protect their sources in much the same way as intelligence officers have. As far as the intelligence officer is concerned, he himself may be perceived as a 'source' by the journalist – an extremely dangerous situation to be in. From the army's perspective, the real problem of military intelligence officers talking to journalists is that most journalists are far better 'intelligence' gatherers than the often bewildered military intelligence officials, and so information may flow *to* the press rather than *from* it. Ethical concerns also prevent journalists from giving tactical information that could be used to kill people, or that could compromise their neutrality in any way. The whole point of a more holistic approach is that 'find, fix, finish' should no longer be considered to be the central aim of intelligence collection. Journalists not only have an almost unique feel for 'atmospherics', but they also play a part in creating them. Atmospherics, formerly considered somewhat *infra dig* by military intelligence officers, are now a vital part of the environment in which the force operates. In Northern Ireland, background information tended to be collected by 'green army' (i.e. non-intelligence/special forces), while secret material was collected and handled by 'specialists'. It may well be that intelligence operators simply got out of the habit of regarding it as important.

In January 2010, the former chief of intelligence of the US army in Iraq, Michael Flynn, published a groundbreaking paper that was a pure breath of fresh air for those who sought a more effective and outward-facing military intelligence or informational system. Undoubtedly such a paper could not have been published in the UK. It would have been classified and issued to a select group – partly because that is usually the fate of reports that implicitly or explicitly criticize British actions (to be followed invariably by a leak to the press) and partly because it contained the word 'intelligence'. Though essentially a bureaucratic task that may be enlivened by a little travel and adventure, the word 'intelligence' (or the 'I word', as I was taught to call it in my basic intelligence training) tends to conjure up images of James Bond, shady operators and shadowy derring-do rather more readily in the UK than it does in the US. The report derides the attitude that 'secret is best':

> The Cold War notion that open-source information is 'second class' is a dangerous, outmoded cliché. Lieutenant General Samuel V. Wilson, former director of the Defense Intelligence Agency, captured it perfectly: 'Ninety percent of intelligence comes from open sources. The other 10 percent, the clandestine work, is just the more dramatic.'[27]

Provenance, in other words where the intelligence came from, whether dramatically acquired in the course of a secret operation or taken from the local newspaper, has no impact upon utility. As Flynn and his colleagues put it, intelligence is 'a culture that is emphatic about secrecy but regrettably less concerned about mission effectiveness'.[28]

Flynn speaks of 'the mission'. Yet what is 'the mission'? One significant common feature of both Iraq and Afghanistan is indeed 'the mission'. We saw in Basra how a fragile, almost diaphanous objective was ditched in favour of force protection. In Helmand, a similar pattern has developed, driven by the desire to reduce politically damaging casualties, as well as by the more immediately appealing wish for the force and its members to protect itself. While the Helmand force is by no means in thrall to the 'self-licking lollipop' syndrome of existing to protect itself, as the troops in Basra became, the focus has shifted in that direction. When casualties from IEDs became too high, the response was to create an elite group of intelligence and special forces personnel to become a 'counter-IED task force', whose mission was self-explanatory.

This mission does not sit well with the proclaimed 'population-centred' approach espoused by 'counterinsurgency' advocates. Highlighting this contrast, Flynn speaks of the experience of the 1st Battalion, 5th Marines in the village of Nawa, in Helmand province, who took over from a beleaguered British force in June 2009. When they arrived, no soldier could venture more than one kilometre from the base without being attacked. No information was offered to soldiers, and indeed no one made eye contact. Five months later, the centre of the town, formerly ghostlike, was bustling. And crucially – from every perspective, but especially from that of the soldiers – IED attacks were down by 90 per cent. What did the US Marine Corps do or know that the British did not? Was it vast numbers of troops? No. About 1,000 men replaced close to 600.

Flynn ascribes the improvement to a combination of a dynamic commander, who worked very well with the local political leaders, and a change in the intelligence focus. Instead of deploying analysts and operators (as the British would call them) to the battalion or usually brigade HQ, these people were devolved to the company, where they became very familiar with the environment in which they worked. There was no primary emphasis on 'finding, fixing and finishing' the enemy (although, being marines, that was certainly on their mind and, equally certainly, would have happened in due course). The focus was on 'understanding the environment'. Crucially, Flynn says, this would ultimately make the marines safer than would concentrating overmuch on the IED threat. These intelligence teams looked at what caused grievance, what disputes there were between villages, and what made the villagers believe they were safer. In other words, they asked questions of the 'vital ground' before acting to influence it. As we have seen, a similar effort by the UK's 52 Brigade, though less well developed, resulted in an appreciable diminution of British casualties.[29] Although causality cannot be proven in either case, the evidence is compelling that trying to see yourself as the civilian population sees you bears military fruit.

This is the very reverse of the 'counter-IED task force' approach espoused by the British in Helmand, a centralized strike force supported by highly skilled analysts and addressed towards a purely tactical threat to the force rather than a threat to the *mission* – protection of the 'people' – the 'vital ground', the 'prize', etc. Implicit in the approach advocated by Flynn is treating the 'people' not as an inert body to be won or lost, or taken as ground. The 'people' are human beings who require a far more sophisticated approach to intelligence than that offered by the traditional 'enemy-focused' systems derived from Cold War ideas, with which the British are so well equipped. Such an approach might provide the 'two-way street' that Stephen Grey stresses as an avenue to effective influence.

This, in turn, requires an awareness on the part of commanders that the mission must have a far more wide-ranging approach to intelligence: 'Meaningful change will not occur until commanders at all levels take responsibility for intelligence. The way to do so is through devising and prioritizing smart, relevant questions – "information requirements" – about the environment as well as the enemy.'[30] This may well involve intelligence officers dealing with people they (particularly the highly secretive operators of the British army) have hitherto preferred to avoid – the much-feared NGOs and journalists. These two groups are, without question, the best informed of all in any theatre of war. In the perfect Darwinian world that limited war can be, awareness of matters relevant to safety and life are literally vital to aid workers and journalists. The same is, of course, true of soldiers, but they often have the advantage of numbers and an extensive suite of weaponry to deter or repel attack.

Clearly, aid workers and journalists have to be seen to be neutral. To a very great degree, this neutrality guarantees their security, which is initially provided by their awareness of the environment. Intelligence collectors need to be acutely aware of this basic fact, but, with that limitation, they should be given a licence to roam far wider and, as General Flynn puts it:

> leave their chairs and visit the people who operate at the grassroots level – civil affairs officers, PRTs, atmospherics teams, Afghan liaison officers, female engagement teams, willing NGOs and development organizations, United Nations officials, psychological operations teams, human terrain teams, and staff officers with infantry battalions.[31]

One might add to this list doctors and medical staff. And the intelligence collected should be used to ensure that casualties are properly compensated – soft power in its best form, ameliorating the savagely destructive and largely pointless use of 'kinetic' force in 'counterinsurgencies' or civil wars. In Northern Ireland, the ethos was that 'every soldier was an intelligence collector'. No doubt this mantra is preached to this day. However, the kind of information they should be trained to seek must be far wider in scope. Instead of long periods of training in increasingly archaic and irrelevant techniques of 'agent-handling mechanics', 'humint' operators might be taught how properly to approach and appreciate the problems of the much-reviled (or feared) aid workers or journalists. Officers might take an interest in how disputes are solved. It would be a caricature to suggest that no officers do this: undoubtedly some of them do. But the cultural change, reflected in doctrine, is neither present nor envisaged. The seeds may be present in some forward-thinking officers, such as Major General Andrew Mackay (now retired). What they are advocating is the use of what has become known as 'soft power', some of which comes very close to the 'human security' focus argued by Mary Kaldor and US army Lieutenant Colonel Shannon Beebe in *The Ultimate Weapon is No Weapon*.[32]

Explorers not conquerors: bringing in the civvies

If the peace is to be won, the changes advocated here will, as Flynn says, require a departure from the comfort zone of very many officers. It will necessitate a change in focus of mission and a move away from inward-looking, enemy-focused fighting to an outward-looking concentration on a broad spectrum of activity.

Soldiers should act, as Stephen Grey says, as 'explorers not conquerors'.[33] Until soldiers can offer more than 'kinetic influence' or transparent 'consent-winning activities', then, in the words of the officer who opened this chapter: 'I doubt if anyone would listen to us in Southern Afghanistan if we were unarmed.' Captain Simpson has a point. Perhaps that is because, without weapons, we have very little to say.

So what? As the perennial question goes, what can we do about it? Here we arrive once again at the central thesis of this book – armed forces 'opening up' their culture. Rupert Smith called this 'opening networks'. If we are to continue to fight, or indeed prepare for, 'war among the people', we need to understand the civilian perspective intimately. This is particularly vital where the military meets its civilian 'hosts' in circumstances that are not lethal. As we saw, concessions are made to the 'comprehensive approach', with its deployment of contractors (such as me) or diplomats of varying motivation or suitability for the task. Drawing in 'civilians', many of whom are anyway recently retired military men, is one thing; changing the perspective of the force is another.

There are many areas that are often perceived as involving warlike roles where purely civilian expertise far outstrips military knowledge. An example close to my own heart, both as a lawyer and as a former intelligence officer, is interrogation. The UK armed forces got themselves into a terrible mess over what is a day-to-day activity for thousands of policemen. Legal boundaries were allegedly transgressed, prompting a constant drip of press stories and legal inquiries, which gave the inaccurate impression of extensive ill-treatment.

British police officers spend entire careers asking sometimes hostile questions of sometimes extremely hostile people while staying within legal boundaries. Let no one claim that somehow interrogation – defined as the extraction of information from an unwilling subject – of a hardened armed robber is conceptually different from interrogation of a 'terrorist' or a captured soldier. The likelihood is that the armed robber will be very familiar indeed with police procedures and techniques, having faced them many times before, which makes the police officers' task arguably more difficult. In my experience of both criminals and 'terrorists', the armed robber is highly likely to be every bit as tough as an average resistance fighter. Yet how many police officers have served as military interrogators? No doubt a few have; but I am certain that their involvement was incidental rather than intentional. Yet in Northern Ireland and Malaya, two campaigns where the civilian lead was apparent (at least in the far more successful later stages of the campaigns), military interrogation was emphatically subordinate to civilian. Indeed, in Northern Ireland, when large numbers of military interrogators were involved, the result was highly damaging. The outcome is well known to anyone who is remotely familiar with the law relating to torture and ill-treatment – the leading case of *Ireland* v. *UK* in the European Court of Human Rights.[34] Later in the campaign, as a rule, all interrogation in Northern Ireland was handled by police officers, with far greater success.

The area of interrogation and detention is, of course, a huge topic. Inquiry after inquiry will report on this matter. The reason they are convened at all is that matters clearly went so badly wrong with the result that what was once the province of a relatively clandestine and extremely closed world – that of the military interrogator – became a regular front-page topic of informed comment. This has not served the armed forces well, to put it mildly. I am not suggesting that my former military colleagues are incapable of carrying out this task; I am suggesting that trained and highly experienced police interrogators might be, if not better, then at the very least as effective.

A less clandestine world is that of the civil affairs officer, another relatively unknown and under-resourced province of activity, confined largely to the (until recently) despised world of the reservist – the STAB[35]– where arguably it belongs. Under-resourced and unknown it may be, but in my experience, in every one of the four theatres of operation where I have served as a civilian and a soldier, these men and women have been the single best-informed and most useful group of military personnel – be they American, British or indeed, in Kosovo, German – not excepting the vastly better resourced intelligence teams. Trained and brave soldiers, their focus is on precisely those matters that this book has addressed. With an effect out of all proportion to their numbers, their job is to ensure that the occupying military force acts positively on and with its host population. They do this by building links with key leaders, companies, schools and organizations – the sinews of any society anywhere. They then seek ways whereby the army can assist constructively. However, they comprise a tiny number of operators, and are almost entirely reservists. If any concept points the way to a more successful, more 'open-networked' future it is civil affairs. It embodies the much-preached ground of 'comprehensive approach'.

Advances are being made by the British army in this respect. The Military Stabilisation Support Group (MSSG), the descendant of the civil affairs units of the Second World War that implemented Operation Eclipse (see above), was set up in 2008. It is largely, though not exclusively, composed of reservists, many of them with civilian skills that are directly relevant to the civilian communities within which they work – police officers, engineers and surveyors. They draw on the substantial expertise of the more constructive elements of the 'line army', such as the Royal Engineers and the Royal Army Medical Corps. They have conducted exercises in close cooperation with other armed forces – not in the tired, repetitive and hugely expensive re-enactment of military operations which dominates the normal run of 'military cooperation', but in relieving natural disasters. Real work, in other words. As matters stand, the MSSG is a small and not especially well funded outfit, occupying, at best, the periphery of the awareness of senior military officers. It represents, however, a very positive start.

Building real professionalism

In any other profession, the idea of 'professionalism' is deeply embedded. In the UK armed forces, there are very many highly professional individuals, who treat the 'profession of arms' with the seriousness it demands. The structures, however, do not support the aspiration. It will be clear from the foregoing that the kind of critical, informed and free discourse that characterizes 'true' professions, such as law, medicine, nursing or accountancy, is simply not present in the military field. That in itself is a major problem. However, the way in which the careers of service officers are structured presents a serious block to the development of deep professional knowledge.

While young officers are – indeed must be – specialist infantrymen, artillerymen, pilots or seaman officers, when they reach the rank of major (or its equivalent) they start to become 'generalists', at a time when the reverse should be the case. Officers change their postings every two or three years, and on each posting they may be required to take on jobs in areas in which they have not the slightest experience. It may well seem that if this happens to be a staff job within the Ministry of Defence, little harm may be done. However, Mackay and Tatham speak particularly of the need to understand the deep background of a topic.[36] All officers at that level are aware of the phenomenon whereby they are posted to a job for which they are not in the slightest degree qualified and told to get on with it. One acquaintance of mine was posted as senior desk officer for a remote part of the world with fairly considerable British interests. He was only vaguely aware of the location on the map of this region, but, two days after he took up the job, a war broke out there. Briefing senior officers and politicians on the political nuances of the area proved a challenge. Needless to say, in the military world, no excuse is available along the lines of 'I only started yesterday.'

At best, this approach serves as an incentive to quick learning. Clearly, in areas where professional expertise is absolutely necessary, military officers are at least as competent as most of their civilian counterparts:

military lawyers and doctors, for example, are highly competent and professional by any standards. After all, that is their profession, and they will be 'found out' quickly if they are not up to the job. They train and practise their profession constantly.[37] This is not the case for 'line' officers in many fields, who can find themselves responsible for 'influence operations' for an entire theatre of operations on the back of a two-week course in media and psychological warfare.

It should by now be clear that the issue is not so much that of individual professionalism, but of a culture that promotes a 'part-time' approach. This coexists well with a 'cracking on', 'no nonsense' culture that values action over considered thought. Ironically, considering their image as 'part-time soldiers', it is often the case that reservists have a far more informed and professional approach to their military tasks than regulars, for the straightforward reason that their military job often is and has been their 'day job' for many years. In a world of increasing technical, political and human complexity, the day of the generalist – the person who can turn his hand to anything for a few weeks or even years, the 'instant expert' – has long passed. Given that most commentators see British military involvement within the context of interventions in failed states – with complex, wicked[38] problems – the requirement for specialist military expertise is pressing, and there is a commensurate growth in the need for real (as opposed to 'instant') knowledge.

The key role of the reserves

A landmark report, published in October 2010 by two highly experienced and successful officers, recommended a complete rethink of the role of reserves.[39] The authors point out that, in other highly effective armed forces, reservists take a far more central role in national defence. Almost all pilots in the Israeli air force are reservists, as are no less than a third of fighter pilots in the US air force.[40] They observe that, in time of war, all national skills must be utilized, and now is a time of war. This must surely be all the more important in so-called 'wars among the people' where, as we saw in Chapter 7, the division of effort should be 80:20 civilian/military respectively.

Rarely in the UK are the civilian skills of reservists intelligently utilized. I ended my military career as head of a reserve intelligence unit. Earlier in this chapter I observed that it was surprisingly rare for police officers (or barristers such as myself, for that matter) to be recruited as interrogators. I was never given a good reason why these professional questioners should not be hunted out and recruited to use their ample and regularly practised skills in the defence of their country. The same applies in almost every military field of activity.

I used to give recruiting talks to other reservists, to encourage them to apply to my unit. This was accompanied by a slide show, with pictures showing our activities in Iraq and Afghanistan. In the background of some of these pictures, the observant might see the equipment we and our sister units used. After one such talk I was approached by a young naval reserve officer, who asked me if a piece of communications hardware was a particular make and type. I had not the slightest idea and said so. He described how the communications network he had seen in the slide presentation was set up and said that such equipment could be readily tracked. I said I doubted this: 'we only have the best', 'it can't be tracked' and so on. 'We' had our own experts. In fact, I doubted whether any of our 'expert' officers – who might have been working on a piece of sonar last year and next year be in a staff job responsible for ordering the army's food – knew half as much as this man about the current market in personal communications. The young officer opened a laptop, tapped a few keys and showed me where in the world every such item of communications equipment was being used, apparently freely available to anyone with the right knowledge.

So what? Whether our equipment was or was not secure – and I have no idea, maybe it was an entirely different kind – this was a young man who knew his business, communications. Yet he was not working part time for special forces and contributing his expertise. He was serving in a tertiary support capacity, occasionally getting on board ships for a few days a year, whenever the navy would condescend to have reservists on board its vessels – generally to fill gaps left by those on leave. Every reserve unit in the country is a potential repository of such professional, civilian skills in every field.

In the two world wars it was men and women who were *civilians first* that won the battles for survival. More than 50 per cent of pilots in the

Battle of Britain were reservists. Almost all bomber crews who led Britain's main offensive efforts were taken from civil life. The naval forces that won the Battle of the Atlantic, so vital for national survival, were largely officered and crewed by men serving only for the duration of the war. The only time the British army was truly world class, in the last year of the First World War, was when it was almost entirely composed of officers and men who had, two years before, been working as civilians in towns and on farms. Indeed, arguably the single most successful national commander of that war – certainly on the allied side – Australia's General Sir John Monash had been a civilian engineer and colonel in a territorial regiment at the start of the war. There is surely a simple and incontrovertible reason for this: the population as a whole contains far more expertise and skill – and indeed potential to develop both – than the rather narrow sliver of society that comprises the regular and reserve forces.

We are regularly assured that the wars we are fighting now are in our crucial national interest. They are fought among civilians, and yet they are fought by a narrow, often self-regarding 'elite' warrior class whose civilian brothers in the reserves are allowed to participate only to 'fill gaps', or provide expertise that does not attract 'regular' interest – such as the civil affairs units we met earlier in this chapter. Yet surely it is when fighting war among civilians that the approach of the reservists is most keenly required and, I would argue, most profoundly missed. The US armed forces regularly send formed reserve units on operations; in the case of the Territorial Army, this is rarely the case – with one or two noble exceptions, Territorials tend to be sent as individuals. But then, the US is a country whose very existence is founded upon the skills of the most famous of all reserve officers, George Washington – a former colonel in the Virginia Militia and a man whose application for a regular commission in the British army had been turned down; surely the most significant such rejection in history.

Aside from the clear cost advantage of reservists (who cost about an eighth of their regular colleagues to maintain), there is a skills benefit too. These are not men and women who move from specialization to specialization, job to job every two years. Like the young naval reserve telecoms expert, or the airline pilots of the US Air National Guard for that matter, these are men and women who ply their trade every day. For reservists and civilians to begin to play a really critical part in defence, we will need a very deep shift of attitudes from the 'regulars'.

There is another component of the population that lies untapped – rather astonishingly, given the lessons of history. Britain has always been blessed with large numbers of willing immigrants from all parts of the world. Such communities have almost always become major assets to the larger British society, usually within a single generation. We have seen that, during the Second World War, it was quickly realized that victory would have to involve occupation and control of the enemy's heartland. Once this was clearly recognized, great efforts were made to ensure that all relevant human assets were mobilized. Prior to the start of the war, Britain had welcomed large numbers of mostly Jewish German refugees (not large enough, but nonetheless considerable). In due course, many thousands of them were absorbed into the British armed forces, initially in the Pioneer Corps doing manual work. In 1943, they were given permission to apply to any regiment or arm of the service. The contribution they, as a group, made not only to military victory but to what we would now call post-conflict stabilization is only now being realized.[41] These men (and in special forces women too), fluent German speakers all, were utterly central to British efforts to assist in all aspects of the occupation of Germany, from the hunt for war criminals to the development of a democratic media.

Today, Britain is host to even more thousands of exiled Iraqis, Afghans and Pakistani Pashtuns. Vanishingly few of them have had their skills or knowledge utilized either in assisting the military or in the stabilization efforts. Why this may be is beyond the scope of this book. It took a mere two years of the Second World War for the British authorities to understand that not all refugee Germans – most, but by no means all, Jewish – were potential fifth columnists, worthy of distrust and internment. The day may – indeed must – come when British Muslims are regarded less as potential 'terror suspects' and more as assets.

When that day dawns, the UK may find, as it did during the Second World War and throughout the days of empire, that such people add immeasurably to any effort that is undertaken in countries such as those in which the UK and its armed forces work today. It is worth mentioning in this context that the US has been quick to appreciate the benefit of such people. Indeed, the former US ambassador to Afghanistan, and more recently Iraq – Zalmay Khalilzad – is an Afghan Pashtun, born in Mazar i Sharif. Of course, the will of British Muslims to work with the British armed forces is, to some degree understandably, dependent on a perception that the wars embarked upon are just. I would add one personal note: those few expatriate Afghans or Iraqis with whom I have worked (incidentally, they were mainly with the US forces) left me with an abiding respect for their loyalty and courage.

A friend of mine was serving in Afghanistan, in the disastrous early campaigns of the war in Helmand. On his return, I asked him what at the time seemed a reasonable question: 'Are we winning?' He answered with another question: 'Is the nation at war?' to which, of course, the answer is 'no'. His point was more subtle than simply a reference to the lack of public support for the war. He was saying that success is unlikely until the country becomes willing to engage all its resources, and not simply the military or those parts of government contingent to it, as happens now with the 'comprehensive approach'. This is particularly important in environments, like southern Iraq and Afghanistan, where the assistance of the supposed 'legitimate' government cannot be relied upon. For example, it was only in early 2010 that anyone thought of involving well-known academic experts in informal justice on an institutional basis, in the effort in Helmand. Until then, this was regarded as essentially an ancillary matter. By 2010, even the army was beginning to see it as central. By that time, the Taliban had emphatically established itself as the arbiter (in every sense) of disputes in Helmand.

In a fine paper produced by the Development, Concepts and Doctrine Centre in preparation for the 2010 Strategic Defence and Security Review – *The Future Character of Conflict* – 'influence' is said to be central to future conflict.[42] 'Influence operations' are currently 'flavour of the day' in the military. It is to be expected that the enthusiasm for this term (as for other formerly fashionable concepts and buzzwords[43] that are now anathema) will wane. The concept, however, is sound, provided it is part of the idea that the application of influence must involve a step change on the part of military men, who need to spend time seeing themselves as others see them. This is not simply a question of morality: it is a hard-edged question of effectiveness. By taking the easy way – of talking from behind the cloak of weapons and ignoring what is said to us – we are failing. This reluctance to engage with the human environment of modern war is one of the most damaging legacies of the old ways of war.

It is true that outmanoeuvring opponents physically is less important than outmanoeuvring them mentally. As the strategist Lawrence Friedman put it, 'superiority in the physical environment is of little value unless it can be translated into an advantage in the information environment'.[44] But the converse is also true: rhetoric is for home consumption and will not cut it on the ground, where fact has more traction. What happens on the ground is rather more important, and that depends on having a true appreciation of what one is doing. In turn, that appreciation must be founded on hard fact, not on the kind of wishful thinking that passes for military assessments of 'effect'. Even if a capability to understand the whole environment within which we operate is nurtured and developed, conflicts may arise that require different skills. This will require flexibility and lateral thinking. As Rupert Smith has said, the opponent may very well simply use weapons below our radar, like justice, for example. Those who claim that these are not now matters of relevance to the military have failed to understand the key lessons of recent conflicts. We need to have men and women who are able to adapt quickly and, where necessary, to transform. It may well be, as Mary Kaldor and an increasing number of commentators have suggested, that armies are simply not the right organizations to deal with problems thrown up in places such as Afghanistan. It may be that we need to be looking at entirely new entities.

However radical the transformation on the horizon, it will require a real step change in the abilities of British servicemen to adapt – to be Stephen Grey's explorers rather than conquerors. In the next chapter, we look at how that capability might be developed.

CHAPTER 11

Opening Networks

The old saying 'live and learn' must be reversed in war, for there we 'learn and live'; otherwise we die.

US War Department, 1945

Officers are recruited from the best classes in society, are active in body and have a practical education and great personal smartness. Their knowledge of military science and general education are not so good.

General von Kuhl, *Die deutsche Generalstab*[1]

Published by the Royal United Services Institute (RUSI), the *RUSI Journal* is the in-house journal of the British military establishment. While the debates in it can be vigorous, the tone is generally subdued. In spring 2009, a very different article appeared. It was written by a recently retired army officer who, significantly, had served at the Development, Concepts and Doctrine Centre in Shrivenham, on the same campus as the Joint Command and Staff College we visited in Chapter 6. Patrick Little writes about what he regards as the development of an insular, conformist culture in the British army:

The UK and its military are therefore at a critical moment – one in which an urge to protect individual (political and senior military) and collec-tive legacies will either follow one of two routes. The route of least resist-ance is to pass blame for all shortcomings on to a lame duck government.

The second option in the case of the British army specifically and defence more generally, is to turn the critical mirror on itself. This mirror will lead to an acknowledgement of shortcomings.[2]

A former syndicate leader, an experienced officer who leads discussions at Shrivenham, told me that he was deeply disappointed with the attitude of many of his students, particularly to questions of motivation and principle. They were simply not interested in discussing, for example, why they were fighting in Afghanistan.[3]

This unfortunate attitude is borne out by research. A study conducted in 2009 on 114 British army and Royal Marine officers of the rank of captain and major found that 27 per cent knew neither what the British government wished to achieve in Afghanistan nor what the role of the army was there. Those who offered 'correct' interpretations of the reasons for the Afghan campaign in most cases only identified subsidiary or peripheral objectives.[4] The effect of this is critical and plays into much of what has been discussed. Without a clear understanding of what one is doing fighting a war, for what one is fighting and how, the mission is highly unlikely to succeed. It is highly unlikely that enlisted soldiers, who in any event rely heavily on being well briefed by their platoon and company commanders, are any better informed. One highly regarded academic and former army officer told me: 'We recruit graduates because we expect them to think. When they join the army, they stop thinking; the system does not encourage independent critical analysis.' A crucial reason for the poor performance of the UK armed forces in Iraq and Afghanistan has been their inability to see themselves as others perceive them – specifically the unfortunately (but all too often aptly) named 'target-populations'. This needs to change, and networks need to open. This chapter is about how that change might come about.

Future conflict

Arguably the greatest general of the eighteenth century, Frederick the Great, had clear ideas about how soldiers should use their time: 'For those who are destined for the military profession, peace must be a time of meditation, and war the period where one puts his ideas into practice.'[5]

In the aftermath of Iraq, and as the ragged endgame of Afghanistan plays out, such meditation is under way within the British defence establishment. The *Future Character of Conflict* paper produced by the Development, Concepts and Doctrine Centre (DCDC) reflected exactly the sort of critical and forward-thinking analysis that is required. It examines how war may look five and twenty-five years ahead, in 2014 and 2029. Conflict may result from climate change, globalization, failed states, ideology. Conflict, it says, is an 'unpredictable and uniquely human activity' where quantitative advantage may no longer be assumed. The sense of amazement inherent in the idea that, in future, the UK 'may actually be more likely to use the military instrument for reasons of fear and interest' is as surprising as the sentiment itself. For implicit in that statement is the notion that force has been used for reasons *other than* perceived threat or national interest. In other words, the idea is being floated that the Ministry of Defence may well return to its advertised role of defence.

In a world of free-flowing and unpredictable human behaviour, 'Human Intelligence and Civil-Military cooperation will ... be battle-defining'.[6] Computer Network Operations wielded by extremist non-state actors are only one of the so-called 'hybrid threats' that may loom in what, by 2029, may be a multipolar world, where UK qualitative or quantitative supremacy may not be guaranteed. Future wars will be different, and we need to be prepared. So far so good. In conclusion, the paper argues that: 'The UK must make its people the edge.'[7] Unfortunately, it says, the 'capacity to educate to the required level is under-resourced'.

Training and education

There is no better *training* organization in the world than the British armed forces. There is little need for more training, however. What is required is a culture of lifelong learning – of *education*. As matters stand, the approach is that once one has 'done the course' in any given field, one is trained and sufficiently expert not only to operate, but to advise or indeed instruct. If one has practised the skills in operations, so much the better. Dovetailing with a requirement for better education is a need for the introduction of a concept of institutional openness and honesty. As matters stand, the culture is closed and at times less than entirely honest.

Strategic education within a military environment naturally has the tendency to produce a self-referential and reinforcing intellectual environment, and the UK armed forces certainly do not need to be any more self-referential than they are today. Shrivenham is not always an institution where dissent is readily encouraged. I completed my (Reserve) Advanced Command and Staff Course (ACSC) at Shrivenham in 2006. Every student is part of a 'syndicate' – essentially a study and discussion group.

One day my syndicate was required to discuss the legal foundations of the Iraq War. At that time, our group was being observed by a member of the college staff, a hard-charging, very senior officer. He ordered us to stop the discussion, as it was not going in what he considered to be a productive direction. When I objected (privately, of course – to contradict such an officer in public is absolutely not done), I was told that if I or any of my colleagues had a serious problem with national policy, the solution was not to complain about it, but to resign. This is not as unreasonable a suggestion as it may at first seem to an outsider. Clearly there are risks in having dissent among officers in a fighting organization. We were not, however, on operations at that time. Not a single one of my syndicate would have begun to consider that kind of conversation on operations – after all, what would be the point? But, to reiterate, we were not on operations: we had been directed to discuss this topic in what purported to be an institution of academic integrity.

No doubt, as I have been told and believe, this was a highly unusual and irregular occurrence. Nonetheless the kind of difficulty I encountered would be completely unheard of in most serious civilian institutions. The former US army officer and academic Andrew Bacevich is right when he says that 'to my mind real education requires an environment where free inquiry is not only permitted but encouraged'.[8] One former officer, now an academic very familiar with the ways of Shrivenham, had strong views on this. His language was a little more earthy and emphatic, but his point may be summarized thus: 'Why don't they just give them a little book, order them to learn what is in it and tell them to go away?'

Building a critical soldier?

The general intellectual hinterland of the US armed forces is far deeper and richer than that in the UK. There is a constellation of military universities, colleges and academies, all of which are manned by highly qualified men and women. Some of these institutions are of the highest calibre. West Point Military Academy, where the intellectual and leadership elite of the army is educated and initially trained, was named by *Forbes* magazine and the Center for College Affordability and Productivity (in its flagship annual list of the finest US universities) as 'America's best college' in 2009. In a field that includes the likes of Yale, Harvard, Stanford and Princeton, as well as 600 or so other institutions, this is a telling accolade and is highly indicative of the value the US military places on academic achievement.[9] The results were 'based on the quality of the education they provide, the experience of the students and how much they achieve'.[10] Clearly, these institutions need to be staffed, and staffed they are largely by serving or retired military academics. There are about 400 academic staff at West Point alone, 75 per cent of whom are military officers, and about 30 per cent of them have PhDs.

US military education should not – and indeed does not – stop at the initial training academies. The US armed forces take far more seriously the adage that training and doctrine must be founded on good education. It is a mistake, though, to presume that such continuing training should take place only in military institutions. This is a particularly important point to consider for the senior levels of the military, as they are taught strategy. Andrew Bacevich raises a problem, which, he says, churches come up against all the time: 'There is a tension between genuine education and advancing overarching institutional agendas ... how do you square the pursuit of truth with the conviction that truth is already known?'[11]

The roots of one solution may lie in the US practice of sending senior military officers to civilian academic institutions. As US military officers (and indeed other ranks) progress, so they are offered the opportunity of joining the Advanced Civil Schooling programme – a fully funded and supported opportunity for qualified officers to gain advanced degrees at civilian institutions. This is the way General Petraeus and hundreds of other officers gained their doctorates. The programme takes more than

400 officers annually from the army alone.[12] General David Petraeus's own thoughts on this form of education are worth relating: 'The most powerful tool any soldier carries is not his weapon but his mind. These days, and for the days ahead as far as we can see, what soldiers at all ranks know is liable to be at least as important to their success as what they can physically do.'[13]

Petraeus takes the view that attendance at civilian graduate programmes draws officers out of their intellectual and social comfort zones, a process far more violently apparent in operational theatres:

> They are exposed to diverse and sometimes hostile views, and sometimes diverse cultures. Just as the best way by far to learn a foreign language is to live in the culture where the language is spoken, so the best way to learn about other worldviews is to go to and live in another world: grad school forces a person to redefine upward one's own internal standards of excellence.[14]

Brigadier General H.R. McMaster, author of *Dereliction of Duty*,[15] wrote his controversial and lacerating criticism of the joint chiefs of staff in the Vietnam War initially as a PhD thesis, while being funded by the US army to do so at the University of North Carolina at Chapel Hill. In a talk to graduate students at that university, he said that his time studying at Chapel Hill had prepared him for combat in Iraq: 'It was here that I think I learned to ask the right questions . . . about complex issues.'[16] His tour in Tal Afar as commander of the 3rd Armored Cavalry Regiment stands as one of the very few success stories of the US armed forces in pre-2007 Iraq. Just in passing, a comment: it is unlikely that a British officer, even if a system similar to the Advanced Civil Schooling programme was made available, would be permitted to spend three years reflecting on (and writing so devastatingly about) the failures of recently serving British generals.

The (comparatively) lamentable position of graduate military education in Britain is summed up by retired General Sir John Kiszely:

> The army's Defence Fellowship programme has largely fallen into abeyance, relying on the charity of individual commanders to find funding 'at risk' to their own budget. Each year, two officers undertake an MPhil at

Cambridge, but whereas in the past such programmes were awarded to potential high-flyers, in the last decade this has been very much the exception rather than the rule. As for doctorates, there is little official incentive for officers to undertake these – they must be undertaken in an officer's own time and, apart from at Cranfield University (one of the Defence Academy's academic partners), largely at the officer's expense.[17] Little recognition seems to be given to the award of a doctorate.[18]

Plenty of opportunities exist for gaining advanced degrees. The one-year MPhil at Cambridge, regularly threatened with being cut, represents the only real opportunity for the 'high flyer' to develop academically on a full-time basis. Very few are available in any event – numbers vary every year but rarely exceed half a dozen. Single services, with the RAF offering the best selection,[19] offer some scholarships for very senior officers to reflect upon their profession. For those slightly less senior there is a series of Master's degrees offered by King's College London, These include the MA in Defence Studies, offered as an option to all studying on the ACSC at Shrivenham. It requires a limited input from students over and above the course itself, 'eight Wednesday afternoons and a dissertation' as one officer put it to me.

There are no funded full-time opportunities, outside the medical professional branches, for officers to undertake research degrees – although in fairness there are several part-time scholarships. Unfortunately, funding for part-time study for the excellent 'War in the Modern World' MA at King's College London was cut for serving officers in 2010. The contention here is that the funded and supported education on offer is narrowly focused. None of it involves extensive exposure to non-military viewpoints such as are available to their US counterparts. As matters stand, *in British universities* there are far more American military officers studying for research degrees than British officers.

It is not only officers' in-service education that is in urgent need of serious consideration. Every British TV viewer will have seen recruiting advertisements for the military services. The central message is 'join up and get a trade', rather as it would have been in the 1960s. The class system in the UK military is necessarily entrenched in the officer/other rank distinctions. However, rarely do old presumptions creep in more clearly than in educational presumptions attached to rank: no consideration appears to be given to people who wish to join one of the services for any reason other than that they are unemployed and need a 'trade' or because they need to have 'the best brought out of them'. The usual presumed route for anyone who is already a graduate or a member of a trade or profession (or who aspires to become so) is for them to apply to become an officer. There is rarely, if ever, a serious effort to encourage graduates, or indeed those who might aspire to go to university to join 'the ranks'. Yet many branches of all armed forces would benefit from such people. I am thinking particularly but not solely, of the intelligence and various technical trades.

In the United States, there is active and highly attractive encouragement for those officers or enlisted service personnel who have aspirations to become university students. The system is usually simply referred to as the GI Bill,[20] after a congressional Act of 1944, which was intended to assist reintegration of Second World War veterans.[21] The GI Bill is not short of its critics or problems, largely because it is not perceived to go far enough in helping veterans.[22] Nonetheless, it is rightly considered a key foundation stone of the astonishingly extensive structures of care and development for veterans in the US. It must also be said that, although originally designed as a reward for service, the GI Bill is considered to be an excellent and vital recruiting tool for those who would otherwise not be able to afford a university education.

The system, introduced as it was after the Second World War and improved over the last few years of the 'war on terror', ensures that any serviceman (or woman) who has served a prescribed minimum term (in the region of five years) is entitled to have his university tuition fees paid, plus a sizeable contribution towards living expenses. In a society where college education is (at times literally) prohibitively expensive, this is a major incentive for high-quality eighteen-year-olds to serve, against the promise that they will not need to concern themselves with paying for their university education for much of the rest of their lives. The result of this system is readily visible on many US campuses. Columbia University, for example, is an Ivy League college and therefore comparable to Oxford and Cambridge. It has something of a radical reputation, and so is perhaps not a natural home for ex-servicemen; yet it has no fewer than 210 veterans on its books.[23]

Some 300,000 servicemen and their dependants (who, under certain circumstances, can also benefit) take advantage of this system, ensuring a higher quality of intake of young recruits into both the officer and the enlisted cadres and, just as importantly, ensuring the possibility of a smooth reintegration into civilian life for those who have served. One wonders how many UK veterans of Iraq or Afghanistan are currently students at Oxbridge or Russell Group universities, or indeed at any institution of higher education. Needless to say, no figures are available. Certainly no one is having their fees fully paid.

There is a system in the UK called Enhanced Learning Credits, which allows long-service soldiers up to £2,000 per year while they are in the armed forces. It is a poor and sick relation of the GI Bill.

The debate about education rages in the US, and the view of the system is by no means rose-tinted. Fewer US officers are now being educated in civilian graduate schools than in 1970, and there is a debate about an anti-intellectual strain in the US army. There are, as in the UK, strong arguments for suggesting that the 'training mentality' has infected those who have attended civilian institutions. For example, an expert in 'counter-insurgency' may delude himself that he is also, by virtue of having 'taken a course', an authority on development. Further, there is sometimes said to be a 'qualification mentality', whereby the importance of gaining degrees is not the education itself but what, in British parlance, might be called 'the tick in the box', fulfilling a requirement.

Of course the sceptic might say, so what? What advantage does all this education accrue to an effective armed service? Are we trying to make soldiers into academics? In an age where every pound spent on education is a pound not spent on something else, how do we quantify its value?

We have seen above that Generals Petraeus and McMaster were clear about the operational value of elite-level education for soldiers. However, there is certainly a serious debate to be had about these questions. That notwithstanding, in Iraq in 2006–7, the US military was quick, relative to the British, to realize that it needed to change direction radically. Unburdened by useless shibboleths of the past, such as Malaya or even Northern Ireland, it was able to identify the simple and robust actions required successfully to protect what remained of vulnerable populations.

It achieved this quickly and, within the terms of the operation's objectives, successfully. Was this due to the critical faculties deployed by a few highly educated officers who realized what needed to be done? Or were other factors at play?

It is important in all of this not to lose sight of the overall difficulty. Without any adequate strategy or serious knowledge of the situation they were about to create, both the US and the UK entered operations that they have found exceedingly hot to handle. The US, like the UK, essentially failed in its objectives overall (or such objectives as there appeared to be). The US army has proved itself to be a bludgeoning instrument, lacking much of the necessary knowledge – and, more importantly, the awareness that such knowledge was required. It has been responsible for the unnecessary killing of thousands of Iraqis, Afghans and others. There is little mitigation for this.

However, at the very least the US military machine, or that part of it under the command of General David Petraeus, showed itself capable of changing course, admitting mistakes and learning from them in the middle of a fierce war. The strategy deployed by Petraeus in the 'Surge' was coherent, its purpose being to buy time for political dialogue to take effect, and the resources were sufficient. Whether the improvement in the situation in Iraq was incidental to, or caused by, the shift in direction by the US army and marines is a topic for studies other than this one.[24] What really distinguished the team that developed the Iraq strategy was that all of them had received advanced research degrees from the finest civilian institutions in the country and abroad – Petraeus himself from Princeton, and others from such universities as Stanford, Columbia and Oxford. They had, at least partially, been formed in an atmosphere of free debate.

Opportunities for officers or senior NCOs to experience that broad-based relatively free-flowing debate outside the British military world are almost entirely absent. One very senior officer I spoke to, who had extensive recent front-line experience, placed this problem into an operational perspective:

A lot of officers do a lot of reading before deployment. They read deeply into the history, anthropology and social make-up of the country or campaign to which they will deploy. The trouble is that they do not have the educational context, the breadth of knowledge required to place that knowledge into its proper context. They have a tendency to go down intellectual rabbit holes. Their knowledge of the broader context of counterinsurgency can be rather limited.[25]

It was this syndrome which, arguably, produced the constant, irrelevant and highly damaging comparisons of Basra and Helmand with Malaya.

This officer took the view that promising future military thinkers should be selected and nurtured early. The first selective course within the UK armed forces is the ACSC, usually when an officer is approaching forty years old. 'This is too late. We should select promising high flyers much earlier, perhaps as early as their mid- to late twenties.'

This is an avenue down which the US is beginning to travel with the introduction of the 'soldier scholars program' at the Army War Command and General Staff College at Fort Leavenworth. Of the class of about a thousand future majors, eight are selected to conduct in-depth case studies of twenty-six campaigns. Each soldier scholar arranges interviews with leading scholars and experts. It is regarded as an intense and very tough programme. These officers are seen as the future leaders of the army. Interestingly, the course is directed by Dr Daniel Marston, a former lecturer at Sandhurst who had been a critic of UK achievements in Iraq. One of the in-depth studies enquires into the UK's thirty-year war in Northern Ireland. Astonishingly, nowhere in the UK military academic establishment is that campaign systematically analysed in such detail.

The point here is not to question the intellect of British military officers;. There should be no caricature of the education of senior officers in the UK military services. Let there be no doubt about it, British officers are highly intelligent, often very well-educated men and women. The purpose here is to compare the intellectual *culture* of the British military establishment with that of the US. It might well be argued, in response, that the officer cadre of the armed forces in the United Kingdom is predominantly (85 per cent) made up of university graduates, but that is hardly the point. The intellectual element is an integral, vital part of a very great number of junior officers' initial training in the United States, and this has created a culture where academic endeavour is, or may be, respected and supported.

While no one would seriously suggest that the United States military services are the ideal habitat for research academics or intellectual discourse, the fact is that time and space are given to those who wish to engage in that activity and are suited to it. This is emphatically not the case in a UK defence establishment where ambitious officers are pushed up a promotion ladder which allows very little (if any) meaningful time for reflection on what they have been doing throughout their career. The result is that even promising officers remain in the same environment throughout their careers, with minimal exposure to other perspectives. This is a process reminiscent of the 'Venturi effect': the narrower the perspective, the faster one can move through the process. It is not only our allies who have an eye to education. Consider this statement:

> The human factor will be more prominent in high-technology warfare. Making the most of the combat effectiveness of high-technology weapons and application of correct strategy and tactics will depend on the calibre of military personnel ... This means that the education and technical skills of military officers in the future information society will have to be higher than that those of civilians [sic]; otherwise, even with information-intensified weapons, defeat in war will be possible.[26]

The writer is Chang Mengxiong, a noted Chinese military theorist. The Chinese military has taken these words and the sentiments behind them to heart. The implications behind the fact that there are now said to be more Chinese than US military officers doing PhDs in the United States will be clear to all readers.[27] While the Chinese armed forces undoubtedly have their 'generalists', there is no room for amateurism or 'instant expertise' in Chang's sentiment.

Healthy discourse

The editor of the US army's *Military Review* must be accorded a great deal of credit for helping to bring about something of a minor revolution, with a series of occasionally subversive (by US military standards) articles. Equally importantly, the *Military Review* and its sister publication, *Parameters*, the journal of the US Army War College, have a very dynamic readership. Anyone can read articles from the entire archive online; indeed they may do so in Arabic and Spanish, as well as English.[28] Debate is vigorous, respectful but robust. Most of all, the publications are widely read. Indeed, Petraeus used *Military Review* to get his ideas into the US army mainstream – particularly his fourteen observations for counterinsurgency,[29] and his later 2008 'guidance'[30] – on the basis that soldiers *would read it.*

Military debate is not quite so dynamic in Britain. It is not only at Shrivenham that dissent is often unwelcome. The nearest equivalent to the *Military Review* is the *British Army Review*. In 2009, under its editor, the impressive Colonel John Wilson, one of a series of critical pieces attracted what the army's higher echelons considered to be the wrong sort of attention. Major Sergio Miller wrote a quite remarkably critical article on the 'comprehensive approach' in Afghanistan. He took the view that the British had 'sleepwalked' into the 'unmitigated disaster' of the effort in Helmand, an effort which had had the remarkable effect of turning the province into the opium centre of the world. The strategy of 'clear, hold and build' had become a 'parody of itself', and the British forces in the province were engaged in self-protection, reinforced by air strikes that further undermined the mission. 'We need to win a war, not spin one.'[31] There was much more in that vein.

Matters did not improve in the next issue, when an article by US Colonel Peter Mansoor, another of Petraeus's 'brains trust' (and another PhD from the Advanced Civil Schooling programme), opined:

> Rather than protecting the Iraqi people in Basra and thereby insulating them from militia violence and intimidation, British political and military leaders had abdicated responsibility for their security – the exact opposite of what was happening in Baghdad and elsewhere, as US forces were moving off their large forward operating bases to position themselves among the Iraqi people where they lived.[32]

Professor Anthony King and founder of the US soldier scholars program Dr Daniel Marston, leading experts in military reform and counterinsurgency respectively, also provided articles in that issue, looking critically but constructively at recent British military performance. This was too much. Shortly afterwards, David Betz, a leading academic expert on counterinsurgency (and, incidentally, a contributor to the British Stabilisation doctrine JDP 3–40), and his colleague Anthony Cormack submitted an article to the *Review*. It had already been published in the prestigious American journal *Orbis*,[33] but it was blocked by officials at the Ministry of Defence, along with two other critical pieces. The reason given was as follows: 'In order to avoid giving such propaganda gifts to the enemy in future we have found that, regrettably, we need to be a bit more cautious about what we publish or – in this case – republish. Hopefully, this will not always be the case.'[34]

Surely this is reasoning such as would make any censor in the Soviet Union proud; especially as it is far from clear that the Taliban (or indeed any other enemy of the United Kingdom) reads the *British Army Review*: they would need to be subscribers to the very limited print edition, as it is only otherwise available on the army intranet.[35] It may well be that the 'enemy' spoken about is rather nearer home in the shape of those who do not see eye to eye with the Ministry of Defence concerning the wars being fought.

With a scholar-editor such as Colonel John Wilson, and without the censorship exercised by interfering military bureaucrats, the *British Army Review* has very great potential. There is no doubt that the incident above and the publicity attached has resulted in an improvement in the situation and the *British Army Review* retains a somewhat idiosyncratic approach. What might have been, however, can easily be seen by anyone with access to the internet. There the US *Military Review* and its sister publication *Parameters* contain vigorous and often highly critical debate. A free press is one thing; however, a free-thinking, intellectually vigorous officer corps is quite another. The kind of critical contributions and debate found in these and other journals is almost unimaginable in the British army's officer corps. The idea of serving officers publicly (if debate in journals with a niche readership may be described as public) criticizing current strategic theory is not only unwelcome, it is unheard of – partly because officers are almost untrained in such theory.

There is the occasional flash of hope. The army's Counterinsurgency Centre, part of the Land Warfare Centre at Warminster, was set up in 2009. This small organization convenes seminars and produces military doctrine. By army standards, it is a forward-thinking, open-networked organization. The reader will not be surprised to learn that there are no civilians in this set-up, which deals with an area of warfare that, according to every single credible commentator for the past fifty years, requires an 80:20 civilian–military proportion for success. It is also, famously, funded on a shoestring – unable, as one officer commented to me, to buy lunch for visiting lecturers.

Or again, the organization that produced the *Future Character of Conflict* is led by a general who is well known for his intellect and broad-minded approach to necessary reform. Major General Paul Newton is 'Commander, Force Development and Training'. He is one rather lonely voice at that level.

Professor Anthony King, a sociologist highly respected in military circles, has suggested that there are three essential ingredients for military transformation, should it become necessary.[36] First, there is the need to identify a clear and distinct role. As we have seen, that was previously supplied by 'expeditionary warfare' ideas encouraged, if not engendered, by the 1998 Strategic Defence Review. Those ideas have proved to be misguided and are now rather stale. New thinking is required, and that must come from outside the military establishment as much as from within it. Second, there needs to be a (small) group of reformers. And finally, there must be institutional support for them from policy makers, academics and the media.

It is these last two conditions that are seriously lacking in the UK. Of the hundreds of general officers in the UK armed forces (and the army specifically), very few are 'reform-minded'. As we have seen, the ethos within the army is avowedly and understandably 'warfighting'.[37] That ethos has tended to subsume all else. There is also the subsidiary difficulty that generals, as it were, reproduce in their own image. Dissidents do not prosper. Major General Andrew Mackay, the most successful but least 'kinetic' of the Helmand commanders, has left the army, along with many forward-thinking as well as highly militarily effective veterans. These include General Graeme Lamb, who led the effort to co-opt insurgents in the Iraqi 'Awakening', and Lieutenant Colonel Richard Williams, the former Commanding Officer of 22 SAS regiment. Dozens of more junior, promising and, most importantly, extensively experienced officers have left the service. There is nothing in the British army to compare with the 'brains trust' that Petraeus gathered around him, both in the US, as he worked to shift the army's perspective, and in Iraq, as he tried to 'slow down the Washington clock' in Iraq in 2007 with his 'Surge'. There is little institutional pressure for profound change from the media or a political nation that is poorly informed about military affairs, and that has tended, with noble exceptions, to lionize the UK armed forces.

Is intervening in civil wars a military role?

Yet surely a deeper question remains: should the military be involved in this kind of operation at all? If we are to intervene in civil wars, there is one principle that must be paramount – the overriding principle of all humanitarian work: 'do no harm'. It may seem trite to raise that 'fluffy' idea at this juncture. Yet, given that the British military played a role (at the very least) in starting one civil war in Iraq and in exacerbating another in Afghanistan, its value should be luminously clear, not only in humanitarian terms, but in a purely military, selfish context. Of course, ultimately any strategy depends on the policy it is intended to achieve, and in neither theatre of operations was this ever clear.

'No matter how clearly one thinks, it is impossible to anticipate precisely the character of future conflict. The key is to not be so far off the mark that it becomes impossible to adjust once that character is revealed.'[38] Iraq and Afghanistan were racked by problems and were actually in the midst of civil wars (into which 'we' crashed as participants). However, by treating them as though they were in the midst of *insurgencies*, we created far more problems than we solved. It has been shown conclusively that it is hopeless to attempt a 'comprehensive approach' in the absence of meaningful state government.

Major General Mackay and Commander Stephen Tatham argue, 'Since 1800 the results of conflicts are increasingly favouring the actor willing to make conceptual jumps in thinking.'[39] They are right. One such jump may well be traversing the whole concept of intervention – from enemy-centred counterinsurgency to 'human security'. This might be described as a Kuhnian 'paradigm shift', a complete change of approach. Human security requires the intervener to switch his perspective from the 'enemy' to the people who host him. It does not take a cultural anthropologist to work things out: all too often what the 'people' want is for you not to be there in the first place. A human security approach requires an intervener who is willing to 'open networks', so that he is capable of understanding exactly the sort of conflict he is in, and who is prepared to use measures that will 'do no harm' either to the mission or, commensurate with the mission, to the host population. Such measures will generally not include artillery and jet bombers. All of this must, above all, be underpinned by clear policy, backed by realistic strategy that links ends to means. That is to say, it requires the appropriate resources. If Clausewitz tells us nothing else, he tells us this: overriding all is the political element. No amount of military nostrums or principles will make up for the lack of a workable political objective, backed by a firmly realistic appreciation of national interest. That requires the ability to reassess what exactly we might be capable of achieving with armed force in countries not our own.

Conclusion

Nobody likes an armed missionary.

Robespierre

It's the occupation, stupid.

Professor Robert Pape[1]

It was only in 2009, when General David Richards, a considered, highly intelligent officer, took over as chief of the general staff and head of the army, that the latter was placed on a 'campaign footing'. Almost incredibly, up until that point the operations that were taking place were deemed formally secondary to 'normal' activities of training and administration. The implication of the new 'campaign approach' was that training and equipment would be directed primarily to Afghanistan. At a speech to the Royal United Services Institute, General Richards said something that resonates with history:

> If this, arguably at least our generation's horse and tank moment, is not gripped, our armed forces will try, with inadequate resources, to be all things to all conflicts and perhaps fail to succeed properly in any. The risks of such an approach are too serious for this any longer to be an acceptable course, if ever it has been.[2]

General Richards was appointed chief of the defence staff in 2010.

The reference to a 'horse and tank moment' harks back to the 1920s and 1930s when, or so the common belief goes, supporters of archaic and useless cavalry obstructed the introduction of a new type of armoured mechanized force.[3] The German army, on the other hand, realized the significance of the new developments and acted, much to British discomfiture.

Cavalry and tanks both exist to reconnoitre and apply speed and power to the weak points of enemy formations. They were simply mechanically different ways of achieving the same effect. I would contend that our more recent struggles have been of an entirely new and deeply problematic character for our military forces. The problem may be summed up thus: the old ways of 'cracking on' and then muddling through, using a combination of wishful thinking, old myths and 'initiative', are (or should be) long gone.

Strangers in strange lands

Changes are afoot. No longer do the most senior officers in divisional headquarters or their staffs serve for only six months. They now do a year in theatre, which produces a far greater sense of continuity. There are some glimmers of a culture that is more open to criticism. Since plenty of criticism is now beginning to be voiced, this is useful.

But the essential problems remain. We do not currently have armed forces that are at all equipped for conflicts (characterized as 'insurgencies') where, brutally put, they are actually invaders in lands far away and of which they know really very little. We will need to do a great deal more than simply exchange our attitudinal horses for tanks.

As well as a useful summary of the 'can-do', culture which has proved so damaging, Richards' comments are genuinely profound: our armed forces will find themselves in that position unless it is absolutely clear what they are for and what they can do. Determining this must be a symbiotic task undertaken by politicians and generals. If we have been taught nothing else by recent entanglements, we must have learned that, at the highest levels, there is no place for ill-considered 'cracking on'. Indeed, there is a very real question as to whether armed forces are the right instrument for the kind of intervention that has been undertaken. That point, which underlies much of what this book has been about, in turn strongly implies that these are not struggles we should become involved in at all. This, of course, is primarily a political question; as we have seen, however, it is for generals to advise political leaders appropriately, and this has not been done. Air Marshal Jock Stirrup, at the time chief of the defence staff, spoke a deep truth when he said: 'We have lost an institutional capacity for and culture of strategic thought.'[4] This capacity can only be developed when the fact and cause of its absence has been internalized. That will require a culture shift involving far greater self-criticism and the commensurate assumption of responsibility. Signs of that shift are not yet wholly apparent.

It is open to serious doubt whether similar adventures on the scale of those in Iraq and Afghanistan will be undertaken. Unfortunately, military doctrine, equipment and capability are, and will remain, geared to 'expeditionary warfare'. And there is little doubt that the armed forces will retain their enthusiasm for 'expeditionary warfare': the preservation of 'big-ticket' equipment items and units depends upon it. The public, however, has, for the moment, lost its appetite for foreign adventurism. Unfortunately the hasty British involvement in Libya in April 2011 suggests that – contrary to Templer's example – generals may still be failing to advise that before any military commitment it is essential that a political objective be set and sufficient resources made available.

The defeats – let us not mince words – in the civil wars – the 'counter-insurgencies' in Helmand and Basra need not have been so comprehensive; indeed, they need not have happened at all. Unlike Malaya, in Basra the British started with a 'winning hand' and played it poorly. In Helmand, they managed to ignore several factors to which any Afghan could and would have drawn their attention (and to which several soldiers did) – this was the single worst possible province into which the British could crash.

The form of 'expeditionary warfare' on which Britain's armed forces staked their future has proved to be beyond their commanders' capabilities. A failure to adapt, antediluvian structures and intelligence systems, deployment schedules that ensured a lack of continuity, a cavalier attitude to post-entry planning, a mentality geared to an excessive readiness to use extreme violence, an attachment to archaic traditions and imagined histories – all of these factors played their part. Inadequate equipment and a dearth of personnel coexisted alongside a vastly swollen command structure that was proportionately eight times the size of that of the US marines.

This produced armed forces that were 'simultaneously bloatedly fat and dangerously lean'.[5] The commensurate lack of accountability and the 'all must have prizes' approach resulted in a failure of accountability, with a consequent lack of incentive to change track.

Taken in by their own legends of triumph in Malaya, Kenya and Cyprus, as well as Northern Ireland, our military leaders failed to extract from those wars any relevant lessons – the most notable of which would be that insurgencies and rebellions – civil wars all – can only be fought if there is not just government, but also all the frameworks that government implies. The shibboleths of Malaya and Northern Ireland have the most limited relevance in the face of the totally different problems we have created for ourselves in Iraq – and even more in Afghanistan. Indeed, 'far from being the recognised authority in these countries, with all that implies in terms of broad control over governmental security forces and a pre-existing bureaucratic structure, the army operates as a "guest" of the host nation, while being further subordinate to allies'.[6] The 'comprehensive approach' is little more than a fiction.

There have been some temporary palliatives – notably a more broadminded approach to culture, with the creation of a British equivalent of the US Human Terrain Systems.[7] These address some current problems, but they do not even acknowledge deeper problems. Attractive at first blush, all the notions of protecting the people or of population-centred 'counterinsurgency' exist on the presumption that the 'people' want to be protected in the way the British presume they do. The assumptions inherent in these approaches are of a war being done *to* the people. More nuanced ideas of using soft 'influence' are effective only when some effort is made to ensure that influence moves in both directions. Intelligence needs to move beyond a focus on 'finding, fixing and finishing' the 'enemy'.

Finally, the lie has been given to the seductive myth of 'punching above our weight' militarily. As anyone even remotely familiar with boxing will readily acknowledge, punching above one's weight is to be avoided if at all possible. There is no virtue in entering a fight at a disadvantage. Heroic, outnumbered actions are not primarily accounts of courage; they are often testaments to inadequate contingency planning and poor strategy. The purpose of military action backed by well-thought-out strategy is to apply maximum force to an enemy's key centres of gravity, not to allow forces too small for the task to be in a position where they can be overrun or fail.

So what now?

It is clear what will happen in the medium term. By 2015, most, if not all, British combat troops will be out of Afghanistan and the Taliban or groups very like it will continue to fight with warlords over control of the rich poppy fields of the South. The Iraq war is effectively over for the British. As with Vietnam, arguments will trickle on for decades about the causes, conduct and results of both wars. One thing is certain, though: the reputation of the British army has been seriously damaged. The British were at sea in both places, devoid of viable doctrine, without awareness of their environment, lacking adequate forces and minus any coherent strategy to pursue. All this was coupled with a hubris which attracted its inevitable riposte – nemesis. Blood, treasure and reputation have been liberally spent. The inevitable inquiries into the disasters will have troops of generals united in sticking to the same line, which might be summarized thus: 'Things did not go quite according to plan, but it all worked out fine in the end.' This has been very much the pattern of evidence given by many senior military officers to the Chilcot Inquiry, the declared purpose of which is 'not to apportion blame'. One notable exception to this 'sticking to the line' was General Sir Graeme Lamb, who led the successful 'key leader engagement' strategy for the entire coalition in Baghdad, bringing Iraqi leaders 'back' from insurgency. He was asked at the Iraq Inquiry what lessons had been learned from Iraq. 'A raft of lessons', he replied, 'few of them learnt I sense.'[8]

One alternative to admitting the truth – of failure if not defeat – is to rewrite what happened, making out that it was all part of an overall failing coalition effort. It was not the British that did not come up to the mark: it was the fault of the US or our NATO allies; or 'we were part of a wider effort'. Besides, the politicians did not dedicate the right resources. As we saw, that last argument is decidedly double edged: it is for generals to balance aims and capabilities and to advise on what can be done. As we have seen in this book, the shortfalls of Basra and Helmand were indeed specifically *British* failures, not coalition failures.

There is nothing unusual or new about this process of assessment of failure, or lack of it. Britain avoided a sensible and comprehensive analysis of what went right and what went wrong in the Second World War by the simple expedient of ignoring the need for one. Once the absolute requirements of national defence recede, the amateurs go back to their civilian lives, the 'professionals' take over and we get 'horses and tank moments' without the knowledge, awareness or open-mindedness to deal with them.

It is important now that the truth of British involvement in these last two disastrous wars is acknowledged. Only then can there be a really effective rethink of what UK forces, and particularly the army, are truly capable of doing, and only then can a brutally honest, outward-facing effort be made to calibrate its aims to its capabilities. This is not a question of kit, but of approach.

Another option for senior officers is to blame everything on inadequate resources. This, as we have seen, is the 'stab in the back' story. Yet the truth is far worse than that. What really happened was that generals, ill-trained and inadequately educated in the basic elements of strategy, failed in their role as speakers of truth to power.

Three suggestions

There has been no shortage of problems outlined in this book. Commanders are fond of telling their subordinates that they do not wish to hear problems, only solutions. I offer here three reforms which would, in my view, begin to arrest the symptoms, and indeed the cause, of our failures. I believe that they would assist in opening the networks of the British military machine.

First, our generals have not proved up to the task. We need better ones. There is no point in tiptoeing around this: let us reduce the number of generals and take steps to increase their diversity and quality. We should cut the number of officers with one star or more, across all three services, from 500 to 150. This would make the corps of generals 'only' twice the size, proportionately, of the complement of general officers in the US marines, and about three times the size of the Israeli equivalent. How the numbers might be apportioned would be a matter for debate. Why do we need more than one four-star general officer, for example? The seventeen three-star officers could be cut to one for each of the services. The 130 major generals (and equivalent admirals and air marshals), sufficient to command many dozens of divisions, might surely be reduced to forty or so. Why do we need a rank of brigadier at all? The command of much larger brigades was usually assumed by full colonels (who were given the *appointment* of brigadier-general) until 1920. We have 800 full colonel equivalents in all services, surely enough to command twelve brigades and the very, very few remaining naval seagoing squadrons and RAF air groups.

By diversity, I do not mean racial or social – although the racial and social homogeneity of the very senior ranks of all services is a marvel in itself. Indeed, it was only in 2009 that the first woman completed the Higher Command and Staff Course (HCSC) at Shrivenham, and she was a civilian. Lindy Cameron, a DfID official, later successfully took on the post of Head of the Provincial Reconstruction Team in Helmand. Generals reproduce in their own image, and it is therefore not surprising that this process produces so few free-thinking senior officers. It is time that promotion to brigadier and above was governed by more than the 'tick in the box' approach adopted now. *All* general officer aspirants should be required to complete a course in basic strategic thought as part of the selection process. Such a course should not be run by the current Defence Academy, which admits a very small number every year in any event. The HCSC is designed to produce commanders of operations. The course is intended to deal with the nuts and bolts of day-to-day command and decision making. It contains very little, if any, strategy.

A board of experts might be convened to provide training in this key art and to establish where generals should and do fit in. Such a board should have on it the best thinkers in the UK and the world – people such as Hew Strachan (Oxford), Colin Gray (Reading) or Paul Rogers (Bradford), all of whom come from very different perspectives. There is no reason why masters from other countries should not be invited to give seminars – such as Eliot Cohen or Edward Luttwak. Why not include some highly effective business leaders and thinkers as well? Such a (virtually cost-free) exercise has the potential to be world leading. The need for greatly improved strategic education is now being realized. A recent parliamentary report by the House of Commons Public Administration Committee characterized the recent wars as 'strategic failures' and recommended a 'cultural change' with an attendant educational programme for military officers and their civil service colleagues.[9] The former chief of the defence staff Sir Jock Stirrup has also identified a deficit in strategic thinking and has set up a 'strategic forum' for promising senior officers 'to engage in virtual debate'.[10] This is alongside another initiative, under which a strategic advisory group has been set up, composed of exactly the sort of academic and other experts advocated here. A promising start, but only a start. The next step might be to bring the two groups together. One (needless to say retired) former senior officer and highly innovative strategist, Commodore Steven Jermy, has even proposed the establishment of a new strategic politico-military 'school' or system of strategic thought.[11] A new mechanism for the development of generals might be the occasion to explore such ideas.

One-star officers, with their myriad staffs and secretaries, may truly be regarded as 'million-pound men' (they are, of course, mostly men). I suggest, as a second reform, that over time the savings that accrue from this cull of hundreds of million-pound officers should be invested in setting up a UK equivalent to the US Advanced Civil Schooling programme. This would allow officers and warrant officers with the potential and the will to do so to get out of their social and intellectual comfort zones and explore new thought in graduate research study in *civilian* institutions. The British are falling far behind the US and other nations in this respect, and that needs to change. At the very least, a British equivalent to the US Command and General Staff College's 'soldier scholar' programme, involving half a dozen promising officers per year, is surely not beyond even current resources. There is certainly a realization in the higher reaches of the army that this has to happen. General Sir Richard Dannatt, the recently retired chief of the general staff, says as much in his thoughtful and blunt autobiography *Leading from the Front*. Referring to the crop of superbly educated US officers he comments: 'We need to look closely at how we can re-invest in education for this generation of officers, if we wish to identify the next generation of military thinkers.'[12]

Finally, I suggest a wholesale review of how the British military machine functions in civil and internal conflict. It is simply inadequate to label its activities 'counterinsurgencies' or 'stabilization operations' and write hefty manuals about them. It may well be that the kind of civil wars and quasi-occupations in which the UK armed forces have become involved are indeed 'the only show in town'. Time will tell. If that is the case, the British soldier needs to be recalibrated to deal with ideas like human security, in the absence of resources for traditional counterinsurgency. Such a review must involve a wide community of civilian and military thought, unlike the 2010 Strategic Defence and Security Review, which in many respects was an ill-thought-out reheat of its 1998 predecessor. It took no account of the excellent *Future Character of Conflict* paper, and is rightly regarded as an exercise in capability reassessment, rather than one with any true strategic coherence.[13] A review of the kind I suggest would address such questions as force structure, deployments, expertise and training. Previous chapters will, I hope, have illustrated the need to ensure that realistic consideration is given to the nature of the wars that might need to be fought.

A good starting point for such a review might be the ideas derived from discussions of senior commanders convened by General Sir Richard Dannatt during his time as chief of the general staff. It was clear to these senior officers that the army will need to develop very different skills if it is to be able to function in new environments. Accordingly, officers' training could and should involve a far more diverse range of training and development than is now generally available. This might include postings to DfID, police forces in Africa or equally useful if less exotic attachments to local authorities. As General Dannatt put it in his autobiography:

> Alongside combat operations, the availability of a multi-disciplined and inter-agency organisation capable of both fighting alongside local forces and delivering reconstruction and development tasks in areas where the civil agencies cannot operate, is extremely attractive ... This is the stuff that was second nature to our grandfathers and great-uncles.[14]

As I argued in Chapter 10, the corollary of this entirely sensible proposal is that officers will need to become far more specialized and professional. Such a radical re-alignment of military training, approach and education, however, will require more than a few informal discussions. Nonetheless there do appear to be signs of an appreciation at senior levels of the need for a true opening of networks.

There is a danger that this approach will be misunderstood – there may well come a time when we need the conventional capabilities that the armed forces possess in such depth. Overconcentration on 'wars among the people' might easily result in these 'high-end' skills atrophying or in entirely new skills not being developed. Yet, as matters stand, the ruinous war in Afghanistan is 'the only show in town'. The fall-out from the longest foreign engagement undertaken by British forces since the end of Empire will take decades to settle. It may also define the army and other services for decades.

There are very clear and very dangerous indications that the focus on the army and its needs in fighting its small wars is subsuming many of the warfighting skills of the other services, which resent the army's 'Falklands Moment' approach to the recent conflicts. The briefest conversation with naval or RAF officers (or indeed many clear-thinking army officers) reveals a real concern that the armed forces will not be ready for forms of 'strategic shock', other than those involving ill-armed peasants or suicide bombers. This is the danger of which US army academic Colonel Gian Gentile constantly warns.[15] There may come a time when the threats we face require our defence forces to take far more literally their advertised role of defence.

Threats may take forms at least as damaging as conventional war, such as cyber attack.[16] Now that transport systems, bank transactions, food, energy and fuel delivery all depend on highly complex computerized systems, even a medium-scale cyber attack could do more damage to a country's infra-structure in a few minutes than the Luftwaffe managed to inflict over several years. The well-publicized capability of the Chinese or Russian armed forces in cyber warfare represents their equivalent of Bomber Command.

We return to Michael Howard's often quoted comment: 'I am tempted to declare dogmatically that whatever the doctrine the Armed Forces are working on now, they have got it wrong. What matters is their capacity to get it right quickly when the moment arrives.' That capacity must lie not in expensive kit but in the minds of its leaders. Less often quoted is Howard's view (in the same article) that in future conflicts there may be limited opportunity to learn from mistakes:

> If there were to be another conflict the first battle may be the last ... the social changes of our time may so transform the whole nature of warfare that the mode of thought of the military professional today will be, at

best, inadequate or, at worst, irrelevant. This is the kind of change for which we must today be prepared and able, if necessary, to adjust ... the alternative is disappearance and defeat.[17]

Getting it right

The 'capacity to get it right quickly when the moment arrives': the British armed forces as a whole need to begin seriously to consider the development of that capability to adapt and learn at all levels. If nothing else, the last ten years have shown that relying on your reputation and falling back on self-congratulation will not suffice. There are some encouraging signs that very many of the rising cadre of middle-ranking British officers – lieutenant colonel and below – who have seen at first hand much of what has been described in this book, recognize the depth of the problems within the senior officer corps. These promising leaders need to be cherished *now*. They need to be given the chance, as the best of their American (and evidently Chinese) colleagues already have, to develop their approaches and innovate in environments far removed from the officers' mess or wardroom.

Unfortunately many of these middle-ranking officers are retiring early. It is to be hoped that the fine, highly experienced younger officers who decide to press on are not 'selected out' at key points, and that new generations of senior officers are not composed of ciphers of the old. The few years following the wars of Iraq and Afghanistan will be pivotal in the development of the armed forces as a whole, and the army in particular. The Strategic Defence and Security Review of late 2010 changed little in the posture of the armed forces as 'expeditionary'. Lessons have been 'identified'. Only time and future operations will determine whether they have been 'learned'.

The consequence of failing to act on the lessons of failure in Iraq and Afghanistan may be that the next 'strategic shock' proves devastating for Britain as a whole, not simply for some hundreds of soldiers, or thousands of citizens of the countries they occupy. Unlike Iraq and Afghanistan, the next war that is fought – whatever form it takes – may well not be a war of choice.

Abbreviations and Acronyms

ACSC	Advanced Command and Staff Course
AH	attack helicopter
AOR	area of responsibility
AOSB	Army Officer Selection Board
CIGS	chief of the imperial general staff
COIN	COunterINsurgency
CPA	Coalition Provisional Authority
DCDC	Development, Concepts and Doctrine Centre
DCDS(C)	deputy chief of the defence staff with responsibility for commitments
DfID	Department for International Development
DOCEX	document intelligence
F3EA	find, fix, finish, exploit, analyse
FCO	Foreign and Commonwealth Office
FOO	forward observation officer
FRL	former regime loyalist
IED	improvised explosive device
IMINT	imagery intelligence
IPB	intelligence preparation of the battlefield
IRA	Irish Republican Army
ISAF	International Security Assistance Force
ICSC	Initial Command and Staff Course

ISTAR	Intelligence Surveillance Target Acquisition and Reconnaissance
IWPR	Institute for War and Peace Reporting
JAM	Jaish al-Mahdi
JDAM	Joint Direct Attack Munition
JSCSC	Joint Services Command and Staff College
LEI	locally employed interpreter
MASINT	measurement and signatures intelligence
MITT	Military Instruction and Training Team
MND N	Multi-National Division North
MND SE	Multi-National Division South East
MoD	Ministry of Defence
MOG	Mobile Operational Group
MRLA	Malay Races Liberation Army
MSSG	Military Stabilisation Support Group
NCO	non-commissioned officer
OMLET	Operational Mentor Liaison Team
OMS	Office of the Martyr Sadr
OSINT	open source intelligence
PIFWC	person indicted for war crimes (Piffwick)
PJHQ	Permanent Joint Headquarters
PRT	Provincial Reconstruction Team
RMP	Royal Military Police
RUSI	Royal United Services Institute
SAS	Special Air Service
SCU	Serious Crimes Unit
SDR	Strategic Defence Review
SIGINT	signals intelligence
SIS	Secret Intelligence Service
SMA	Sher Muhammed Akhundzada
SOE	Special Operations Executive
TECHINT	technical intelligence
UAV	unmanned aerial vehicle
WMD	weapons of mass destruction

Notes

Introduction

1. Professor Sir Michael Howard, *Captain Professor*, Continuum, 2006, p. 155.
2. John Mockaitis, *The Iraq War*, p. 11, cited in Alexander Alderson, 'The validity of British Army counterinsurgency doctrine after the war in Iraq, 2003–2009', PhD thesis, available at: https://dspace.lib.cranfield.ac.uk/bitstream/1826/4264/1/100126-Alderson-PhD%20 Thesis.pdf
3. The best of these is Lewis Page, *Lions, Donkeys and Dinosaurs*, Heinemann, 2006. Frequently sniffed at by senior British military officers as 'polemic', much enjoyed by more junior officers, it is in fact a very well researched and informed critique of procurement and equipment matters. It is also highly readable.
4. See Professor Sir Michael Howard, 'The use and abuse of military history', Lecture to the Royal United Services Institute in 1961, *RUSI Journal*, 138:1 (1993), pp. 26–30.
5. James Fergusson, *One Million Bullets*, Bantam Press, 2008, p. 160.
6. Evidence of Sir Sherard Cowper-Coles to Parliamentary Committee on Foreign Affairs, 9 November 2010: www.publications.parliament.uk/pa/cm201011/cmselect/ cmfaff/c514-iii/c51401.htm
7. Page, *Lions, Donkeys and Dinosaurs*.
8. Richard North, *Ministry of Defeat, the British in Iraq 2003–2009*, Continuum, 2009.
9. Patrick Cockburn, *The Occupation: War and Resistance in Iraq*, Verso, 2007.
10. Fergusson, *One Million Bullets*; James Fergusson, *Taliban*, Bantam Press, 2010; David Loyn, *Butcher and Bolt*, Hutchinson, 2008; Stephen Grey, *Operation Snakebite*, Viking/ Penguin, 2009.
11. For a fine overview of the strategic mistakes from an insider's perspective, see Steven Jermy, *Strategy for Action: Using force wisely in the 21st century*, Knightstone Publishing, 2011.
12. Report of the Public Administration Select Committee of the House of Commons, *Who Does UK National Strategy?* October 2010, p. 10, available at: www.publications. parliament.uk/pa/cm201011/cmselect/cmpubadm/435/435.pdf
13. See, for example, Patrick Porter, 'Why Britain doesn't do grand strategy', *RUSI Journal*, 155:4 (2010), pp. 6–12.

14. Dannatt, General Sir Richard, *Leading from the Front*, Bantam, 2010, p. 122.
15. At the height of their involvement, British military forces comprised about 9 per cent of foreign forces in Afghanistan. Now the figure is closer to 7 per cent. They make up much less than 2 per cent of total security forces, once the Afghan police and army are taken into account. In Iraq, the figures are similar: after the invasion itself, the proportion of UK forces was 5 per cent or less of the total numbers engaged.
16. The impressive Captain Leo Docherty was effectively dismissed for some relatively mild critical remarks about his time in Afghanistan in 2006. Fortunately, it enabled him to write the outstanding *Desert of Death* (Faber, 2008).
17. For a master class in perceptions of strategy, see the evidence given at the UK Parliament's Public Administration Committee as it discussed 'Who Does Grand Strategy?' on 9 September 2010 with Professors Lindley-French, Hennessy and Strachan. Available at: www.publications.parliament.uk/pa/cm201011/cmselect/cmpubadm/435/10090901.htm The full report is available at: www.publications.parliament.uk/pa/cm201011/cmselect/cmpubadm/435/43502.htm#evidence
18. An excellent account of the confusion as to exactly where responsibility lies for the creation of national strategy from the perspective of a political insider is to be found in Matt Cavanagh, 'Inside the Anglo-Saxon war machine', *Prospect*, December (2010), pp. 69–71.
19. General Sir John Kiszely, *Post-Modern Challenges for Modern Warriors*, Shrivenham Papers no. 5, September 2007.

Chapter 1: 'Ridiculous Expectations'

1. *The Times*, 22 August 1919.
2. Rod Thornton, 'Countering Arab insurgencies: The British experience' in Tim Benbow and Rod Thornton (eds), *Dimensions of Counter-Insurgency: Applying experience to practice*, Routledge, 2008, p. 7.
3. Thornton, 'Countering Arab insurgencies', p. 9.
4. David Omissi, *Air Power and Colonial Control 1919–1939*, Manchester University Press, 1990.
5. Thornton, 'Countering Arab insurgencies', p. 9.
6. Cockburn, *The Occupation*, p. 14.
7. Evidence of Lieutenant General Sir Peter Wall to the Iraq Inquiry, 14 December 2009.
8. Colonel Tim Collins, speaking on the BBC *Today* programme, 14 September 2010, report available at: www.bbc.co.uk/news/uk-politics-11296829
9. For a full account of their involvement, see Helen Fry, *Denazification*, History Press, 2010.
10. An excellent article on this is: Kenneth McCreedy, 'Planning the peace: Operation Eclipse and the occupation of Germany', *Journal of Military History*, 65:3, pp. 713–39.
11. *Ibid.*
12. Similar planning took place prior to Operation Husky, the taking of Sicily. Later in the war, the Soviet army prepared a similar operation to ensure the rapid restoration of basic services to a devastated Berlin. See Antony Beevor, *Berlin: The Downfall*, Viking, 2005, p. 321 (cited in Cockburn, *The Occupation*).
13. Evidence of Commodore Steven Jermy to the Public Administration Committee in its inquiry into UK strategy, 16 September 2010, Q 219, available at: www.publications.parliament.uk/pa/cm201011/cmselect/cmpubadm/435/10091602.htm

14. Cf. Norman Dixon, *On the Psychology of Military Incompetence*, Pimlico, 1976, *passim*.
15. Statement of Major General Tim Cross to the Iraq Inquiry, 7 December 2009.
16. Evidence of Major General Tim Cross to the Iraq Inquiry, 7 December 2009.
17. Evidence of General Sir Anthony Piggott to the Iraq Inquiry, 4 December 2009.
18. He was asked at one point by Professor Friedman: 'The general criticism is not that the plan was wrong, but that there wasn't any plan at all?' Viggers: 'Correct.'
19. Evidence of General Viggers to the Iraq Inquiry, 9 December 2009.
20. Interview with senior special forces officer, 2 October 2010.
21. Interview with senior member of 7 Armoured Brigade staff during Kosovo operations in 1999 (October 2010). One of those innovations was ensuring that potentially violent action could be forestalled by the simple expedient of allowing essentially blockaded Serbian populations to have protected bus links between each other and with the 'outside world'. These ideas spread throughout Kosovo, and were copied by other nations' security forces.
22. Evidence of General Graeme Lamb to the Iraq Inquiry, 9 December 2009.
23. John Keegan, *The Iraq War*, Hutchinson, 2004, pp. 175–6.
24. 'The smug superiority of the British over their peacekeeping efforts in Iraq is an insult to those of us who live there', *Guardian*, 16 February 2006.
25. A good account of this chaotic period from the point of view of an outlying office of the CPA is Rory Stewart, *Occupational Hazards*, Picador, 2007.
26. Patrick Cockburn, 'The real scandal is Blair's ignorance', *Independent*, 21 January 2011, available at: www.independent.co.uk/opinion/commentators/patrick-cockburn-the-real-scandal-is-blairs-ignorance-2190107.html
27. Cockburn, *The Occupation*, p. 112.
28. The Fourth Geneva Convention of 1949, Articles 47–78 (indeed the entire Fourth Convention) and the Fourth Hague Convention of 1907, Articles 42–56, deal explicitly and in fairly simple terms with duties of occupying powers.
29. The US, UK and Spain drafted UN Security Council Resolution 1483 of 22 May 2003, which explicitly recognized the US and UK as 'occupying powers' and recognized their 'responsibilities and obligations'. See: http://daccess-dds-ny.un.org/doc/UNDOC/GEN/N03/368/53/PDF/N0336853.pdf?OpenElement
30. Hague Convention 1907, Article 43.
31. See: www.iraqinquiry.org.uk/media/47679/iraq-theaftermath-militaryoptions-4March 2003.pdf (declassified 10 July 2010).
32. *Ibid.*, p. 5.
33. James Meikle, 'Iraq inquiry hears Washington called the shots on postwar government', *Guardian*, 10 December 2009, available at: www.guardian.co.uk/uk/2009/dec/10/chilcot-inquiry-iraq-war-sawers
34. Colonel Richard Iron, 'Northern Ireland: a case study of institutional learning and unlearning', *British Army Review*, 152 (Spring 2011).
35. Evidence from General Stewart to the Iraq Inquiry, 9 December 2009.
36. Senior British officer with extensive first-hand knowledge of Iraq, in communication with the author, November 2010.
37. 'Switched off in Basra', *New York Times*, 31 July 2005.
38. 'Rogue police officers seized in Basra', *Daily Telegraph*, 23 December 2006.
39. Adam Holloway in: http://www.defenceviewpoints.co.uk/articles-and-analysis/the-failure-of-british-political-and-military-leadership-in-iraq (article first published in Firstdefence.org.uk).

40. Royal Air Force personnel generally did only four months.

41. Conversation with intelligence officer, January 2010.

42. General Sir Richard Dannatt, interview with *Daily Mail*, 12 October 2006.

43. A brigade is intended to be a balanced, largely self-sustaining force of about 6,000 soldiers. The current order of battle includes 16 Air Assault, 1 Mechanized, 4 Mechanized, 11 Mechanized, 11 Light, 12 Mechanized, 19 Light, 7 Armoured, 20 Armoured, 52 Infantry and 3 Commando Brigade (Royal Marines).

44. Commodore Steven Jermy, 'Back to an offshore future: past and present lessons for Britain's future defence policy', in Alessio Patalano (ed.) *Maritime Strategy and National Security in Japan and Britain: From the First Alliance to Post 9/11*, University of Hawai'i press, 2010.

Chapter 2: 'Defeated, Pure and Simple'

1. British general, speaking off the record, in Paul Wood, 'Uncertainty follows Basra exit', BBC News Online, 15 December 2007, available at: http://news.bbc.co.uk/1/hi/world/middle_east/7145597.stm

2. Evidence of General Richard Shirreff to the Iraq Inquiry, 11 January 2010.

3. Interview with senior officer, February 2010.

4. General Sir Robin Fry, interviewed on BBC TV's *Secret Iraq*, October 2010.

5. See Mark Urban, *Task Force Black*, Little, Brown and Company, 2010.

6. Niel Smith and Sean MacFarland, 'Anbar awakens: the tipping point', *Military Review*, 88:2 (March–April) (2008), pp. 410–52.

7. International Crisis Group (ICG), *Iraq After the Surge*, ICG report, 30 April 2008. See Executive Summary.

8. General Erwin Rommel, cited by Eliot Cohen, *Military Misfortunes*, Free Press, 2006, p. 235.

9. Evidence of General Jonathan Shaw to the Iraq Inquiry, 11 January 2010.

10. James K. Wither, 'Basra's not Belfast: the British army, "small wars" and Iraq', *Small Wars and Insurgencies*, 20:3 (2009), pp. 611–35.

11. Hew Strachan, 'Want to understand war? Ask the generals', *The Times*, 17 March 2010.

12. This quotation is usually attributed to 'a senior American intelligence officer'. David Kilcullen, Petraeus's Australian adviser on 'counterinsurgency', said in 2008: 'it is fair to say that in 2006 the British were defeated in the field in Southern Iraq'. In 'US accuses Britain over military failings in Afghanistan', *The Times*, 16 December 2008.

13. *Where is Iraq Heading? Lessons from Basra*, Middle Eastern Report no. 67, International Crisisi Group, 25 June 2007: http://www.crisisgroup.org/en/regions/middle-east-north-africa/iraq-syria-lebanon/iraq/067-where-is-iraq-heading-lessons-from-basra.aspx

14. Howard, *Captain Professor*, p. 167.

15. '"British Forces useless in Basra", say officials', *Daily Telegraph*, 19 August 2007.

16. Urban, *Task Force Black*, p. 247.

17. *Ibid.*, p. 248.

18. 'UK has left behind murder and chaos, says Basra police chief', *Guardian*, 17 December 2007.

19. 'UK troops return Basra to Iraqis', BBC News, 17 December 2007, available at: http://news.bbc.co.uk/1/hi/uk/7146507.stm

20. Evidence of General Barney White-Spunner to the Iraq Inquiry, 9 January 2009.
21. Charles Gwynn, *Imperial Policing*, Macmillan and Co., 1936, p. 19.
22. Evidence of General Jonathan Shaw to the Iraq Inquiry, 11 January 2010.
23. Evidence of Sir Jock Stirrup to the Iraq Inquiry, 1 February 2010.
24. For an excellent account of the methods used by the legendary anti-mafia police chief Cesare Mori, see Tim Newark, *Mafia at War: Allied collusion with the mob*, Greenhill Books, 2007.
25. Evidence of Sir Jock Stirrup to the Iraq Inquiry, 1 February 2010.
26. 'Basra betrayed: when the British Army leave will the Mahdi Army replace them?', *Independent*, 25 February 2007.
27. Interview with British officer present at the time, February 2010.
28. Patrick Cockburn, *Muqtada al Sadr and the Fall of Iraq*, Faber, 2008, p. 244.
29. Interview with army officer present at the time and familiar with the situation.
30. Interview with senior British officer, February 2010.
31. 'British accused of appeasing Shi'a militia in Basra', *The Times*, 8 April 2008.
32. Interview with member of British civilian mission in Basra, February 2010.
33. Wither, 'Basra's not Belfast', p. 628.
34. Evidence of Major General Andy Salmon to the Iraq Inquiry, 20 July 2010.
35. Communication with senior British officer, April 2011.
36. *Ibid.*
37. Written statement of Mark Etherington to the Iraq Inquiry, available at: www.iraq inquiry.org.uk/media/49551/etherington-statement.pdf
38. Memorandum of Dr Eric Herring dated 28 September 2007 to the United Kingdom Parliament, House of Commons Select Committee on Defence inquiring into UK land operations in Iraq: http://www.publications.parliament.uk/pa/cm200708/cmselect/cmdfence/110/11006.htm. Cited in Wither, 'Basra's not Belfast', p. 622.
39. '"British forces useless in Basra" say officials', *Daily Telegraph* 17 August 2007.
40. General Sir Richard Dannatt, lecture to Chatham House 'Perspectives on the nature of future conflict'; 15th May 2009 available at http://www.chathamhouse.org.uk/files/14009_150509dannatt.pdf
41. Interview with senior officer, October 2010.
42. Written evidence of Sir Sherard Cowper-Coles, 23 December 2010, available at: www.publications.parliament.uk/pa/cm201011/cmselect/cmfaff/writev/afpak/afpak17.htm
43. Interview for the BBC *Today* programme, 21 January 2011, available at: http://news.bbc.co.uk/today/hi/today/newsid_9369000/9369141.stm

Chapter 3: 'Where's Helmand?'

1. www.publications.parliament.uk/pa/cm201011/cmselect/cmpubadm/435/10091602.htm at Q206.
2. See:www.mod.uk/DefenceInternet/FactSheets/OperationsFactsheets/Operations InAfghanistanWhyWeAreThere.htm
3. Fergusson, *A Million Bullets*, p. 172, quoting General Richards.
4. *Ibid.*, p. 173.
5. The battle took place on 27 July 1880. There is to this day a memorial in the form of a huge statue of a lion to those lost at 'Gereshk-Maiwand' in Reading, Berkshire. The 66th (Berkshire) Regiment was largely wiped out in the battle.

6. Colonel Ali A. Jalali and Lester W. Grau, 'Expeditionary forces: superior technology defeated – the Battle of Maiwand', *Military Review*, May–June (2001).

7. Loyn, *Butcher and Bolt*, p. 120.

8. Abdul Zaeef, *My Life with the Taleban*, Hurst, 2010, p. 242.

9. Fergusson, *One Million Bullets*, p. 174.

10. Victoria Schofield, *Afghan Frontier*, Tauris Paperbacks, 2010, p. 230.

11. Evidence of Air Chief Marshal Sir Glen Torpy to the Iraq Inquiry, 18 January 2010.

12. A good account of this period can be found in Docherty, *Desert of Death*.

13. Fergusson, *Taliban*, p. 134.

14. Damien McElroy, 'Afghan governor turned 3,000 men over to Taliban', *Daily Telegraph*, 20 November 2009, available at: www.telegraph.co.uk/news/worldnews/asia/afghanistan/6615329/Afghan-governor-turned-3000-men-over-to-Taliban.html

15. Interview with Jean Mackenzie, February 2010.

16. Interview with senior British officer, October 2010.

17. Interview with Jean Mackenzie, February 2010.

18. Fergusson, *Taliban*, p. 134.

19. Interview with UK Special Forces soldier, October 2010.

20. Grey, *Operation Snakebite*, p. 51.

21. Stuart Tootal, *Danger Close: Commanding 3 PARA in Afghanistan*, John Murray, 2009, p. 22.

22. *Ibid.*, p. 21.

23. The Israelis procured these helicopters 'off the shelf' from the US for about £14 million each. The British decided to make their own version, which did not at first work – their missile system had the unfortunate effect of damaging the aircraft's rotors when fired. Eventually the cost rose to nearly £50 million for each helicopter. For a detailed description of the story of waste, corruption and incompetence of this and other UK procurement disasters, see Page, *Lions, Donkeys and Dinosaurs*.

24. See Anthony King, 'Understanding the Helmand campaign: British military operations in Afghanistan', available at: www.chathamhouse.org.uk/files/16165_86_2king.pdf

25. The British version of the AH-64 'Apache' helicopter system had recently been cleared for operational use after very lengthy and costly delays.

26. Interview with UK senior officer involved in the planning of this stage of the operation.

27. Statement of Afghan intelligence officer to Afghan human rights organizations, Lashkar Gah, October 2007.

28. Email from Lieutenant Tom Burne, quoted in Fergusson, *A Million Bullets*, p. 157.

29. Conversation with senior special forces officer, October 2010. In fairness, the officer qualified this by saying that, as a combat soldier not averse to challenge, he may well have made the same decision.

30. Interview with senior officer, March 2010.

31. Interview with Jean Mackenzie, February 2010.

32. 'Officers attack MOD muddle', *The Times*, 22 March 2009, available at: www.timesonline.co.uk/tol/news/uk/article5950402.ece

33. Grey, *Operation Snakebite*, pp. 90–1.

34. *Ibid.*, p. 91.

35. Interview with British military intelligence officer, 2010.

36. Interview with Dan Jarman, February 2010.

37. Loyn, *Butcher and Bolt*, p. 294.

38. Tootal, *Danger Close,* p. 282.
39. Interview with Dan Jarman, February 2010.
40. Interview with a UK aid official.
41. Loyn, *Butcher and Bolt,* p. 297.
42. International Crisis Group (ICG), *Countering Afghanistan's Insurgency: No quick fixes,* Asia Report 123, ICG, 2006, available at: www.crisisgroup.org/en/regions/asia/south-asia/afghanistan/123-countering-afghanistans-insurgency-no-quick-fixes.aspx. Cited by Loyn, *Butcher and Bolt,* p. 301.
43. Frank Ledwidge, 'Justice and counter-insurgency in Afghanistan: a missing link', *RUSI Journal,* 154:1(2009), pp. 6–9.

Chapter 4: 'A Bleeding Ulcer'

1. General McChrystal of Marjah district, Helmand, 29 May 2010.
2. US army soldiers do twelve-month tours, although US marines typically do less, reflecting their history of short, sharp operational tempo.
3. Written evidence of Sir Sherard Cowper-Coles, 23 December 2010, available at: www.publications.parliament.uk/pa/cm201011/cmselect/cmfaff/writev/afpak/afpak18.htm
4. Operation Panchai Palang ('Panther's Claw', June 2009), Operation Moshtarak ('Together').
5. Grey, *Operation Snakebite,* p. 55.
6. Evidence of Sir Sherard Cowper-Coles to Parliamentary Committee on Foreign Affairs, 9 November 2010, Q99, available at: www.publications.parliament.uk/pa/cm201011/cmselect/cmfaff/c514-iii/c51401.htm
7. Andrew Mackay and Stephen Tatham, *Behavioural Conflict: from general to strategic corporal: complexity, adaptation and influence,* Shrivenham Papers no. 9, 2009, p. 13.
8. Evidence of Jolyon Leslie to Parliamentary Committee on Foreign Affairs, 13 October 2010, Q30, available at: www.publications.parliament.uk/pa/cm201011/cmselect/cmfaff/c514-i/c51401.htm
9. House of Commons Foreign Affairs Committee: Fourth Report. 'The UK's foreign policy approach to Afghanistan and Pakistan', available at: www.publications.parliament.uk/pa/cm201011/cmselect/cmfaff/514/51402.htm at para 33
10. Gordon Brown in General Election TV debate, 16 April 2010.
11. Conversation with the author, August 2007.
12. Warren Chin, 'Colonial warfare in a post-colonial state: British military operations in Helmand province, Afghanistan', *Defence Studies,* 10:1 (2010), pp. 215–47, at p. 226.
13. Mackay and Tatham, *Behavioural Conflict,* p. 14.
14. Interview with senior officer, July 2010.
15. 'Triumph for British forces in Boy's Own-style Kajaki mission', *The Times,* 3 September 2008.
16. www.mod.uk/DefenceInternet/DefenceNews/MilitaryOperations/KajakiDamTroopsReturnToBase.htm
17. 'Afghanistan's insurgents on brink of defeat', *Daily Telegraph,* 2 June 2008.
18. '"We can't defeat the Taleban"' says Brigadier Mark Carleton Smith', *The Times,* 6 October 2008.
19. King, 'Understanding the Helmand campaign', p. 324.
20. John Nagl interview for PBS *Obama's War,* available at: www.pbs.org/wgbh/pages/frontline/obamaswar/interviews/nagl.html

21. Rory Stewart, interviewed for PBS *Obama's War*, available at: www.pbs.org/wgbh/pages/frontline/obamaswar/interviews/stewart.html

22. 'Afghan Operation is "worthless"', BBC News, 7 March 2009, available at: http://news.bbc.co.uk/1/hi/uk/7929785.stm

23. Conversation with Jean Mackenzie, head of IWPR and regular visitor to Helmand.

24. Channel 4 documentary, 'Panther's Claw: on the Front Line with the Black Watch', 19 August 2009 available at: http://www.channel4.com/news/panthers-claw-on-the-front-line-with-the-black-watch

25. Ian Pannell, reporting for the BBC, 5 August 2010.

26. Interview with senior special forces officer, October 2010.

27. A new Helmand Plan was eventually adopted.

28. Evidence of Professor Lindley-French to the Public Administration Committee in its inquiry into UK strategy, 9 September 2010, Q17, available at: www.publications.parliament.uk/pa/cm201011/cmselect/cmpubadm/435/10090901.htm Whether being 'ally of first resort' is an appropriate objective is, of course, a difficult political question, the answer to which depends heavily upon whether a close assessment of national priorities has been made. Such an assessment has not yet taken place.

29. www.mod.uk/DefenceInternet/FactSheets/OperationsFactsheets/OperationsIn AfghanistanWhyWeAreThere.htm

30. Adam Holloway at: www.defenceviewpoints.co.uk/articles-and-analysis/the-failure-of-british-political-and-military-leadership-in-iraq. Article first published at Firstdefence.org.uk

31. *The UK's Foreign Policy Approach to Afghanistan and Pakistan*, Report of the UK Parliamentary Committee on Foreign Affairs (March 2011), para 209, available at: www.publications.parliament.uk/pa/cm201011/cmselect/cmfaff/514/51413.htm#a56

32. *Ibid.*, para 182.

33. *Ibid.*, para 210.

34. http://blogs.abcnews.com/politicalpunch/2010/06/cia-at-most-50100-al-qaeda-in-afghanistan.html

35. 'British al-Qaeda hub "is biggest in West"', *Daily Telegraph*, 15 January 2010.

36. Claudia Harvey and Mark Wilkinson, 'The value of doctrine: assessing British officers' perspectives', *RUSI Journal*, 154:6 (2009), p. 26. Junior officers tended to provide better answers.

37. Evidence of Sir Sherard Cowper-Coles to Parliamentary Committee on Foreign Affairs, 9 November 2010, Q92, available at: www.publications.parliament.uk/pa/cm201011/cmselect/cmfaff/c514-iii/c51401.htm

38. *The UK's Foreign Policy Approach to Afghanistan and Pakistan*, Report of the UK Parliamentary Committee on Foreign Affairs, note 119 at para 74, available at: www.publications.parliament.uk/pa/cm201011/cmselect/cmfaff/514/51409.htm

39. Letter from Matthew Hoh to US Secretary of State, available at: www.washingtonpost.com/wp-srv/hp/ssi/wpc/ResignationLetter.pdf?sid=ST2009102603447

40. Interview with British official, June 2009.

41. Rodric Braithwaite, *Afgantsy*, Profile Books, 2011, p. 332.

42. *Ibid.*, p. 335.

43. The best example of this technique used successfully was the 3rd Armored Cavalry Regiment under Colonel H.R. McMaster in Tal Afar, 2005–6.

44. There was an especially savage massacre of Soviet civilian advisers and their families in Herat in 1979.

45. Interview with senior British official, June 2010.
46. 'A soldier writes from Afghanistan', *Independent on Sunday*, 20 February 2011.
47. Interview with senior retired army officer, February 2010.

Chapter 5: Dereliction of Duty: The Generals and Strategy

1. 'MOD faces questions over why Army majors on generals', *The Times*, 29 December 2009. Official UK defence statistics for 2009, available at: www.dasa.mod.uk/modintranet/UKDS/UKDS2009/c2/table206.html
2. There are six divisions, although the other four act as administrative formations with, at best, a very limited active operational capability. See: www.army.mod.uk/structure/1592.aspx
3. Official UK defence statistics for 2009, available at: www.dasa.mod.uk/modintranet/UKDS/UKDS2009/c2/table206.html
4. There are about 160 helicopters in the army, including 48 training aircraft. See: www.armedforces.co.uk/army/listings/l0051.html
5. There are 345 Challenger II tanks 'available'. See: www.armedforces.co.uk/army/listings/l0023.html Many of these, however, have been mothballed – held in 'storage'.
6. Although the US Marine Corps relies for much of its support – logistics and transport – on the other services.
7. Forty brigadiers, twenty-three major generals, seventeen lieutenant generals and four full generals.
8. 10 USC 526.
9. http://seattletimes.nwsource.com/html/nationworld/2012735296_generals27.html
10. Figures taken from Monthly Army List, February 1910, available at the library of the Joint Services Command and Staff College, Shrivenham.
11. This figure presumably included less operational officers, such as three dukes and the king of Spain.
12. The same was the case for commodores in the navy, an appointment for naval captains posted as commanders of *squadrons* of ships.
13. Page, *Lions, Donkeys and Dinosaurs*. Chapter 9, 'Brass hats and rear echelons', provides an excellent account of the eccentric structure of the armed forces in its higher reaches.
14. Further down the scale there are also two forms of lieutenant and two grades of colonel.
15. Similar numbers apply for the other two services.
16. Grey, *Operation Snakebite*, p. 51.
17. Interview with retired two-star general, June 2010.
18. Navy commanders or air force wing commanders.
19. There are a total of 187,000 in the armed forces. All figures are from UK defence statistics for 2009, available at: www.dasa.mod.uk/modintranet/UKDS/UKDS2009/c2/table206.html. See also Andrew Dorman Smith, 'Rank nonsense', *Parliamentary Brief*, 12:8 (April 2010), p. 15.
20. None of this talent comes cheap, of course. Each officer employed by the armed forces will cost several million pounds over the twenty or so years of his career and the decades of his pension. Each of the 500 general officers is paid at least £94,467 per annum (for one-star officers), rising to £164,281 for full generals. That, of course, is in pay alone – those figures do not include the substantial benefits they enjoy.

21. The same pattern, by the way, is evident in the contemporary US armed forces, where successful officers are regularly recycled into the line.
22. Communication to the author, November 2010.
23. See Field Marshal Sir Alan Brooke, *War Diaries 1939–45*, ed. Alex Danchev and Daniel Todman, Phoenix, 2002.
24. 'Sir Jock Stirrup's exit points to defence changes', BBC News, 13 June 2010, available at: www.bbc.co.uk/news/10304840
25. The 'Jamiat Incident', October 2005.
26. Former major generals, now lieutenant generals.
27. 'General's 10 point plan for Cameron', Channel 4 News, www.channel4.com/news/afghanistan-10-point-plan-for-uk-strategy
28. Interview with senior British officer, February 2010.
29. Theo Farrell and Stuart Gordon, 'COIN machine: the British military in Afghanistan', *Orbis*, 53:4 (2009), pp. 665–83.
30. Written evidence of Sir Sherard Cowper-Coles, 23 December 2010, available at: www.publications.parliament.uk/pa/cm201011/cmselect/cmfaff/writev/afpak/afpak18.htm
31. Paul Robinson, 'The generals must share the blame', *Spectator*, 13 October 2009.
32. *Ibid*
33. Cf. Hutton Inquiry into the death of David Kelly, Butler Inquiry into WMD, the first Bloody Sunday 'Widgery' inquiry.
34. Cf. www.iraqinquiry.org.uk/faq.aspx#O01: 'The Inquiry is not a court of law. The members of the Committee are not judges, and nobody is on trial. But if the Committee finds that mistakes were made, that there were issues which could have been dealt with better, it will say so.'
35. General Karl von Clausewitz, *On War*, translated and edited by Professor Sir Michael Howard and Peter Paret, Everyman edition, 1993, Book 8, Chapter 2, p. 700.
36. Commonly articulated by, for example, Mackubin Thomas Owens, 'Strategy and the strategic way of thinking', *Naval War College Review*, Autumn 2007, available at: www.usnwc.edu/getattachment/d73f1c33-649a-41e4-93e5-28ce624fd041/Strategy-and-the-Strategic-Way-of-Thinking—Commen
37. Hew Strachan, 'The lost meaning of strategy', *Survival*, 47:3 (2005), pp. 33–54.
38. Colin Gray, *Modern Strategy*, Oxford University Press, 1999, p. 60.
39. *Ibid*.
40. Extracted from Major General Sir John Kennedy, *The Business of War*, William Morrow, 1958. I am obliged to Colonel John Wilson for referring this extract to me.
41. Gray, *Modern Strategy*, p. 61.
42. H.R. McMaster, *Dereliction of Duty*, Harper Collins, 1998.
43. His tour in command of the 3rd Armored Cavalry Division in 2004 in the Iraqi town of Tal Afar is rightly regarded as a model of 'counterinsurgency' operations.
44. Anthony Loyd, 'Is that the sound of donkeys in Whitehall', *The Times*, 9 June 2010.
45. Minute by Sir G. Templer to Mr Churchill PREM 11/639, from *British Documents on the End of Empire*, HMSO, 1995, p. 361.
46. Directive issued by Mr Lyttleton on behalf of HMG PREM 11/639, from *British Documents on the End of Empire*, HMSO, 1995, p. 372.
47. A full discussion of the failure to understand the very fundamentals of strategy in this context is contained in Strachan, 'The lost meaning of strategy'.
48. Rupert Smith, *The Utility of Force*, Penguin, 2005, p. 215.

49. Winston Churchill, *The Gathering Storm*, 1948, p. 462, cited in Eliot Cohen, *Supreme Command*, Simon and Schuster, 2005, p. 254, n16.
50. See Field Marshal Sir Alan Brooke, *War Diaries 1939–45*.
51. Cohen, *Supreme Command*, p. 13.
52. *Ibid.*, p. 14.
53. 'Part of the problem was obsequious officers telling ministers what they wanted to hear'; Colonel Tim Collins on the BBC's *Today* programme, 14 September 2010, reported at: www.bbc.co.uk/news/uk-politics-11296829
54. Evidence of Major General Tim Cross to the Iraq Inquiry, 7 December 2009.
55. *Ibid.*
56. Evidence of Admiral Michael Boyce to the Iraq Inquiry, 3 December 2009.
57. *Ibid.*
58. Evidence of Sir Kevin Tebbit to the Iraq Inquiry, 3 February 2010.
59. Evidence of Admiral Michael Boyce to the Iraq Inquiry. Sir Kevin Tebbit glosses on this with a statement that there were such submissions.
60. Lt Col Richard Williams and Lt Gen Graeme Lamb, *Upgrading Our Armed Forces*, Policy Exchange, 2010, p. 41, available at: www.policyexchange.org.uk/images/publications/pdfs/PX_A5_Defence.pdf
61. Evidence of Sir Sherard Cowper-Coles to Parliamentary Foreign Affairs Committee, 9 November 2010, Q99, available at: www.publications.parliament.uk/pa/cm201011/cmselect/cmfaff/c514-iii/c51401.htm
62. Evidence of Tony Blair to the Iraq Inquiry, 29 January 2010.
63. Evidence of John Reid to the Iraq Inquiry, 3 February 2010.
64. Evidence of Air Chief Marshal Sir Jock Stirrup to the Iraq Inquiry, 1 February 2010.
65. Interview with senior army officer, February 2010.
66. 'British hand over Basra Command to US', *Daily Telegraph*, 31 March 2009.
67. Urban, *Task Force Black*, p. 248.
68. Evidence of Sir Kevin Tebbit to the Iraq Inquiry, 3 February 2010.
69. Evidence of General Sir Robert Fry to Public Administration Committee in its inquiry into UK strategy, 16 September 2010, Q 191, available at: www.publications.parliament.uk/pa/cm201011/cmselect/cmpubadm/435/10091602.htm
70. Max Hastings, *Finest Years: Churchill as Warlord 1940–45*, Harper Press, 2010, p. 129.
71. Interview BBC *World at One* programme, 14 October 2010.
72. Evidence of General Sir Peter Wall to the Iraq Inquiry, 14 December 2009.
73. Cf. James T. Quinlivan, 'Force requirements in stability operations', *Parameters*, Winter (1995), pp. 59–69. Available at: www.carlisle.army.mil/usawc/Parameters/Articles/1995/quinliv.htm A more recent, shorter, but rather prophetic update can be found at James T. Quinlivan, 'Burden of victory: the painful arithmetic of stability operations', *Rand Review*, Summer (2003), available at: www.rand.org/publications/randreview/issues/summer2003/burden.html
74. 'UK soldiers killed in Afghanistan', BBC News Online, 2 July 2006, available at: http://news.bbc.co.uk/1/hi/5137956.stm
75. Cited in a letter from Lieutenant Colonel Peter Richards in *British Army Review*, 144, Spring (2008), p. 103.
76. Evidence of General Sir Richard Shirreff to the Iraq Inquiry, 11 January 2010.
77. Smith, *The Utility of Force*, p. 402.
78. David Betz and Anthony Cormack, 'Hot war, cold comfort', *RUSI Journal*, 154:4 (2009), pp. 26–9, at p. 27.

79. Clausewitz, *On War*, Book One, Chapter One, section 27.
80. Evidence of Tony Blair to the Iraq Inquiry, 21 January 2011.

Chapter 6: Cracking On: British Military Culture and Doctrine

 1. 'Chaos theory', Jerome Monahan quoting Gary Sheffield, *Guardian*, 27 November 2001.
 2. For an interesting analysis by an expert sociologist of exercises at Shrivenham, see Anthony King, 'Unity is strength: staff college and the British officer corps', *British Journal of Sociology*, 60:1 (2009).
 3. In 1939 it was 84.3 per cent. In the Second World War, 34 per cent of officers were from public schools. Between 1947 and 1958 it was roughly 66 per cent. In the 1970s it was approximately 40 per cent (Jeremy Paxman, *Friends in High Places: Who runs Britain?* Penguin, 1991, pp. 225–7).
 4. www.army.mod.uk/join/selection/15305.aspx
 5. For an excellent discussion of these issues, see King, 'Unity is strength'.
 6. This phrase is emblazoned above the entrance to the Joint Staff in the Pentagon in Washington.
 7. King, 'Unity is strength'.
 8. Anthony King, 'Why we're getting it wrong in Afghanistan', *Prospect*, 156 (March 2010).
 9. General Sir John Kiszely, 'Thinking about the operational level', *RUSI Journal*, 150:6 (2005), pp. 38–43.
10. For an outstanding extended summary of the legacy, both attitudinal and particularly material, see Lewis, *Lions, Donkeys and Dinosaurs*.
11. Commander 1 (BR) Corps and NATO Northern Area commander, 1981–5.
12. Simon Ball, 'Unchanging lessons of battle', in Hew Strachan (ed.), *Big Wars and Small Wars*, Routledge, 2006, p. 147.
13. See Anthony King, 'Beyond the crisis: critical requirements for successful military transformation', *British Army Review*, 147 (Summer 2009), p. 24.
14. Development, Concepts and Doctrine Centre, *British Defence Doctrine* (JDP0-01), August 2008, pp. 5–7.
15. King, 'Understanding the Helmand campaign', p. 323.
16. For a fine discussion of this, see King, 'Why we're getting it wrong in Helmand'.
17. Development, Concepts and Doctrine Centre, *British Defence Doctrine*, pp. 5–7.
18. William F. Owen, 'The manoeuvre warfare fraud', available at: http://smallwarsjournal.com/blog/journal/docs-temp/95-owen.pdf
19. See Colin McInnes, 'The Gulf War', in Strachan (ed.), *Big Wars and Small Wars*, p. 168.
20. Williams and Lamb, *Upgrading Our Armed Forces*, p. 18.
21. As time went by, informed by experience and common sense, the orders would be reduced to a straightforward 'we are going to A to speak to B to try to find out C – Usual precautions, here is the route; any questions?'
22. Williams and Lamb, *Upgrading Our Armed Forces*, p. 18.
23. Michael Howard, 'Military science in an age of peace', *RUSI Journal*, 19:2 (1974), p. 7.
24. Iron, 'Northern Ireland: A case study of institutional learning and unlearning'.
25. See Williams and Lamb, *Upgrading Our Armed Forces*.

26. *Ibid.*, p. 22. It is instructive that the commander of this small but significant operation in Congo in 1996, Brigadier Graeme Lamb, was also the (lieutenant) general responsible for one of the more significant (and very positive) British contributions to the situation in Iraq. He coordinated the coalition initiative to 'reconcile' Sunni tribes to the Iraqi government and helped convert this low-level tactical development into a major strategic success. He was subsequently selected by General McChrystal to attempt the same role in Afghanistan, prior to the latter's self-immolation in the media in July 2010.

Chapter 7: 'Tactics without Strategy?' The Counterinsurgency Conundrum

1. 'Tactics without strategy; the noise before defeat' – Sun Tzu.
2. Jermy, *Strategy for Action*, p. 91.
3. Clausewitz, *On War*, Book One, Chapter Seven, p. 140.
4. *Ibid.*, Book One, Chapter Eight, p. 141
5. Thomas Mockaitis, *British Counterinsurgency in the Post-Imperial Era*, University of Manchester Press, 1995, p. 12. Examples of scholars extolling the 'British approach' were plentiful – prior to 2005.
6. Rear Admiral Chris Parry, speaking on the BBC *Today* programme, 10 June 2010. The speaker was director of the Development, Concepts and Doctrine Centre (2006–8). The interview is available at: http://news.bbc.co.uk/today/hi/today/newsid_8736000/8736814.stm
7. Byron Farwell, *Queen Victoria's Little Wars*, Wordsworth Edition, 1999, p. 364.
8. General Charles James Napier, cited in Farwell, *Queen Victoria's Small Wars*.
9. *Duties in Aid of the Civil Power*, HMSO, 1923, p. 3, cited by Thomas Mockaitis, *British Counterinsurgency 1919-1960*, Macmillan, 1990, p. 18.
10. Only four years before, in 1919, there had been a disgraceful departure from the concept of minimum force at Amritsar, when General Reginald Dyer had given the order for soldiers to open fire on a demonstrating crowd, killing 379 and wounding over a thousand others.
11. Matthew Hughes, 'The practice and theory of British counterinsurgency: the histories of the atrocities at the Palestinian villages of al-Bassa and Halhul, 1938–1939', *Small Wars and Insurgencies*, 20:3 (2009), pp. 528–50.
12. See also David French, 'Big wars and small wars between the wars, 1919–39', in Strachan (ed.), *Big Wars and Small Wars*, p. 36.
13. Mockaitis, *British Counterinsurgency in the Post-Imperial Era*, p. 133 cited and criticized by T.R. Moreman, ' "Small wars" and "imperial policing": the British army and the theory and practice of colonial warfare in the British empire, 1919–1939', *Journal of Strategic Studies*, 19:4 (1996), pp. 105–31, at p. 126.
14. Michael Crawshaw, 'The evolution of British COIN', MOD JDP 3–40, paragraph 3, available at: www.mod.uk/NR/rdonlyres/365FD263-1F10-4842-8929-D2491EEA8DA9/0/JDP340TheEvolutionofBritishCOINbyMichaelCrawshaw.pdf
15. See *Human Security Report 2005*, available at: www.hsrgroup.org/human-security-reports/2005/text.aspx. This reports states that Britain was involved in twenty-one 'international conflicts' between 1946 and 2003, ahead of France (19), the United States (16) and the Soviet Union.
16. Army Staff College, *Handbook on Counter-Revolutionary Warfare*, Army Staff College, 1995. In chronological order: Greece (1945–6), Palestine (1945–8), Egypt (1946–56), Malaya (1948–60), Eritrea (1949), Kenya (1952–6), Cyprus (1954–8), Aden (1955,

1956–8), Togoland (1957), Brunei (1962), Borneo (1963–66), Radfan (1964), Aden (1965–7), Dhofar (1970–6), Northern Ireland (1969–2007), Afghanistan (2001 to date) and Iraq (2003 to date). I am grateful to Martin Bayly for allowing me to read his thesis for his Oxford MPhil – 'COINing a new doctrine' (unpublished MPhil thesis, Oxford 2009) containing this information, and for the insights gained from extensive conversations with this emerging scholar.

17. Alum Gwynn Jones, quoted in Andrew Garfield *et al.*, *Succeeding in Phase IV: British Perspectives on the US Effort to Stabilise and Reconstruct Iraq*, Foreign Policy Research Institute, 2006.

18. Many of these are now critical of using Malaya as any kind of 'leading case'. See, for example, Karl Hack, 'The Malayan insurgency as counterinsurgency paradigm', *Journal of Strategic Studies*, 32:3 (June 2009), pp. 383–414; Hew Strachan, 'British counterinsurgency from Malaya to Iraq', *RUSI Journal*, 152:6 (December 2007), pp. 8–11; Wither, 'Basra's not Belfast'; Ashley Jackson, 'British counterinsurgency in history: a useful precedent?', *British Army Review*, 139 (2006), pp. 12–22.

19. Christopher Griffin, 'A revolution in colonial military affairs: Galieni, Lyautey and the "tache d'huile"', Paper prepared for the 2009 British International Studies Association Conference, Leicester, 14–16 December.

20. Evidence of Sir Suma Chakrabati to the Iraq Inquiry, 22 January 2010.

21. None of the end-of-empire campaigns were described officially as wars. They were 'emergencies', in order to ensure that insurance claims were not compromised by awkward clauses excluding claims for damage incurred in war. Special provisions existed for emergencies.

22. I am obliged to the Arabist Colonel Richard Iron who kindly pointed this out to me.

23. The 1947 census of Malaya found 2,403,000 Malays and 1,883,000 Chinese, from a population of 4,878,000 – the remainder being composed of Indians.

24. A fine account of investigations concerning this massacre and the ensuing efforts at cover-up and deception may be found in Ian Ward and Norma Miraflor, *Slaughter and Deception at Batang Kali*, Media Masters, Singapore, 2009.

25. K.R. Brazier-Creagh, 'Malaya', *RUSI Journal*, 99:594 (1954), pp. 175–90.

26. Imperial War Museum interview with Sir Robert Thompson (IWM DSR 10192/6 Sir Robert Thompson).

27. Simon C. Smith, 'General Templer and counter-insurgency in Malaya: hearts and minds, intelligence, and propaganda', *Intelligence and National Security*, 16:3 (2001), pp. 60–78, at p. 69.

28. David Benest, 'Aden to Northern Ireland', in Strachan (ed.), *Big Wars and Small Wars*, p. 118.

29. And its predecessor journals, the *British Army Journal* (1949–54) and the *British Army Annual* (1954–5).

30. I am obliged to Colonel John Wilson for lending me the entire run of *British Army Review* on disk.

31. Cited in *Army Field Manual* Volume 1 Part 10 – *Countering Insurgency* (January 2010) CS5-2 para 6.

32. Strachan, *Big Wars and Small Wars*, p. 8.

33. I am obliged to Colonel David Benest for referring me to this saying of Templer's.

34. Mockaitis, *British Counterinsurgency 1919–1960*, p. 8. It is fair to say that Mockaitis – probably the strongest proponent of British mastery of 'counterinsurgency' – deals persuasively with this argument later in his book.

35. Although the French avoidance of serious conflict in Tunisia at the same time as Malaya was being fought deserves respect.
36. Imperial War Museum interview with Sir Robert Thompson (IWM DSR 10192/6 Sir Robert Thompson).
37. Hack, 'The Malayan insurgency as counterinsurgency paradigm'.
38. David Galula, *Counterinsurgency Warfare Theory and Practice*, Praeger Security International, 1964.
39. Strachan, 'British counterinsurgency from Malaya to Iraq', p. 10.
40. *Ibid.*, p. 8.
41. For excellent discussions of the relationship between the techniques used in Malaya and those in the wars in Iraq and Afghanistan, see James Pritchard and M.L.R. Smith, 'Thompson in Helmand: comparing theory to practice in British counter-insurgency operations in Afghanistan', *Civil Wars*, 12:1 (2010), pp. 65–90; Chin, 'Colonial warfare in a post-colonial state'; Gian Gentile, 'A strategy of tactics: population centred COIN and the army', *Parameters*, 39 (Winter 2009), available at: www.carlisle.army.mil/ USAWC/Parameters/Articles/09autumn/gentile.pdf
42. His taped interview with Imperial War Museum staff is available at the Imperial War Museum's sound archive (IWM DSR 10192/6 Sir Robert Thompson).
43. See *Ireland* v. *UK* (European Court of Human Rights case number 5310/71), available at: http://cmiskp.echr.coe.int/tkp197/view.asp?action=html&documentId=695383&p ortal=hbkm&source=externalbydocnumber&table=F69A27FD8FB86142BF01C116 6DEA398649
44. General John Kiszely, 'Learning about counterinsurgency', *RUSI Journal*, 151:6 (December 2006).
45. Benest, 'Aden to Northern Ireland', p. 115.
46. Iron, 'Northern Ireland: A case study of institutional learning and unlearning'.
47. Strachan, 'British counterinsurgency from Malaya to Iraq', p. 11.
48. Benest, 'Aden to Northern Ireland', p. 140.
49. Iron, 'Northern Ireland: A case study of institutional learning and unlearning'.
50. John Nagl, *Learning to Eat Soup with a Knife*, University of Chicago Press, 2002, p. 205.
51. See Headquarters Department of the Army, *Counterinsurgency*, December 2006 (henceforth FM 3–24), pp. 1–148 to 1–158.
52. Colonel I.A. Rigden, *The British Approach to Counter-Insurgency: Myths, realities, and strategic challenges*, USAWC Strategy Research Project, March 2008.
53. http://usacac.army.mil/blog/blogs/coin/archive/2010/08/02/general-petraeus-issues-new-comisaf-coin-guidance.aspx, dated 1 August 2010.
54. David Petraeus *et al.*, *US Army/USMC Counterinsurgency Field Manual*, Chicago University Press, 2007, p. 38.
55. Originally published in the *Arab Bulletin* of 20 August 1917. Available (*inter alia*) at wwi.lib.byu.edu/index.php/The_27_Articles_of_T.E._Lawrence
56. *British Army Field Manual*, Volume 1, Part 10, *Countering Insurgency* (henceforth AFM 1–10), p. 2.
57. www.nato.int/cps/en/natolive/topics_51633.htm
58. Quoted *in extenso* from an article I had written.
59. Hanson Baldwin, quoted in Fall, *Street Without Joy*, p. 372.
60. Martin van Creveld, *The Changing Face of War: Combat from the Marne to Iraq*, Ballantine, 2008, p. 268.

61. Gentile, 'A strategy of tactics'.
62. Gentile, Gian, 'Time for the deconstruction of FM 3–24', *Joint Force Quarterly*, 58 (July 2010), available at: www.ndu.edu/press/deconstruction-3-24.html
63. Andrew Bacevich reviews David Kilcullen's *Accidental Guerrilla* in *The Nation*, March–April 2009, quoted in 'Rolling Stone Article's True Focus: counterinsurgency', *New York Times*, 23 June 2010.
64. Marshall, Alex, 'Imperial nostalgia, the liberal lie and the perils of postmodern counterinsurgency *Small wars and Insurgencies*, 21:2 (June 2010), pp. 233–58.
65. Colin Gray, *Another Bloody Century*. Phoenix, 2005, p. 222.
66. Crawshaw, 'The evolution of British COIN', paragraph 1.

Chapter 8: Doing no Harm? The Question of Force

1. Father of a victim of British forces, available on: www.channel4.com/news/articles/uk/afghan+casualties+uk+payouts+for+civilian+deaths+apostrebleapos/3690482
2. See: www.iwpr.net/report-news/helmand-precision-strike-or-reckless-bombing. The sums seemed to have no element of predictability: $950 for a ten-year-old boy killed by UK forces and $875 for a nine-year-old girl, rising to $40,000 for eight deaths in a mistaken killing.
3. 'British army officer arrested over military secrets leak', *Daily Telegraph*, 4 February 2009, available at: www.telegraph.co.uk/news/newstopics/onthefrontline/4510438/British-Army-officer-arrested-over-military-secrets-leak.html
4. Conversation with government official, February 2009.
5. Hamit Dardagan, John Sloboda and Richard Iron, 'In everyone's interest: recording all the dead, not just our own', *British Army Review*, no. 150 (Summer 2010).
6. Wither, 'Basra's not Belfast', p. 617.
7. Rod Thornton, 'The British army and the origins of the minimum force philosophy', *Small Wars and Insurgencies*, 15:1 (2004), p. 86.
8. For example Jackson, 'British counterinsurgency in history'.
9. Humanitarian law is the term used for law relating to the use of force and war in general.
10. John Tonkin, cited in Paul Fussel, *The Boys' Crusade*, Weidenfeld and Nicolson, 2003, p. 116.
11. Charles Townsend, *Britain's Civil Wars: Counter-insurgency in the twentieth century*, Faber and Faber, 1986, p. 20.
12. Admiral Sir Michael Boyce, quoted in 'Lawyers besiege army over Iraq abuse', *Guardian*, 25 July 2005.
13. 'Chief of Defence Staff demanded assurance Iraq war was legal', *Daily Telegraph*, 4 March 2004.
14. Address by Defence Secretary John Reid to RUSI, 3 April 2006.
15. Senior officer's communication with the author, November 2010.
16. See 'Introduction' to this book and also Fergusson, *One Million Bullets*, p. 160.
17. Interview with witness present at that meeting, March 2010.
18. Private conversation with the author, November 2007.
19. Interview with infantry company commander recently returned from Afghanistan, February 2010.
20. Discussion with senior training officer, June 2010.
21. Interview with former senior artillery officer, February 2010.

22. Interview with UK military intelligence officer, July 2010.
23. The cost of this equipment is well known to the troops. The Javelin anti-tank missile is regularly used to attack positions from which a few men are firing rifles. These missiles cost roughly £70,000 each. Soldiers refer to this as 'firing a Porsche'.
24. Interview with Colonel John Wilson, March 2010.
25. Colonel John Wilson, in a review of Kevin Myers' *Watching the Door*, in *British Army Review*, 144 (Spring 2008), p. 110.
26. Interview with Colonel John Wilson, February 2010.
27. *Ibid.*
28. Quinlivan, 'Burden of victory'; 'Force requirements in stability operations'.
29. Interview with former company commander who had served in Helmand, February 2010.
30. AFM 1–10.
31. '"Courageous Restraint" putting troops lives at risk', *Daily Telegraph*, 10 July 2010.
32. *Ibid.*
33. *Ibid.*
34. *Ibid.*
35. David Betz and Anthony Cormack, 'Afghanistan and British strategy', *Orbis*, 53:2 (2009), pp. 319–36, at p. 327.

Chapter 9: Civvies

1. See Michael Asher, *The Real Bravo Two Zero*, Phoenix, 2003, for a credible alternative view of the events contained in *Bravo Two Zero*.
2. Patrick Porter, 'Good anthropology, bad history: the cultural turn in studying war', *Parameters*, Summer (2007), p. 1, available at: www.carlisle.army.mil/USAWC/Parameters/Articles/07summer/porter.pdf
3. Patrick Porter, *Military Orientalism*, Hurst, 2010, p. 9.
4. http://armedservices.house.gov/comdocs/openingstatementsandpressreleases/108thcongress/04-07-15Scales.pdf
5. Porter, 'Good anthropology, bad history', p. 3.
6. *Ibid.*
7. Montgomery McFate, 'Anthropology and counterinsurgency: the strange story of their curious relationship', *Military Review*, March–April 2005, p. 24, available at: http://www.au.af.mil/au/awc/awcgate/milreview/mcfate.pdf
8. *Ibid.*, p. 27.
9. *Ibid.*, p. 25.
10. Jacob Kipp, Lester Grau, Karl Pinslow, Don Smith, 'The Human Terrain System: a CORDS for the 21st century', *Military Review*, September–October 2006, p. 8, available at: http://usacac.army.mil/CAC2/MilitaryReview/Archives/English/MilitaryReview_20061031_art005.pdf
11. Roughly equivalent in size to a British army brigade.
12. Interviews of the author with two such experts, June 2010. The last academic post in Afghan Studies (at the London School of Oriental and African Studies) was discontinued in 1984.
13. Development, Concepts and Doctrine Centre, *The Significance of Culture to the Military*, UK Joint Doctrine Note 09/1, available at: www.mod.uk/NR/rdonlyres/85A05A02-B2FE-4965-B1CD-E9DF1E913A0B/0/20090219JDN_1_09UDCDCIMAPPS.pdf

14. '60 Iraqi interpreters murdered working for UK', *Daily Telegraph*, 12 August 2007.

15. Interview with British military intelligence officer, August 2008.

16. Thornton, 'Countering Arab insurgencies', p. 13, citing Bernard Fergusson.

17. Porter, *Military Orientalism*, p. 193.

18. Cited by Tamara Duffey, 'Cultural issues in contemporary peacekeeping', *International Peacekeeping*, 7:1 (2000), pp. 142–68, at p. 149.

19. H.R. McMaster quoted by Thomas Ricks, *The Gamble*, Penguin, 2009, p. 161.

20. Evidence of Professor Hew Strachan to the Public Administration Committee, in its inquiry into UK strategy, 9 September 2010, Q6, available at: www.publications. parliament.uk/pa/cm201011/cmselect/cmpubadm/435/10090902.htm

21. Mackay and Tatham, *Behavioural Conflict*, p. 11.

22. Evidence of Major General Andy Salmon to the Iraq Inquiry, 20 July 2010.

23. Written statement of Mark Etherington to the Iraq Inquiry, available at: www. iraqinquiry.org.uk/media/49551/etherington-statement.pdf

24. House of Commons Defence Committee, *The Comprehensive Approach: The point of war is not just to win but to make a better peace*, Seventh Report of Session 2009–10, para 42, available at: www.publications.parliament.uk/pa/cm200910/ cmselect/cmdfence/224/224.pdf

25. Stephen Grey, in evidence to House of Commons Defence Committee: *The Comprehensive Approach: the point of war is not just to win but to make a better peace*, Seventh Report of Session 2009–10, Ev 55.

26. Interview with Dan Jarman, September 2010.

27. Daniel Korski, in evidence to House of Commons Defence Committee: *The Comprehensive Approach: the point of war is not just to win but to make a better peace*, Seventh Report of Session 2009–10, Ev 57.

28. Sir Olaf Caroe, interview for Imperial War Museum (IWM DSR 4099).

29. Christian Tripodi, 'Peacemaking through bribes or cultural empathy: the political officer and Britain's strategy towards the North West Frontier 1901–1945', *Journal of Strategic Studies*, 31:1 (February 2008), *passim*.

30. Civilian 'advisers' in Helmand today generally serve less than a year in total. This onerous period is, however, broken up with 'breather breaks' *every six weeks*. Very, very few speak any language other than English.

31. Christian Tripodi, 'Cultural understanding: its utility and influence: the British experience on the North West Frontier 1918–1939', *British Army Review*, 144 (Spring 2008), p. 25.

32. *Ibid.*, p. 26.

33. See Tripodi, 'Peacemaking through bribes or cultural empathy', p. 123.

34. Tripodi, 'Cultural understanding', p. 29.

35. British Library MSS EUR D879/1RHD Lowis Diaries 1927–44 (1937), cited in Tripodi, 'Cultural understanding', p. 29.

36. Tripodi, 'Cultural understanding', p. 29

37. Interview with Dan Jarman, September 2010.

38. Smith, *The Utility of Force*, p. 214.

39. Words from an interview given to Sean Smith by Captain Eldouard Plunkett of the Duke of Lancaster's Regiment, during Operation Black Prince. Video report 'British troops in Afghanistan: "We try to help them . . . but it just seems pointless"', *Guardian* online, 6 August 2010, available at: www.guardian.co.uk/world/video/2010/aug/06/ afghanistan-taliban

40. From Sean Smith's video report 'British troops in Afghanistan: "We try to help them ... but it just seems pointless"'; interview given by unnamed infantryman.
41. Interview with Dan Jarman, September 2010.

Chapter 10: Bad Influences

1. For example, Emile Simpson, 'Gaining the influence initiative', *British Army Review* 147 p. 67.
2. See: http://www.da.mod.uk/colleges/arag/document-listings/monographs/091216%20FINAL.pdf/view
3. Mackay and Tatham, *Behavioural Conflict*, citing at p. 9 David Galula, *Pacification in Algeria 1956–1958*, RAND, 1963, new edition available at: www.rand.org/pubs/monographs/2006/RAND_MG478-1.pdf
4. AFM 1–10, pp. 6–4.
5. *Ibid.*, pp. 6–5.
6. Thomas Withington, 'Night of the flying hooligans: Soviet army aviation and air force operations during the war in Afghanistan 1979–1989', in *Air Power, Insurgency and the 'War on Terror'*, ed. Joel Hayward, Royal Air Force Centre for Air Power Studies, 2009, p. 133.
7. SO is NATO shorthand for Staff Officer. The numbers relate to the rank of the officer concerned, 1 being lieutenant colonel or equivalent, 2 – major or service equivalent, and 3 – captain.
8. AFM 1–10, pp. 6–11.
9. *Ibid.*
10. Interview with author, July 2010.
11. Evidence of Major General Andy Salmon to the Iraq Inquiry, 20 July 2010.
12. Rob Johnson, *Spying for Empire: The Great Game in Central and South Asia 1757–1947*, Greenhill Books, 2006, p. 200.
13. Mackay and Tatham, *Behavioural Conflict*, p. 13.
14. Theo Farrell, 'Appraising Moshtarak', RUSI Briefing Note, 2010, p. 9, available at: www.rusi.org/downloads/assets/Appraising_Moshtarak.pdf
15. *Ibid.*, p. 10.
16. Stephen Grey, in evidence to House of Commons Defence Committee: *The Comprehensive Approach: the point of war is not just to win but to make a better peace*, Seventh Report of Session 2009–10, Ev 60.
17. The practice is spreading throughout all three services.
18. AFM 3–40, 3.8.
19. 'No friendly waves, only hatred for British troops in Afghan town', *Guardian*, 22 April 2010.
20. The British army considers it to be a single campaign under the name Operation Banner. Beginning in August 1969, Banner was officially discontinued in July 2007. It is the longest continuously running formal campaign in the British army's history.
21. Frank Kitson, *Bunch of Five*, Faber and Faber, 1977; and *Low Intensity Operations*, Faber and Faber, 1971.
22. Subsequent events in Afghanistan, with SIS being implicated in politically damaging and professionally embarrassing debacles such as the misidentification of Mullah Mansour in late 2010, have not improved its reputation.
23. Williams and Lamb, *Upgrading Our Armed Forces*, p. 20.

24. Johnson, *Spying for Empire*, p. 254.
25. *Ibid.*, p. 256.
26. Sir Peter Heap, former UK ambassador to Brazil, 'The truth behind the MI6 facade', *Guardian*, 2 October 2003.
27. Major General Michael T. Flynn, Matt Pottinger and Paul Batchelor, *Fixing Intel: A blueprint for making intelligence relevant in Afghanistan*, Centre for a New American Security, January 2010, p. 23.
28. *Ibid.*, p. 9.
29. Mackay and Tatham, *Behavioural Conflict*, p. 34.
30. Flynn, et al., *Fixing Intel*, p. 23.
31. *Ibid.* p. 17.
32. Mary Kaldor and Shannon Beebe, *The Ultimate Weapon is No Weapon*, Public Affairs, 2010.
33. Interview with author, July 2010.
34. ECHR 5130/71. This case decided that Britain had been guilty of treatment that amounted, taken as a whole, to torture. It placed close limits on the techniques to be used in interrogation of suspects, defining five 'forbidden techniques' – namely hooding, starvation, deprivation of food, white noise and stress positions.
35. An acronym popularly thought to stand for 'Stupid Territorial Army Bastard'.
36. Mackay and Tatham, *Behavioural Conflict*, p. 32.
37. The Royal Navy has an interesting system of training logistics specialists as lawyers. They maintain currency in both fields throughout their career and it seems to work well.
38. A 'wicked' problem is one that is difficult or impossible to solve, in which potential solutions often raise other equally tricky issues within a shifting environment.
39. Williams and Lamb, *Upgrading Our Armed Forces*, pp. 47f.
40. More accurately, they are members of State Air National Guard units.
41. A superb account of their role is contained in the various books by Helen Fry, notably *Denazification*.
42. Development, Concepts and Doctrine Centre, *The Future Character of Conflict*, DCDC, February 2010, p. 6, available at: www.mod.uk/DefenceInternet/MicroSite/DCDC/OurPublications/Concepts/FutureCharacterOfConflict.htm
43. Such as 'effects-based operations', 'revolution in military affairs', 'fourth-generation warfare', 'network-centred capability'.
44. Lawrence Friedman, *The Transformation of Strategic Affairs*, IISS Adelphi Paper no. 379, IISS, 2006, p. 20.

Chapter 11: Opening Networks

1. General von Kuhl, in his book *Die deutsche Generalstab*, quoted in 'A German General Staff appreciation of the British Army in 1912', *RUSI Journal*, 65:459 (1920), pp. 605–7.
2. Patrick Little, 'Lessons unlearned – a former army officer's perspective of the British Army at war', *RUSI Journal*, 154:3 (2009), p. 10.
3. Interview with syndicate leader at Shrivenham, March 2010.
4. Claudia Harvey and Mark Wilkinson, 'The value of doctrine: assessing British officers' perspectives', *RUSI Journal*, 154:6 (2009), p. 26. There was a trend for junior officers to be more successful in their answers.

5. Frederick the Great, 'Reflexions sur les projets de campagne', *Oeuvres de Frederic le Grand 1846–56*, in Jay Luvaas (ed.), *Frederick the Great on the Art of War*, The Free Press, 1966.

6. *Ibid.*, para 21.

7. *Ibid.*, para 44.

8. Presentation to the 'Teaching Strategy' conference, US Army War College, May 2010.

9. The Air Force Academy at Colorado Springs was placed seventh and the Naval Academy was thirtieth.

10. www.forbes.com/2009/08/02/colleges-university-ratings-opinions-colleges-09-intro. html

11. Presentation to the 'Teaching Strategy' conference, US Army War College, May 2010.

12. http://myarmybenefits.us.army.mil/Home/Benefit_Library/Federal_Benefits_Page/ Advanced_Civil_Schooling_(ACS).html?serv=147

13. David Petraeus, 'Beyond the cloister', *The American Interest*, July–August 2007.

14. *Ibid.*

15. McMaster, *Dereliction of Duty*, see Chapter 5.

16. See posting on *Foreign Policy*, 12 April 2010, at: http://ricks.foreignpolicy.com/ posts/2010/04/12/bg_hr_mcmaster_being_a_grad_student_at_chapel_hill_prepared_ me_for_combat

17. Medical officers are given time and resources to read for PhDs, should they wish to do so.

18. Sir John Kiszely, 'The educational upper hand', *Defence Management Journal*, 46, available at: www.defencemanagement.com/article.asp?id=399&content_name=Education +and+training&article=12622

19. These are the 'Chief of the Air Staff' fellowships; see http://www.raf.mod.uk/raflearn-ingforces/courseinfo/casfellowships.cfm

20. There was discussion of a British version of a GI Bill – funding higher education opportunities for all servicemen – in Parliament in 1947. It was not pursued.

21. The Serviceman's Readjustment Act 1944.

22. See, for example, John B. White, 'The GI Bill: recruiting bonus, retention onus', *Military Review*, July–August (2004). The author is a lieutenant commander in the US naval reserve and a PhD.

23. 'From battlefield to Ivy League, on the GI Bill', *New York Times*, 8 January 2010, available at: www.nytimes.com/2010/01/09/nyregion/09gis.html?scp=1&sq=columbia%20 university%20iraq%20veterans%20bill&st=cse

24. Patrick Cockburn has built a highly informed and persuasive critique of the 'Surge as Victory' narrative in many articles, e.g. 'Is the US really bringing stability to Baghdad', *Independent*, 15 February 2008, available at: www.independent.co.uk/news/world/ middle-east/is-the-us-really-bringing-stability-to-baghdad-782425.html; 'A stable Iraq is still a very long way off', Gorilla's Guides website, 29 May 2010, available at: http:// gorillasguides.com/2010/05/29/patrick-cockburn-a-stable-iraq-is-still-a-very-long-way-off/; 'Take another look at the Surge', *Counterpunch*, 15 September 2008, available at: www.counterpunch.org/patrick09152008.html

25. Discussion with serving senior officer, March 2011.

26. Cited in Thomas Skypek, 'Soldier scholars: military education as an instrument of China's strategic power', *China Brief*, 8:4 (29 February 2008), available at: www. jamestown.org/programs/chinabrief/single/?tx_ttnews%5Btt_news%5D=4734&tx_ ttnews%5BbackPid%5D=168&no_cache=1

27. United States Joint Forces Command, *Joint Operating Environment 2008*, p. 27, available at: www.jfcom.mil/newslink/storyarchive/2008/JOE2008.pdf

28. Website at: www.carlisle.army.mil/usawc/Parameters/

29. David Petraeus, 'Learning counterinsurgency: observations from soldiering in Iraq', *Military Review*, January–February (2006), available at: http://usacac.army.mil/CAC2/MilitaryReview/Archives/English/MilitaryReview_2006CR1031_art010.pdf

30. David Petraeus, 'Multi-national force – Iraq commander's counterinsurgency guidance', *Military Review*, September–October (2008), available at: http://usacac.army.mil/CAC2/MilitaryReview/Archives/English/MilitaryReview_2008CRII0831_art028.pdf

31. *British Army Review*, 146, Spring 2009. Also reported 'British army officer launches stinging attack on "failing" UK strategy in Afghanistan', *Daily Telegraph*, 20 July 2009.

32. *British Army Review*, 146, p. 11.

33. Betz and Cormack, 'Afghanistan and British strategy'.

34. Reported in www.stephengrey.com

35. A freedom of information request on this matter went unanswered.

36. King, 'Beyond the crisis', p. 24.

37. For example, Development, Concepts and Doctrine Centre, *Future Land Operational Concept*, DCDC, 2008, para 117: 'At the heart of the British approach to military operations is the retention of a warfighting ethos.'

38. Cited in Development, Concepts and Doctrine Centre, *The Future Character of Conflict*, para 3.

39. Mackay and Tatham, *Behavioural Conflict*, p. 25, citing Ivan Arreguin-Toft.

Conclusion

1. Professor Robert Pape, 'It's the occupation, stupid', *Foreign Policy*, 18 October 2010, available at: www.foreignpolicy.com/articles/2010/10/18/it_s_the_occupation_stupid?page=full

2. 'Twenty-first century armed forces – agile, useable, relevant', address by General Sir David Richards to Chatham House, 17 September 2009. The sentiment was repeated in the 2010 Chief of the Defence Staff lecture at the Royal United Services Institute, December 2010, available at: www.mod.uk/DefenceInternet/AboutDefence/People/Speeches/ChiefStaff/2010121411thAnnualChiefOfDefenceStaffLecture.htm

3. There was no review of British performance in the First World War until 1932, with the publication of the 'Report of the Committee on the Lessons of the Great War' – better known as the Kirke Report (WO 33/1297; Reprinted SCSI 2001).

4. Air Marshal Sir Jock Stirrup, RUSI Christmas Lecture, 3 December 2007.

5. Conversation with Dr David Betz, King's College London, June 2010.

6. Betz and Cormack, 'Afghanistan and British strategy', p. 323.

7. The Defence Cultural Specialist Unit based at RAF Henlow in Bedfordshire.

8. Evidence of General Sir Graeme Lamb to the Iraq Inquiry, 9 December 2009. There is indeed a database of 'Lessons Identified' (there is a recognition that a lesson identified does not translate into a lesson learned) from Iraq and Afghanistan. Bizarrely, the detail is classified. By way of comparison, the US military critique of operations 'On Point II' was made available online, publicly and quickly. The British equivalent was also made public, but, in true British fashion, this was achieved by means of leaks to the *Daily Telegraph*.

9. House of Commons Public Administration Committee, 'Who does UK National Strategy?', First Report of Session 2010–11, paras 22, 73, available at: www.publications.parliament.uk/pa/cm201011/cmselect/cmpubadm/435/43502.htm

10. Evidence of Air Chief Marshal Sir Jock Stirrup to the Public Administration Committee, in its inquiry into UK strategy, 16 September 2010, Q260 available at: www.publications.parliament.uk/pa/cm201011/cmselect/cmpubadm/435/10091603.htm

11. Jermy, *Strategy for Action*, Chapter 10.

12. Dannatt, p. 376.

13. Professor Hew Strachan: 'Professor Hennessy mentioned just now the publication last year of a document called "The Future Character of Conflict", which was designed to address precisely what its title says, but its arguments are nowhere evident in current thinking in relation to strategy, let alone in relation to the Strategic Defence and Security Review.' In evidence to the Public Administration Committee, in its inquiry into UK strategy, 9 September 2010, Q23, available at: www.publications.parliament.uk/pa/cm201011/cmselect/cmpubadm/435/10090902.htm

14. Dannatt, p. 339.

15. See, for example, Gentile, 'A strategy of tactics'; and 'Our COIN doctrine removes the enemy from the essence of war', *Armed Forces Journal*, available at: www.armedforcesjournal.com/2008/01/3207722

16. In May 2007, for example, Estonia suffered serious problems from what was in fact a limited cyber attack, allegedly instigated by Russia. The targets were the country's parliamentary and governmental sites. Far more serious results could be expected if, taking one obvious example, a nation's electricity supply grid were attacked.

17. Michael Howard, 'Military Science in an Age of Peace', RUSI Journal 119:1 (1974), pp. 7 and 8.

Select Bibliography

Archive materials

Imperial War Museum London (Department of Sound Records)
IWM DSR 10192/6 Sir Robert Thompson
IWM DSR 4099 Sir Olaf Caroe

Books and articles

Alderson, Alex, 'The validity of British counterinsurgency doctrine after the war in Iraq 2003–2009', Cranfield University PhD Thesis, 2010, available at: https://dspace.lib. cranfield.ac.uk/bitstream/1826/4264/1/100126-Alderson-PhD%20Thesis.pdf

Aylwin-Foster, Nigel, 'Changing the army for counterinsurgency operations', *Military Review*, November–December (2005), originally published as a Seaford Paper with the title 'Operation Iraqi Freedom Phase IV: The watershed', available at: www.au.af.mil/au/awc/awcgate/milreview/aylwin.pdf

Bayly, Martin, 'COINing a new doctrine', unpublished MPhil thesis, Oxford, 2009

Beckett, Ian F.W., *Modern Insurgencies and Counter-Insurgencies*, Routledge, 2001

Benbow, Tim and Rod Thornton, *Dimensions of Counter-Insurgency: Applying experience to practice*, Routledge, 2008

Benest, David, *British Leaders and Irregular Warfare*, Defence Academy, 2007, available at: www.da.mod.uk/journal/journal. . ./defac_journal_britishleaders.pdf

Bennett, Huw, 'The Mau Mau Emergency as part of the British army's post-war counter-insurgency experience', *Defense and Security Analysis*, 23:2 (2007), pp. 143–63

Betz, David and Anthony Cormack, 'Hot war, cold comfort', *RUSI Journal*, 154:4 (2009), pp. 26–9

——, 'Afghanistan and British strategy', *Orbis*, 53:2 (2009), pp. 319–36

Bruce, C.E., *Waziristan 1936–37: The problems of the North West Frontier Province and their solutions*, Aldershot, 1938

Caroe, Olaf, *The Pathans*, Oxford University Press, 1958

Carver, Field Marshal Lord, *Britain's Army in the 20th Century*, Macmillan, 1998

Cavanagh, Matt, 'Inside the Anglo-Saxon war machine', *Prospect*, December 2010, pp. 69–71

Chandler, David and Ian Beckett (eds), *Oxford History of the British Army*, Oxford University Press, 1994

Chin, Warren, 'Colonial warfare in a post-colonial state: British military operations in Helmand Province, Afghanistan', *Defence Studies*, 10:1 (2010), pp. 215–47

Churchill, Winston, *The Story of the Malakand Field Force: An episode of frontier war*, 1898 (reprinted Dover Publications, 2010)

Clausewitz, Carl von, *On War*, translated and edited by Professor Sir Michael Howard and Peter Paret, Everyman, 1993

Clayton, Antony (ed.), *The British Officer*, Pearson, 2006

Cockburn, Patrick, *The Occupation: War and resistance in Iraq*, Verso, 2007

——, *Muqtada al Sadr and the Fall of Iraq*, Faber and Faber, 2008

Cohen, Eliot, *Supreme Command*, Simon and Schuster, 2002

——, *Military Misfortunes*, Free Press, 2006

Cohen, Stuart, *Israel and Its Army*, Routledge, 2008

Dannatt, General Sir Richard, *Leading from the Front*, Bantam, 2010

Dardagan, Hamit, John Sloboda and Richard Iron, 'In everyone's interest: recording all the dead, not just our own', *British Army Review*, 150 (Summer 2010)

De Watteville H.G., 'A hundred years of the British Army', *RUSI Journal*, 76:502 (1931), pp. 285–99

Defence Concepts and Doctrine Centre, *The Future Character of Conflict*, MOD, February 2010, available at: www.mod.uk/DefenceInternet/MicroSite/DCDC/OurPublications/ Concepts/FutureCharacterOfConflict.htm

Dimitrakis, Panagiotis, 'British intelligence and the Cyprus Insurgency, 1955–1959', *International Journal of Intelligence and Counterintelligence*, 21:2 (2008), pp. 375–94

Dixon, Norman, *On the Psychology of Military Incompetence*, Pimlico, 1976

Docherty, Leo, *Desert of Death*, Faber and Faber, 2007

Donnelly, Thomas, 'The cousins' counter-insurgency wars', *RUSI Journal*, 154:3 (2009), pp. 4–9

Dorman Smith, Andrew, 'Rank nonsense', *Parliamentary Brief*, 12:8 (April 2010)

Duffey, Tamara, 'Cultural issues in contemporary peacekeeping', *International Peacekeeping*, 7:1 (2000), pp. 142–68

Fall, Bernard, *Street Without Joy*, Stackpole Edition, 2005

Farrell, Theo, 'Appraising Moshtarak', RUSI Briefing Note, 2010, available at: www.rusi.org/ downloads/assets/Appraising_Moshtarak.pdf

Farrell, Theo and Stuart Gordon, 'COIN machine: the British army in Afghanistan', *Orbis*, 53:4 (2009), pp. 665–83

Farwell, Byron, *Queen Victoria's Little Wars*, Wordsworth Edition, 1999

Fergusson, James, *One Million Bullets*, Bantam Press, 2008

——, *Taleban*, Bantam Press, 2010

Flynn, Michael T., Matt Pottinger and Paul Batchelor, *Fixing Intel: A blueprint for making intelligence relevant in Afghanistan*, Centre for a New American Security, January 2010

Friedman, Lawrence, *The Transformation of Strategic Affairs*, IISS Adelphi Paper no. 379, IISS, 2006

Galula, David, *Counterinsurgency Warfare Theory and Practice*, Praeger, 2006

Garfield, Andrew et al., *Succeeding in Phase IV: British perspectives on the US effort to stabilise and reconstruct Iraq*, Foreign Policy Research Institute, 2006

Gentile, Gian, 'A strategy of tactics: population centred COIN and the army', *Parameters*, 39 (Winter 2009), available at: www.carlisle.army.mil/USAWC/Parameters/Articles/09autumn/gentile.pdf

——, 'Time for the deconstruction of FM 3–24', *Joint Force Quarterly*, 58 (July 2010), available at: www.ndu.edu/press/deconstruction-3-24.html

Gray, Colin, *Modern Strategy*, Oxford University Press, 1999

——, *Another Bloody Century*, Phoenix, 2005

Grey, Stephen, *Operation Snakebite*, Viking/Penguin, 2009

——, 'Cracking on in Helmand', *Prospect*, 162 (August 2009)

Griffin, Christopher, 'A revolution in colonial military affairs; Galieni, Lyautey and the "tache d'huile"', paper prepared for the British International Studies Association Conference, Leicester, 14–16 December 2009

Gwynn, Major General Sir Charles, *Imperial Policing*, Macmillan and Co., 1936

Hack, Karl, 'The Malayan Insurgency as counterinsurgency paradigm', *Journal of Strategic Studies*, 32:3 (June 2009), pp. 383–414

Hastings, Max, *Armageddon*, Macmillan, 2004

——, *Finest Years: Churchill as warlord 1940–45*, Harper Press, 2009

Headquarters of the US Army, *Counterinsurgency*, US Army and Marine Corps Field Manual (FM 3–24), December 2006, available at: http://usacac.army.mil/cac2/coin/repository/FM_3-24.pdf

Hitchcock, William I., *Liberation: The bitter road to freedom, Europe 1944–45*, Faber and Faber, 2008

House of Commons Defence Committee, 'The comprehensive approach: the point of war is not just to win but to make a better peace: government response to the committee's seventh report of session 2009–10', First Special Report, 2010, available at: www.publications.parliament.uk/pa/cm201011/cmselect/cmdfence/347/34702.htm

——, 'The contribution of ISTAR to operations', Second Special Report, 2010, available at www.publications.parliament.uk/pa/cm201011/cmselect/cmdfence/346/34602.htm

——, 'Operations in Afghanistan' (evidence), available at www.parliament.uk/business/committees/committees-a-z/commons-select/defence-committee/publications/

House of Commons Public Administration Committee, 'Who does UK national strategy?', First Report, 2010, available at: www.publications.parliament.uk/pa/cm201011/cmselect/cmpubadm/435/43502.htm#evidence

Howard, Professor Sir Michael, 'The use and abuse of military history', Lecture to Royal United Services Institute in 1961, *RUSI Journal*, 138:1 (1993), pp. 26–30

——, *Captain Professor*, Continuum, 2006

Hughes, Matthew, 'The practice and theory of British counterinsurgency: the histories of the atrocities at the Palestinian villages of al-Bassa and Halhul, 1938–1939', *Small Wars and Insurgencies*, 20:3 (2009), pp. 528–50

Human Rights Watch, *Basra, Crime and Insecurity under British Occupation*, HRW, June 2003, available at: www.hrw.org/en/node/12320/section/1

Jackson, Ashley, 'British counterinsurgency in history: a useful precedent?', *British Army Review*, 139 (2006), pp. 12–22

——, 'The imperial antecedents of the British special forces', *RUSI Journal*, 154:3 (June 2009)

Jalali, Ali A. and Lester W. Grau, 'Expeditionary forces: superior technology defeated – the Battle of Maiwand', *Military Review*, May–June (2001)

Jermy, Steven, *Strategy for Action: Using force wisely in the 21st century*, Knightstone Publishing, 2011

Johnson, Rob, *Spying for Empire: The Great Game in Central and South Asia 1757–1947*, Greenhill Books, 2006

Kaldor, Mary, *New and Old Wars*, 2nd edition, Stanford University Press, 2006

Kaldor, Mary and Shannon Beebe, *The Ultimate Weapon is No Weapon*, Public Affairs, 2010

Keegan, John, *The Iraq War*, Hutchinson, 2004

Kilcullen, David, *The Accidental Guerrilla*, Hurst, 2009

King, Anthony, 'Beyond the crisis: critical requirements for successful military transformation', *British Army Review*, 147 (Summer 2009)

——, 'Unity is strength: staff college and the British officer corps', *British Journal of Sociology*, 60:1 (2009)

——, 'Why we're getting it wrong in Helmand', *Prospect*, 162 (September 2009)

——, 'Understanding the Helmand campaign', *International Affairs*, 86:2 (2010)

Kiszely, Sir John, 'Learning about counterinsurgency', *RUSI Journal*, 151:6 (December 2006), pp. 16–21

——, *Post-Modern Challenges for Modern Warriors*, Shrivenham Papers no. 5, September 2007

Kitson, Frank, *Low Intensity Operations*, Faber and Faber, 1971

——, *Bunch of Five*, Faber and Faber, 1977

Ladwig, Walter, 'Supporting allies in counterinsurgency. Britain and the Dhofar rebellion', *Small Wars and Counterinsurgencies*, 19:1 (March 2008)

Loyn, David, *Butcher and Bolt*, Hutchinson, 2008

Mackay, Andrew and Stephen Tatham, *Behavioural Conflict, from General to Strategic Corporal: Complexity, adaptation and influence*, Shrivenham Papers no. 9, 2009

Mallinson, Allan, *The Making of the British Army*, Bantam Press, 2009

Marshall, Alex, 'Imperial nostalgia, the liberal lie and the perils of postmodern counterinsurgency', *Small Wars and Insurgencies*, 21:2 (June 2010), pp. 233–58

McMaster, H.R., *Dereliction of Duty*, Harper Collins, 1998

Ministry of Defence, *The Aitken Report: An investigation into cases of deliberate abuse and unlawful killing in Iraq 2003 and 2004*, 2008, available at: www.mod.uk/NR/rdonlyres/7AC894D3-1430-4AD1-911F-8210C3342CC5/0/aitken_rep.pdf

——, *British Army Field Manual*, vol. 1 part 10, *Countering Insurgency*, October 2009, available at: http://news.bbc.co.uk/1/shared/bsp/hi/pdfs/16_11_09_army_manual.pdf

——, *Security and Stabilisation: The military contribution*. Joint Doctrine Publication 3–40, November 2009, available at: www.mod.uk/DefenceInternet/MicroSite/DCDC/OurPublications/JDWP/JointDoctrinePublicationjdp340SecurityAndStabilisationThe MilitaryContribution.htm

Mockaitis, Thomas R., *British Counterinsurgency 1919–1960*, Macmillan, 1990

——, *British Counterinsurgency in the Post-Imperial Era*, Manchester University Press, 1995

——, *Iraq and the Challenge of Counterinsurgency*, Praeger, 2008

Moreman, T.R., '"Small wars" and "imperial policing": the British army and the theory and practice of colonial warfare in the British Empire 1919–1939', *Journal of Strategic Studies*, 19:4 (1996)

Morris, James (Jan), *Heaven's Command*, Faber and Faber, 1973

Moyer, Mark, *A Question of Command*, Yale University Press, 2009

Nagl, John, *Learning to Eat Soup with a Knife*, University of Chicago Press, 2002

Nagl, John and Paul Yingling, 'New rules for new enemies', *Armed Forces Journal*, October (2006), available at: www.armedforcesjournal.com/2006/10/2088425

Neusinger, John, *British Counterinsurgency from Palestine to Northern Ireland*, Palgrave, 2002

Newark, Tim, *Mafia at War: Allied collusion with the mob*, Greenhill Books, 2007

Newton, Paul, Paul Colley and Andrew Sharpe, 'Reclaiming the art of British strategic thinking', *RUSI Journal*, 155:1 (2010), pp. 44–50

Nicol, Mark, *Condor Blues, British Soldiers at War*, Mainstream, 2008

North, Richard, *Ministry of Defeat: The British in Iraq 2003–2009*, Continuum, 2009

Omissi, David, *Air Power and Colonial Control 1919–1939*, Manchester University Press, 1990

Page, Lewis, *Lions, Donkeys and Dinosaurs*, Heinemann, 2006

Paret, Peter, *The Cognitive Challenge of War*, Princeton University Press, 2009

Petraeus, David et al., *US Army/USMC Counterinsurgency Field Manual*, Chicago University Press, 2007

Pope-Hennessy, L.H.R., 'The British army and modern conceptions of war', *RUSI Journal*, 55: 403, pp. 1181–204

Popplewell, Richard, 'Lacking intelligence: some reflections on recent approaches to British counterinsurgency 1900–1960', *Intelligence and National Security*, 10:2 (1995), pp. 336–52

Porter, Patrick, 'Good anthropology, bad history: the cultural turn in studying war', *Parameters*, Summer (2007), available at: www.carlisle.army.mil/USAWC/Parameters/Articles/07summer/porter.pdf

——, *Military Orientalism*, Hurst, 2010

——, 'Why Britain doesn't do grand strategy', *RUSI Journal*, 155:4 (2010), pp. 6–12

Pritchard, James and M.L.R. Smith, 'Thompson in Helmand: comparing theory to practice in British counter-insurgency operations in Afghanistan', *Civil Wars*, 12:1 (2010), pp. 65–90

Quinlivan, James T., 'Force requirements in stability operations', *Parameters*, Winter (1995), pp. 59–69, available at: www.carlisle.army.mil/usawc/Parameters/Articles/1995/quinliv.htm

——, 'Burden of victory: the painful arithmetic of stability operations', *Rand Review*, Summer (2003), available at: www.rand.org/publications/randreview/issues/summer2003/burden.html

Rayment, Sean, *Into the Killing Zone*, Constable, 2008

Ricks, Thomas, *The Gamble*, Penguin, 2009

Rigden, I.A., *The British Approach to Counter-Insurgency: Myths, realities, and strategic challenges*, USAWC Strategy Research Project, March 2008

Robinson, Paul, *Doing Less with Less*, Imprint Academic, 2005

Roe, Andrew R., 'British governance on the North West Frontier (1919–1947): a blueprint for contemporary Afghanistan?', MA thesis, US Army Command and General Staff College, Fort Leavenworth, 2005

Rubin, G.R., 'The legal education of British army officers, 1860–1923', *Journal of Legal History*, 15:3 (1994), pp. 223–51

Schofield, Victoria, *Afghan Frontier*, Tauris Paperbacks, 2010

Sheffield, Gary, 'The British army of 1918', *RUSI Journal*, 143:6 (1998), pp. 78–9

Slim, Field Marshal Sir William, *Defeat into Victory*, Cassell, 1955

——, *Unofficial History*, Cassell, 1959

Smith, Rupert, *The Utility of Force*, Penguin, 2005

Smith, Simon C., 'General Templer and counter-insurgency in Malaya: hearts and minds, intelligence, and propaganda', *Intelligence and National Security*, 16:3 (2001), pp. 60–78

Stewart, Rory, *Occupational Hazards*, Picador, 2007

Strachan, Hew, *Politics of the British Army*, Clarendon Press, 1987

——, 'The lost meaning of strategy', *Survival*, 47:3 (2005), pp. 33–54

—— (ed.), *Big Wars and Small Wars*, Routledge, 2006

——, *Carl von Clausewitz's 'On War'*, Atlantic Books, 2007

——, 'British counterinsurgency from Malaya to Iraq', *RUSI Journal*, 152:6 (December 2007), pp. 8–11

Thompson, Sir Robert, *Defeating Communist Insurgency*, Hailer, 1966

Thornton, Rod, 'The British army and the origins of the minimum force philosophy', *Small Wars and Insurgencies*, 15:1 (2004)

——, 'Getting it wrong: the crucial mistakes made in the early stages of the British army's deployment to Northern Ireland (August 1969 to March 1972)', *Journal of Strategic Studies*, 30:1 (2007), pp. 73–107

Tierney John J., *Chasing Ghosts: Unconventional warfare in American history*, Potomac Books, 2007

Titus, Paul, 'Honor the Baloch, buy the Pashtun. Stereotypes, social organization and history in Western Pakistan', *Modern Asian Studies*, 32:3 (1998), pp. 657–87

Tootal, Stuart, *Danger Close: Commanding 3 PARA in Afghanistan*, John Murray, 2009

Tripodi, Christian, 'Peacemaking through bribes or cultural empathy: the political officer and Britain's strategy towards the North West Frontier 1901–1945', *Journal of Strategic Studies*, 31:1 (February 2008)

——, 'Cultural understanding: its utility and influence: the British experience on the North West Frontier 1918–1939', *British Army Review*, 144 (Spring 2008)

Tsouras, Peter G., *Dictionary of Military Quotations*, Greenhill Books, 2005

Urban, Mark, *Task Force Black*, Little and Brown, 2010

Wilson, John, 'Politics, doctrine and the army: fighting the enemy over the same ground', *British Army Review*, 145 (Autumn 2008)

Wither, James K., 'Basra's not Belfast: the British army, "small wars" and Iraq', *Small Wars and Insurgencies*, 20: 3–4 (2009), pp. 611–35

Zaeef, Abdul, *My Life with the Taleban*, Hurst, 2010

Zhukov, Yuri, 'Examining the authoritarian model of counter-insurgency: the Soviet campaign against the Ukrainian insurgent army', *Small Wars and Insurgencies*, 18:3 (2007), pp. 439–66

Index